PLAYING
FOR
PAY

PLAYING FOR PAY

HOW TO BE A WORKING MUSICIAN

Writer's
Digest
Books

CINCINNATI, OHIO

Acknowledgments
Thanks to Julie Whaley for nurturing this idea and for her patience, and thanks to Beth Franks for helping me turn my words into English.

Playing for Pay: How to Be a Working Musician. Copyright © 1990 by James Gibson. Printed and bound in the United States of America. All rights reserved. No part of this book may be reproduced in any form or by any electronic or mechanical means including information storage and retrieval systems without permission in writing from the publisher, except by a reviewer, who may quote brief passages in a review. Published by Writer's Digest Books, an imprint of F&W Publications, Inc., 1507 Dana Ave., Cincinnati, Ohio 45207. First edition.

94   93   92   91   90   5   4   3   2   1

Library of Congress Cataloging-in-Publication Data

Gibson, James R.
   Playing for pay : how to be a working musician / James Gibson.
     p. cm.
   Rev. from author's How you can make $30,000 a year as a musician—without a record contract.
   Includes bibliographical references.
   ISBN 0-89869-403-X
   1. Music—Economic aspects. 2. Music—Vocational guidance.
3. Music trade—United States. I. Gibson, James R., 1944- How you can make $30,000 a year as a musician—without a record contract. II. Title.
ML3795.G525 1990   89-70771
780' .23'73—dc20   CIP
                                                              MN

Design by Clare Finney

To Susan Bennett, Rick Hinkle, and Logan Sisk who make playing for pay so much fun

CONTENTS

You're a musician, or you wouldn't be reading this book. Maybe you're an amateur who's never played a note for pay or perhaps you're a professional looking for ways to make more money. In either case, you, like most freelance musicians, are probably trying to figure out what to do next.

In some professions you begin at the bottom and work your way up the ladder. In a large company you might move from stock clerk to administrative assistant to manager to vice president in a smooth progression. In such "mainstream" careers there is a well-marked path to the top.

Life as a musician is very different. Here, there is no clear road to follow, no blueprint that will guarantee success. It's tempting to think that if you just practice enough and get better and better, success will be automatic—clients will come knocking on your door.

The truth is, with very few exceptions, that you can't just sit back and wait for your phone to ring with lucrative offers. Even if you're very good. Even, in fact, if you're great. You'll still have to let the world know what you have to offer, find paying clients, and convince them to hire *you* rather than another talented musician or band.

No matter how good a musician you are, you still have to create your own career, step by step, job by job. No one will be standing by to tell you what to do next. Even if you do have someone to help direct your career—a manager, for instance—you'll still have to be alert and do much of the thinking yourself. An agent, for example, might book jobs for you, but you'll have to oversee his work, and be sure that he is helping *your* career and not just his own. And, of course, you're the one in the spotlight who'll be judged by the audience or client. No one

else can take that heat for you.

The bottom line is this: everybody who plays for pay faces the same situation—Van Cliburn, Michael Jackson, Waylon Jennings—or you. *You create your career as you go, and you're always searching for people who'll pay to hear you perform.*

That, in a nutshell, is what makes professional music such a challenge—you're always looking for venues, searching for gigs, keeping your eyes and ears open for a deal. If you're rich and famous you're looking for another record contract or concert tour, trying to stay in the fickle spotlight of public attention. If you're a beginner looking for work on a local level, you're doing the same thing: seeking out a paying job. You're just doing it all yourself—and on a different scale, of course.

In fact, you very well may work harder than your friend who goes to work for a large corporation—and you may make less money. You may have less security, and you probably won't get a company car or paid vacation.

But despite all that, you may be happier. You'll be your own boss, set your own hours, and—most important of all—be doing exactly what you want to do with your time and life. You'll be making a living doing what you love—making music.

GETTING THERE

The world of music isn't the same as the marketplace, and that's what this book is about. For many musicians it's very difficult to make the transition from being a *good* musician to being a *successful* musician. How can you move from the garage to a gig, from practice to performance, from amateur to professional?

This book will help you take charge of your career. It will:

■ Show you what professional music is really like—how it differs from "normal" jobs, what to expect from a music career, the rules of etiquette you should know, and the rules for success in the music business. Interviews with four professional freelancers, a psychologist, and a sales expert provide additional advice and insights from their experience.

■ Describe a simple but effective marketing system that you can use to sell your music regardless of where you live or what instrument you play.

■ Give you lots of practical, hands-on advice about the business side of professional music—knowledge that's crucial to your success.

■ Explore key personality traits and attitudes that are helpful—because sometimes how you act is more important than how you play.

This isn't a book about how to play, or what to play. There are other places to learn that. And this book isn't about how to become a star—there are other books that purport to teach you that as well. This book *is* for all the freelance musicians who know they could make money, part- or full-time, from their talents, but who need guidance in moving from practice rooms to professional performing. And, it's for the professional who wants to stay out of those dangerous ruts and find new and exciting places to play. New jobs bring new challenges and a fresh sense of accomplishment . . . and help your bank account as well.

Can you do it? Can you build a career as a successful musician? The methods described in this book will help you on the interesting road to freelance success. Try the *Personal Music Marketing System,* described in Chapter Six, and see if it doesn't lead you to lots more jobs, and a more successful career. I can promise that it works because I've done it, and I have dozens of friends and colleagues around the country who have succeeded in freelance music by working systematically at it, too. You can control your career and create opportunities; you'll find that the music business doesn't have to be a matter of luck. You'll learn to find opportunity where you live, because despite popular misconceptions, the path to success in music does not require a recording contract.

Don't just while your life away, enjoying your music but wishing you could make more money. You can. This book shows you how to move from "wishing" to working.

ONE

FROM GARAGE TO GIGS

Let's say you've played the guitar since you were twelve years old. You're pretty good, too—you know lots of hot licks from today's hits, and dozens of oldies. You've spent hours practicing even though you'd rather jam. You have a stack of guitar magazines and hundreds of records, tapes, and CDs.

You have friends in bands who make pretty good money and have lots of fun with their music. You'd like to do what they do—in fact, you'd like to make a career of performing. You dream about playing music every night. Who knows? Maybe you could even be a star. Surely you're good enough.

But right now you'd just like to get in a band, find some jobs, and make some money. You'd like to become a professional musician, but you don't really know how.

Or maybe you're already a part-time professional; you're in a band that works a night or two a week. Things aren't bad, but you'd like to work more with the band, make more money, and eventually quit your day job for a full-time music career.

Or perhaps you're even playing full-time, but you feel like you're coasting, going nowhere. You know you're not making progress, not moving in any direction but you don't know what to do about it.

Both beginners and professionals need two things to build a music career—a clear, honest view of the business, and a plan of action. We all need to see where we are and know where we're going.

LOOK BEFORE YOU LEAP

If you're just starting your music career you need to know what the music business is *really* like. First of all, forget what you read in *Rolling Stone* and *People,* and what you see on MTV. Those world-famous musicians are not typical. The really famous players at the top of the pop, classical, rock, country, and jazz charts are only a fraction of the hundreds of thousands of working musicians. And, even if your video *does* make it to MTV, that kind of success won't make your career—it's just another step in a lifelong progression. Sometimes striving for fame is like searching for pie in the sky—it may not be there, and even if it is, it may not be the panacea you'd hoped for.

There's a vast difference between being a great musician, or even a *famous* musician, and succeeding in the music business. The key word here is *business.* When you offer your talents for pay, you join a long line of players and singers, stretching back to at least Biblical times, and you'll face the very same pressures that have always affected musicians.

In the Bible, King David calls for his musicians to play a soothing song. It's not mentioned what the musicians wanted to play, but it's clear that they were working *for the King,* playing the kind of music that he needed. Not much has changed; doing the bidding of your employer is still the essence of the professional musician's life. So before you spend days and weeks in seclusion in your garage, working on your chops and developing an attitude that looks awesome in the mirror, review what the professional's life is really like. There's more to it than leaping around the stage, doing the split with your guitar.

The Freelance Musician's Life

A lot is wonderful about the music business, but to be honest there are difficulties and problems as well. Despite electronics and sophisticated instruments, we're still a lot like the vagabond musicians of the Middle Ages who roamed around Europe, playing for their suppers. A drummer in Atlanta calls it "the good, the bad, and the desperate:"

The good:

■ You're doing what you want to do. Playing is the most important thing in your life — and what could be better than doing it for a living?

■ You're making at least a decent living. Maybe the money's not great but it's usually pretty good.

■ There's a chance, though to be honest it's pretty remote, that you could become rich and famous.

■ You're on stage, in the spotlight, and it's exciting to be the center of attention. You don't have to play Carnegie Hall to enjoy applause and appreciation.

■ You're part of a small, very select, group — professional musicians — that values good playing. You either have what it takes to succeed — talent, ability, and hours of practice — or you don't, and it's a

great feeling to belong to a truly exclusive fraternity, bound by talent.

■ You don't have to go to work every day. (As you read on, you'll see that this isn't literally true; you may not go to an *office* every day, but your career will require steady effort.)

The bad:

■ You're not building a career — you're just playing a gig. You're always two weeks' notice away from unemployment.

■ You're always looking for another job, another client, another place to play. Thus, you can never relax.

■ Usually, there are no benefits — no paid vacations, company insurance, and certainly no company car.

■ You're performing for people who will never know as much about music as you do, but they're paying you; your boss is rarely a musician. And the boss' goals probably aren't the same as yours — maybe he wants to fill his nightclub and make money, while you just want to play good music.

■ Often, you're playing music you don't really like — sometimes even music you hate — because that's what the jobs require. You are forced to subordinate your own preferences to the needs of the job.

■ You have to do everything yourself — find jobs, keep up your music, hold the band together, do a lot of paperwork — in short, you're creating a career with very little outside help.

■ Working conditions are not always great — long and late hours, loud music, lots of smoke, poor sound systems, lousy pianos, drunken audiences.

The desperate:

■ Music, especially pop music, changes

very quickly, and you have to keep up. If you dislike what's hot or don't play it well, you can be left far behind.

■ Many musicians just lay back, take it easy, and never develop any business skills. Thus, surviving in the real-world marketplace is a continuing struggle. Being without money, however, isn't noble, and being poor doesn't qualify you for membership in the struggling artist's club. Being without money is depressing and eventually debilitating.

■ The constant stress of finding jobs, keeping up with what's new, and pleasing nonmusical clients often leads to burnout. You've seen musicians who played as if they were asleep, without any spark of enjoyment. It's a danger for all of us.

■ Drugs and alcohol are often a part of the music world, and they have ruined too many talented musicians.

Moving Up

It's not easy to create a career as a professional musician, but that's where this book can help. It can be done.

For hundreds of thousands of self-employed people, including musicians, the difficulties are more than balanced by the freedom to go your own way, create your own lifestyle, and not be bound by the daily grind of a regular job. It's not easy being a freelance musician, but neither is it easy being a carpenter, or an architect, or a freelance interior designer; yet every city is filled with professionals who'd rather work for themselves than for someone else.

If you're interested in this kind of challenge, the next question to ask is, "What does it take to succeed?"

A SUCCESSFUL FREELANCE CAREER

One problem with being a musician is that it's so easy to fall into a fairly successful

pattern that you never really do any long-range planning. One job just leads to another, and another, and pretty soon the years are whizzing by. Suddenly you're forty-five years old, doing the same thing you did at eighteen, with the same amount of money in the bank.

For freelance musicians and other artists, building careers requires awareness, work, and planning. There is no corporate ladder to climb, and no set path to success. Luck plays a part, of course, but mostly you have to figure out what to do to advance your career—and then do it yourself.

Some of the things you'll have to do will be new to you, and some will be difficult. For example, as you build your music career, from time to time you'll wear the following hats:

■ *Salesperson.* You'll find clients who need your music and convince them to buy.

■ *Secretary.* You'll type letters, contracts, and you'll keep up with all kinds of business details.

■ *Accountant.* You'll send invoices, keep up with all your financial matters, tax records, subcontractors, and so on.

■ *Advertising/Public relations specialist.* You'll write brochures and other information about your band, create demo tapes, and think of creative ways to promote your music.

■ *Psychologist/Counselor.* If you work in a band you'll find lots of opportunities to solve personal problems within the group, and with clients and audiences. You must learn to balance creative needs with business roles and personal needs.

These are just a few of the different things you'll do, and you'll have to do them well to keep moving forward and stay ahead of your competition. This book, and others listed in the appendix, will help you develop the skills you need.

Does this sound interesting to you, like a challenge or a puzzle that you'd like to tackle? Or does it scare you or seem like too much work? Actually, you're probably already doing lots of these tasks without thinking about them, and others will come almost naturally as your career progresses.

The Freelance Personality

At the most basic level, there are two approaches to being a musician. You can work for someone else, or you can work for yourself. Musicians who work for someone else include school music teachers, band directors, choral directors, armed forces band members, and symphony musicians. They aren't self-employed (although they may play outside freelance jobs), so their career decisions are usually easier. They have much greater security than other musicians, but in return they usually work a forty-hour week and have to fit into a bureaucratic system.

For many musicians, particularly classical players, this is an excellent career choice, for it allows them to make a living in music without worrying about where the next dollar will come from. On the other hand, most salaried musicians will never get rich, and their paths are pretty cut-and-dried. They don't have the freedom, challenges, and excitement of a freelance career.

Musicians who work for themselves are "freelancers," and this includes almost everyone else who makes money from music. All kinds of bands, single acts, and performers find places to play for pay, and we create our careers as we go along. We don't have the security of regular jobs, and we don't have an easy-to-follow career path, either. But these difficulties are balanced by the satisfaction of doing it our way. We have the freedom to go in any direction, spend our time the way we want to, and work as hard—or as little—as we like.

Most musicians, in fact, are freelancers at least some of the time. We play jobs of every sort—nightclubs, concerts, private parties, recitals, anything at all that pays money. So we all face the same kind of problems, pressures, and decisions.

As you move from amateur status to professional, from the garage to the gig, or from the church choir to the stage, you'll need lots of inner strengths to draw on. It may surprise you, but the most important part of your professional life will probably not be your musical ability, although that's extremely important. The real requirements of the freelance musician's life are the same as those for any self-employed entrepreneur. Because, in fact, that's what you are. You work for yourself, so you are *self-employed;* and you are taking risks to build a career, so you're an *entrepreneur.*

This book will teach you lots of the nonmusical secrets of freelance success. Perhaps the most basic idea is that nobody else is going to take care of your business for you. Welcome to the real world.

Throughout this book, there are certain principles, called "Rules to Remember." Here is the first one.

Rule to Remember:
You must work to build your own career because no one else cares as much about it as you do.

What Does It Take?

You wake up Monday morning with an empty week before you. There's no band job until Friday night . . . so what do you do with all that time? Watch MTV? Listen to music? Jam with your friends? Sleep?

"I think I'll just hang out, today," you say. "Tomorrow we might have a band rehearsal. And, really, I'm not very interested in all this other stuff—I'd rather play my guitar."

Hanging out and playing your guitar is great, but unless you are an intergalactic major talent with lots of luck you can't build a career by just sitting back and waiting for the phone to ring.

What do you need, then, to succeed? You need to:

Be able to produce a marketable product. If what you're selling just isn't needed, or isn't good enough, then you'll have to rethink your plans. Professional competence is the starting point for building a career in performing, and if you don't have the talent or the will to make yourself practice, then you don't have much chance in the music marketplace. You don't have to be a virtuoso, but you have to be good.

Have a realistic view of your music and the market. People have to need, and be willing to buy, what you're selling. There may be very little market in rural Arkansas, for example, for a Renaissance Music Consort, and all the work in the world won't enable you to make a living there with a viola da gamba. You must have a realistic sense of the market and be able to look at the "big picture" and not just your own needs of the moment.

Have a clear goal. You should know where you want to go and keep that goal constantly in mind. Your goal could be financial or musical. In any case, your success depends on clearly understanding what you want to do. See the interview with Dr. Morgan Worthy on page 9 and freelance pianist Lee J. Howard on page 122 for more on realistic goal-setting.

Be willing to work hard. You've practiced many exacting hours, so you know you aren't afraid of hard work, but you'll need to work just as diligently at building your career. Does that mean you won't be able to sleep till noon every day? You'll have to answer that for yourself, but few successful freelancers in any field are lazy.

Be self-motivated. No one else can build your career for you, and nobody else cares as much as you do about what happens to you. In short, if you want to be a successful musician and you have the talent, then it's up to you. You'll have to figure out the path you should take—and get out of bed each morning to work on your plan.

Be willing to take risks. If you're your own boss then you are in control of your own destiny, and that can be scary. The safe way—working for someone else—is often the easiest, but if you're a freelancer then you must be willing to risk your own time, effort, and money to build your career.

Be able to face rejection. You won't always win the audition or get the job. You must be able to learn from each experience and move on, and you must be able to separate your music from the rest of your life.

Be willing to stick to your career plans. Building a career takes time, and success won't happen overnight. If you can hang in there, however, your chances for success are much greater.

Be able to work with people. Musicians provide a service, and when the client pays you, he calls the tune. Your bosses will often be nonmusicians, or musicians in areas other than yours, and you'll have to work with them—even if what they need isn't exactly what you'd prefer.

Working It Out

So, do you have to be a rip-roaring self-starter to succeed as a freelance musician? Of course not. There are exceptions to every rule, and you might be just that rare person who is the only decent keyboard player within a hundred miles. Maybe all you have to do is answer the phone and book as many jobs as you can play.

But that's not the way it usually works. Most freelance musicians will have to work at building a career, finding jobs, creating publicity, and all the other tasks that go into running a successful one-person business.

Here are some reasons that you can't lay back.

■ *Competition* gets more intense every year, as thousands of new musicians graduate from colleges and music schools. And, of course, anyone with a guitar or keyboard who plays a gig at the local bar and grill can be called a "professional."

■ *Your rates may be higher* than those of the new kid in town, and you'll have to work to prove you're worth the extra money. Your clients must be educated (and constantly reeducated) about the value of your music.

■ *Other sources of entertainment are in-creasingly available* to your clients, and they may opt to use recorded music or a nonmusical act for their evening's entertainment. Someone has to convince them to use live music, and further, to use *you*.

■ *Clients have short memories*, and you'll have to remind them of your presence. "What have you done for me *lately*," isn't just a cliché, but a fact of life in the music business.

■ *Music changes constantly*, and you'll have to work to keep up. Reading professional magazines, updating your equipment, and learning current tunes will keep you busy.

If you pursue a freelance music career, you'll find, like any small businessperson, that the more you put into your freelancing, the more you'll get back. If you are self-motivated, hard working, and develop some of the traits Dr. Worthy discusses in the following interview, you'll probably end up working more, making more money, and being a happier person. It's up to you.

SUCCESS STRATEGIES FOR FREELANCE MUSICIANS

INTERVIEW WITH DR. MORGAN WORTHY

Dr. Worthy is a counseling psychologist at Georgia State University who works extensively with entrepreneurs. He has discovered some useful techniques that successful self-employed people often share.

Q *What can self-employed freelance musicians do to establish good work habits?*
A Without the routine of going to an office, establishing regular work routines can be very difficult. It's often helpful to actually make your tasks into daily *habits* that you automatically expect to do—but this isn't easy to accomplish. One thing that helps you establish helpful habits is called the *Premack Principle*. It works like this: you find something you already do every day, and make doing that contingent on doing a new thing. For example, if you want to establish the habit of calling two clients every day, you might link that task to, say, having your morning cup of coffee. You might just stick a note on your coffee maker that says "call clients," and not have any coffee until you've called those clients. If you follow this procedure every day, you'll soon develop the new habit and you'll automatically call clients before you enjoy your morning coffee. It sounds artificial, but it works.

Maybe musicians would link a new task to listening to music, or playing their instruments. Just write "clients," or whatever your new task is, on a piece of tape and stick it to your tape player or instrument—and *do* the new task before listening to music. It works very well to establish new habits, especially if you set yourself a time limit; two or three weeks is often effective.

Q *What about goal-setting? How important is it for self-employed people?*

A Goal-setting can be very important because it is one way to "keep score" of how you're doing. Maybe your goal is to improve your playing through practice. That's a fine desire, but it's too vague, because goal-setting works best when it is *concrete—something you can count*. So, make it specific. You can make your goal to practice two hours a day, call four clients, or write six letters, but it should be a definite number. Further, an effective goal should be relatively narrow and clearly defined. It's easy to get lost in complexity if your goal is too broad or not definite enough. "Improving my business," won't work because it's too vague, but "making two calls to clients every day," will since it's a concrete number—and it will lead, if you do it, to improving your business.

Research has shown that an effective goal-setting method is to devise a way of keeping cumulative records—a chart works well. This sometimes seems contrived, but a chart of your achievements on the wall by your desk will clearly show your progress. Maybe you start your freelance music business on the first of June, and with a chart you can see *exactly* how many phone calls you've made to clients, for example. Or how many letters you've written, how many sales calls you've made, and so on. Make it graphic, use colors, and you'll be able to *see your forward movement*, and that will encourage you to more effort. It gives you a sense of positive direction, and shows you, in concrete form, the results of your actions. It's important, though, to only plot *success* on your graph, to only illustrate your positive achievements. Seeing the graphic results of your efforts moving upward on a chart is always inspiring.

Q *How do you set goals?*

A There's a trick to doing it right. You need to set them high enough that you'll feel good about reaching them, but low enough so that you have a good chance to attain them — and you keep setting those kinds of goals. Thus, cumulatively, you'll be moving up all the time.

If you don't set the right goal, though, this process can be counterproductive. For example, we may start a new project with so much enthusiasm that we set very difficult, even unrealistic goals, stay with it a bit, and then give up. Really, then, the whole idea of setting goals is to set moderate goals so you'll keep at it and pace yourself. It may help to set long-term goals, too, but work actively toward *intermediate* goals, or stepping-stones. Ask yourself, "What can I do *today* to work toward this objective?"

The bottom line is this: if your goal leads you to do something today to reach that goal, then it's useful. If, on the other hand, it's too big to translate into immediate action it won't help you. In that case you should break it down, work on it some more, and say, "Okay, here are some steps I can take now, today."

Q *What can self-employed freelance musicians do to stay motivated?*

A One of the difficult things about working alone is that you don't have other people to build you up. Rarely, someone will be so self-assured that he or she won't need a support structure, but most of us do.

One psychological idea that helps explain why some self-employed people do well and others do poorly is called the "locus of control." That is, do you think that the outcome of your life depends on the outside world or on you? Do you feel that what *you* think and do can make a difference, or do you think that your success depends on uncontrollable factors like luck? I think most of the people who are out there making it as freelance musicians are people who believe that what they do will make a difference. Thus they are motivated to work and achieve. Other people feel that external forces — the market, club owners, booking agents, forces you really can't control — determine their success or failure. Such people would ask, "Why bother to work on my career? It's not in my control, anyway."

If you have an "internal locus of control," you're saying that your goal-setting, your desire and work, your motivation make the difference. Research has shown that successful people — high achievers — tend to perceive themselves as determining the outcome of their lives, whereas people who do not succeed are locked in more to the idea that the outside world determines their course.

Q *Freelance musicians often feel a lot of stress — both in performing and in managing their careers. Do you have any suggestions for managing stress?*

A An effective way to lower stress is to not take complete, total responsibility for everything. If you're an "internal locus of control" kind of person, it is possible for you to overdo that idea and put lots of extra tension on yourself, even to the point where you feel guilty. It's important for these people to realize that, in fact, external events *do* make a difference — business *may* be bad this year, or in your town, or an audience *may* not appreciate the quality of your music. There are just some things you can't control, and you have to realize that.

The trick here is to let this knowledge lower your stress levels without lowering your motivation, and that's a balancing act. You want to take responsibility without getting into self-blame. If you get into a state where you're punishing yourself for failing, that's bad. So, if a few sales calls fail, for example, you might blame yourself — and that will have a very negative impact on your motivation to make more sales calls. Our attitudes influence stress; it's not just what happens, it's also how we interpret it.

Q *What about the kind of stress that comes from overwork, the constant feeling that you have a dozen things to do,* right now?
A One way to handle this kind of pressure is to learn to pace yourself so you're never going at 100 percent speed, never working as hard as you can so that "one more thing" will push you over the edge. Obviously, if you're working as hard as you can, already stretched to your limit, then you're in a dangerous situation because one mistake, one more problem, one more deadline may really make you sick or cause other potentially serious problems.

The key here is to find ways to moderate your activities. We need a certain amount of stress, but we must control it — and when we do it becomes a "challenge" and not a "stress." Here, *pacing* is important. Doing the kind of work that musicians do, especially freelancers, it would be very easy to do nothing at all some days. And if you're working hard sometimes and not at all other times, this inconsistency can become a big problem. That, honestly, is one advantage of having an office job. You are forced to have a certain amount of continuity — to go to work every day, for example. Working alone has lots of advantages, but one deadly disadvantage is that the lack of consistency, of pacing, of regularly done tasks, can put destructive pressure on you if you don't balance all your tasks well.

So, spread them out. Plan what you have to do, get organized, and direct your efforts. For example, if you're busy writing sales letters, you don't have to interrupt that to answer the phone. Let your answering machine do it, and return the call at *your* convenience. That's managing your time and your work — and that way you won't feel the burden of stopping what you're doing, breaking your train of thought, rushing over to the phone, and maybe dealing with that caller's problems. Pace yourself, and you'll

reduce stress.

Q *Musicians have to face frequent rejection, criticism, and maybe failure. What can they do about that?*
A First, remember that failure and criticism can be a learning experience. Of course, they can also be devastating. The fact is, that we're all going to have failures and mistakes, some things just aren't going to work. One way to deal with this is to see such a failure for what it is — a limited event — instead of viewing it as total inadequacy. Thus, if you have a poor performance one night you should say to yourself, "Gee, I didn't play well Saturday night." Maybe you were tired, or got started badly, or were worrying about your car — who knows? But it was just *that* Saturday night, it wasn't your career.

But, if you process that poor performance in a negative way and say, "I'm just no good, I won't ever be good, and my playing tonight proves it," then you make it into something significant about you as a person rather than just Saturday night's performance. Doing that will add stress, tear down your self-image, and reduce your confidence.

So when things are bad, and they sometimes will be, try to limit them in time. Things aren't always bad, they were just bad *at that time*. This way, you limit the depressing results by gaining perspective.

A big problem for musicians and other artists, I think, is learning how to separate your playing from your self, to keep criticism of your performance from destroying your self-confidence. If you're going to improve as a musician you've got to have feedback and criticism; that's one way you grow. A good way to keep your balance during criticism is to see your performance as a kind of "experiment." To grow, you have to get into trial and error, and it helps to think of your performances, then, as trials. "I'll try playing this passage that way and see how it works." And, if it doesn't work or you get criticized, it's not a devastating event for you—after all, it was just an experiment. Next time, perhaps you'll play it differently—another experiment—and see what happens. That way, each performance isn't a life-or-death matter.

Of course, it's difficult not to take criticism personally, but if you know that you don't have to, say, play a song a particular way, that there are various ways to do it and you're trying just one of them, then it's an investigation, an exploration, a sample—and such experiments always generate feedback.

What you gain from that approach is credibility. If your critic knocks you off balance with his comments, then automatically he gains power and you lose it. But, on the other hand, if he says "Don't play that—it sounds terrible," and you respond, "Okay, how about doing it this way?" then you gain power and status. You weren't decimated by his negative comments; in fact, you weren't even fazed by them, and you just cycle on to another way to play that passage. Rather than get angry or hurt, your attitude is thus very professional.

Q *How can freelancers cope with being "on their own" without the support structure of, say, an office, co-workers, and a boss?*
A Networks of people in our lives are helpful. For most people, such networks are passive—they're usually there automatically. Office jobs, for example, come with a built-in network. But independent people, like freelance musicians, may have to go out and create their support networks. They can't be passive about it because that's one of the definitions of being an independent, self-employed person—they work, essentially, alone.

So, you may have to ask yourself, "Who are the people that make me feel good, the people I need? Who is important to me?" Think of your network as an "investment" and work to build relationships with the people you need. That may sound contrived—establishing friendships because we need them—but contrived or not, most of us need networks of other people. You may have to identify and cultivate people you need.

Your own mood, for example, may fluctuate, but other people in your network will help keep you balanced. If you play badly on Saturday night and you go home and you're by yourself, you may continue to brood on everything you did wrong in your performance. On the other hand, if you go out with friends, you're much more likely to keep it in perspective.

Q *How can musicians reduce conflict within bands and groups?*
A If you're always together in situations that are high-pressure and stressful, then you should build in some time to be together that's *not* so stressful. You may find that people are resistant to that and may not want to do it—it may seem artificial—but spending nonstress time together can really help.

My son, for example, plays in a band, and one thing they do together is go out as a group to hear other bands. I think that helps them; they're not on stage, they're not under pressure. They can sit back and relax and I think it helps the camaraderie in their own band to spend that time together. It gives them a chance, in a relaxed setting, to broaden their relationships and defuse tensions before they become problems.

Similarly, large corporations often arrange for their executive staffs to go to special outdoor programs that are very different from the daily office routine so the participants can get to know one another in a totally different way. It helps in day-to-day interaction to occasionally get completely away from the routine, whether it's an every-night band job or an office situation. Such contact eases work pressure, builds deeper and broader relationships, and brings a new perspective to the group.

So, any structure you come up with will help. Support groups, friends, colleagues you can talk with about the business problems you have, help you keep moving and pace yourself. They encourage you. You see, if a freelance musician feels a little bad one day, it's easy to just do nothing at all that day, where if he had an office job, he'd go on to work. If he's not careful, the do-nothing syndrome will take over, and in this sense freelance life isn't especially easy. With care, however, you can cope with the problems and take advantage of the positive aspects of being your own boss.

DO YOU HAVE WHAT IT TAKES?

As a freelance musician you'll always have questions and doubts. Even though you've worked for years to prepare, and you've decided that your personality is up to the challenges, you'll still ask:

"Am I good enough? How will I react if they reject me and hire someone else? Will they like me—or laugh at my performance?"

"How much equipment do I need? Other musicians spend thousands of dollars on new instruments, but I can't really afford that right now. Can I work as a musician without all the latest gear?"

When you're selling something as personal as your own talent, you will always have lots of worries about your ability—questions that are especially difficult for beginning musicians. This chapter offers some answers.

AM I GOOD ENOUGH?

This is the most basic concern you'll face, and ultimately the solution is simple: if people will pay to hear you perform, you're good enough.

But, there's more to it than that, and there's no single answer, either. What's good enough for a rural one-night stand could be inadequate in a big city studio, and many small-town professionals may not be good enough for New York, Las Vegas,

Nashville, or Los Angeles. How can you know if you're good enough? Here are some suggestions.

1. *Visit the kinds of jobs you'd like to play*; listen and watch closely. How good are the players who are doing what you'd like to do? How extensive is their repertoire? Are you close to their performance level, or are they light-years ahead of you in proficiency and musicianship? Notice what and how well they're playing. Which styles should you master? Are the musicians reading or improvising? Could you rely on a "fake book," or must you know the tunes without charts? How do other successful bands do it, with sheet music or without?

2. *Ask questions.* Talk to musicians you know and meet others. Tell them what you want to do and get their advice. Many musical jobs seem more intimidating at first than they really are, and many (though not all) musicians are happy to help new players get started.

3. *Study the repertoire.* Find out what tunes you *must* know, and be sure you have them mastered. (This will be your "core repertoire," and will be discussed further in Chapter Three.) If you're a classical guitarist looking for work in a Spanish restaurant, you know you'll have to play "Malagueña," for instance. If you're a country fiddle

player, you've got to be able to impress them with your "Orange Blossom Special." Pop guitarists, similarly, need to know whatever is on the charts right now.

4. *Master the basics first*, and then work on the flashy, fun stuff. Learning hot licks or showy solos is great—but be absolutely sure that you do the basic things well. For drummers, for example, this means keeping a perfectly steady beat in whatever style you're playing. For keyboard players, being able to comp easily behind soloists in different keys is crucial. Bass players must be able to play steady walking patterns in different feels before working on solos at all. Don't forget, most of the time you're a team player and a three-point shot is worthless unless you can also dribble and pass the ball.

5. *Study the nonmusical keys to performing.* You'll be on stage and in the spotlight whether you want to be or not, so get ready. If you sing, be sure you know the lyrics and how to work a microphone. Understand the basics—by knowing the structure of a song you'll know when to sing and when to leave space for an instrumental solo. Audiences sense nervousness; confidence comes from really knowing what you're doing.

Getting Better

Maybe you think you're ready to play for pay, but you want to work on your music, repertoire, showmanship, or professionalism. Or perhaps you're already a professional musician, but you'd like to improve. Where do you go for help?

High-tech learning is a good place to start. Use home audiovisual equipment to review your performance. Tape record your playing or singing, and listen carefully. Wait a day or two to see how you sound. Don't be too critical, but be realistic about the important aspects of your performance.

Thus, if you're a singer, listen carefully to your pitch, inflections, and phrasing. If you're a drummer, check your time with a

metronome from a performance tape, not a practice session. Flashy solos and expensive equipment won't help if you rush or drag badly. Guitarists, keyboard players, horn players—virtually every musician—can learn from tapes of their performances because you don't always notice your own mistakes and weaknesses while you're playing. But listening to yourself on tape can quickly show you what needs work. You'll probably say, "Oh, no! Do I really sound like that?" Tapes can be brutal but effective aids to improvement.

Next, if possible, use a video camera to see how you look, especially if you're interacting with the audience—and most musicians are. A few videotape sessions will quickly reveal any amateurish habits. (Don't, however, replace your natural approach with a plastic show-biz manner; you certainly don't want to look like Arnie Artificial, the lounge lizard. There is a nice middle ground between amateurish awkwardness and artificial pretension.)

If you don't have a video camera, look for a friend who has one. Maybe you could even find a college student majoring in Communications who could videotape you for class credit. You probably don't need to hire an expensive "image consultant" or professional video producer for this kind of work, though. You aren't after top video quality here; you just need to see yourself as others see you.

A good way to quickly gain playing experience is the use of such "play-along" records as Music Minus One, Drum Drops, or the Jamey Aebersold series (see Appendix C). These recordings feature top-quality players with your part missing; this way you can play along with the best and judge your performance against world-class standards.

All musicians can improve; none of us reach the point of perfection where we're finally good enough to quit practicing—but don't overdo it either. You can practice yourself into paranoia.

Keep your perspective by remembering how pop records are made. Days or weeks of overdubbing, adding tracks and enhancements, and "punching-in" to cover mistakes assure that every recording will be flawless. Even classical piano albums have been pieced together from several recording sessions to get the best possible performance, and it's not fair to judge your performance by this contrived perfection. In fact, it could be dangerous to copy album practices too closely; all the breath sounds are edited out of some female pop stars' recordings, so it sounds as if they never breathe. Not only is it not live—it's not real, so don't set your standards too high.

Learning from Others

There is no need to reinvent the wheel, and finding a good teacher can save you lots of time and wasted effort. In fact, a tutor or coach can move you along faster than many hours in the practice room, but you've got to find the right one.

It may not be enough to just learn your instrument through traditional channels, though you do need to master it, of course. If you're working toward becoming a professional, your teacher should understand your goals, special needs, and your kind of music. Truthfully, most classically trained teachers won't understand or enjoy pop music, so they may have little relevance to your aims.

Finding an appropriate teacher can be difficult. First, define exactly what you need to learn. If you just want to improve your reading, theory, or technique, you'll probably be able to find plenty of capable help. If, however, you want to learn pop, jazz, rock, or computer/MIDI programming, for example, then you'll have a smaller selection of experts, and you may have to interview several teachers before you find one who can really help you.

This is especially true for musicians who need to work on improvisation, which in many commercial situations is a crucial skill. Many traditional music teachers can't improvise themselves, so they certainly can't teach you how to do it. And many excellent professionals just "play naturally" without much conscious effort, and that's not much help.

Often, you may profit by taking lessons from a working professional who isn't primarily a teacher. Be sure, though, that the pro knows how to teach, communicates well, and can demonstrate, step by step, new playing concepts. Talk to the best players in your area to get leads on appropriate teachers, and investigate schools devoted to your kind of music.

Where else can you find teachers? For traditional ones, ask at sheet music stores and local college music departments. There may be a piano teachers' federation, for example, listed in the Yellow Pages, and they can recommend teachers in your area. For nontraditional instruction, ask other musicians, check at music (instrument) stores, and look for ads in alternative newspapers— Atlanta's *Creative Loafing*, for instance, has an entire classified section devoted to musical instruction.

Many college music programs now offer jazz and pop music courses and even degrees, and these may be excellent places to improve your skills. Remember, though, that performing for pay is different from performing in a school setting, and *keep your focus on developing the skills you know you'll need in the marketplace.*

For example, the market for jazz saxophonists who play atonal, complex, nonmelodic solos is not large, so even if your first love is jazz, it will help your career if you also absorb as much as you can about the pop/rock world. It's a hard lesson to learn, but your real-world audiences often won't care about your finely crafted solos; they may want to hear simple, trite, but well-known licks from rock hits.

In finding instructional help, then, be sure that what you learn will be applicable to your career.

Still Worried?

You're working on your playing, your repertoire, and performance details, but you're still anxious. What if they *don't* like you? What if they laugh when you sit down to play? What if you *don't* win the audition?

Rejection is never easy to take, but it's a part of the music business. It's difficult to do, but you have to develop a thick skin and a realistic, street-wise attitude. Once you *know* you're good enough—and eventually you'll know—then rejection won't devastate you. It still won't be pleasant, but you'll survive.

Actors and television talent who go to several auditions a week learn that rejection is simply a fact of life, and for them it may have little to do with ability. Perhaps they're too short, too tall, or don't have the right "look." They survive the meat market without too much trauma—and so can you.

Why would anyone reject your band or your own act? There are lots of reasons, including:

■ *You aren't exactly what the client wanted.* If your kind of music doesn't fit his needs, he won't hire you, and it has nothing to do with your ability or quality.

■ *The economic law of supply and demand.* He could only hire one band, and seven were after the job. Thus, six were rejected. Maybe they were all great, but the client, unfortunately, only needed *one.*

■ *You cost too much.* Sometimes people expect miracles for tiny budgets, and there will be times when you'll be rejected because you won't work cheap. Don't be tempted by those low-budget jobs; they're usually the worst ones, and you won't respect yourself in the morning after playing it, anyway.

■ *The client really doesn't know what's good.* More often than we'd like, music is bought for the wrong reasons—the clients are not educated musicians. Maybe Band X plays out of tune, but the client won't recognize that. He knows they'll get the crowd dancing, and that's all he cares about.

■ *Miscellaneous factors beyond your control.* There are lots of other reasons that you might be rejected. Perhaps Band X's singer is the client's daughter. Maybe they've played this party for three years and the client likes them. Or who knows, maybe Band X is paying a "finder's fee" under the table to get the job.

Who knows why you don't get every job? Ultimately, you must learn that you *will* be rejected. Don't take it personally because most rejection isn't personal. It's just a fact of life in the music business—and in most others, too. Architects don't get every job they bid on either.

Finally, worst of all, what if they laugh at you? That's one of the worst fears anyone has—to be the object of derision. While it won't usually happen, it can. Here are two useful approaches to this nagging worry.

First, most of the time when there's laughter in the audience, it's not directed at you. When you're playing in a nightclub, for example, people are trying to have fun—and that involves lots of laughing. Ninety-nine percent of the time, it has nothing at all to do with you.

Once in a while, though, someone will be ill-mannered enough to make fun of you. It may be a yuppie accountant who is insecure but trying to impress his date. Such laughter is irrelevant to your own self-image, and you must learn to slough it off and ignore it.

And, of course, people who are drinking aren't known for subtlety or impeccable taste. If they harass you, heckle you, or laugh at you, you might learn from watching seasoned comedians perform—but you probably shouldn't try for witty comebacks and devastating repartee unless you're really experienced at such quick-thinking actions. Usually, you can ignore rude audiences, or maybe it's time for the band to take a break.

Remember that many audiences envy you, and they may make fun of you as an attempt to bring you down to their level. You can do something that the audience can't—play an instrument. Many—if not most—people would give a lot to be able to play for pay; if you don't believe it, visit any sing-along piano bar and watch the wistful would-be musicians with the microphone. They can't really do it—and you can. And they have to get up tomorrow and go back to their boring nine-to-five jobs. Let them smirk if they need to, because you're the one who's doing what you want to with your life, and that gives you the last laugh.

AM I FULLY EQUIPPED?

Even if you feel confident of your ability to play music professionally, you may worry about your gear. Do you have the right equipment? Is there just one more device that you absolutely have to have to be accepted as a pro?

In today's electronic, high-tech world, almost any musician could spend thousands of dollars on equipment—and be out of date tomorrow. If you're like most of us, you just don't have much extra money to spend on equipment, especially if it will soon be obsolete and replaced by nearly identical, but "new and improved" models.

The simple answer is that you need just enough equipment to be sure you can play the jobs you book. But again, there's more to it than that.

A better answer is that you need reliable equipment that's as good as the norm in your area for the jobs you do. You may also need a backup system, and possibly some peripheral devices that you'll only use occasionally. Office equipment and dependable transportation count, too.

It helps to have a sense of perspective when you're thinking about equipment and deciding what to buy next. Before you grab your checkbook and head for the local "Music R Us" outlet, stop and think about how this part of the music business operates.

The Music-Store Trap

First, realize that music today is *big business*. Selling instruments, accessories, records, and printed music adds millions of dollars to the U.S. economy and provides a good living for music store owners and their employees. Further, most music store salespeople work on commission, so the more they sell the more they make. Remember when you go into a music store that the salesperson is probably more interested in her paycheck than in your performance. That is truly the bottom line for surviving the music store trap.

Music equipment manufacturers are shrewd businesspeople, and they introduce new models frequently to make you dissatisfied with your old equipment. So, just because there's a new synthesizer out, should you go into debt to buy it? Remember, there will be another model, from another manufacturer introduced in a couple of weeks. Will you need that one, too?

To survive the equipment scramble, you must balance your purchases with a realistic view of your income and the instrument's value. You need top-quality equipment, to be sure, and the better your instrument, the better you'll play. But if you're a sax player, for instance, who sometimes doubles on flute, should you rely on a three-hundred-dollar flute, or go in debt to buy a two-thousand-dollar one? Obviously the more expensive instrument will be better, but if the three-hundred-dollar instrument plays in tune and will do the job when you need it, isn't it good enough?

So spend some time deciding what you need, and be armed with this information before you go to a music store. Don't let the salespeople talk you into buying equipment that's not on your list. Of course it's interesting to connect your synth to a computer—but is that a capability you'll actually use? Do you need to create new sounds of your own this way, or is the library of thousands of prepared synth sounds adequate? High-tech equipment, especially, is alluring, but it takes time to master, is quickly outdated, is expensive, and may not mean much to your career.

Remember that although new equipment may make it possible for you to play better, the difference in your performance may not equal the debit in your bank account. And, will the difference in your performance be noticed by other musicians, by the audience, or is it so subtle that you're the only one who'll know?

Finally, beware of the snowball effect. Here's what happened to a guitar player in Atlanta. A new guitar—the hottest one around—arrived and Eric had to have it, so he emptied his savings account and made the purchase. It was a great playing instrument . . . but to get the best sound he needed a new amp. That made things better, but the amp needed a new speaker cabinet to show what it could do—and then Eric needed a limiter and a couple of other outboard gadgets. Naturally, you can't carry around an eight-hundred-dollar amp in a paper sack, so the next purchase was a new road case. Unfortunately, the complete rig was now so heavy that he had to have a new hand truck to transport it.

With all this new equipment to carry, Eric realized that his car wasn't big enough, so he moved up to a larger size. The story may not be over yet, but at this point, the $1,200 guitar has needed musical accessor-ies that cost $2,000—and the car to carry it was $12,000.

That is a true story, and it's probably repeated in lots of forms every day around the country. Does Eric's new rig sound better than his old one? Of course it does. But does it sound $14,000 better? Does the financial burden help Eric be a happier, more successful person, or does it raise his level of stress and worry? Those are subjective questions, but they should be considered before you plunge deeply into debt.

Don't be seduced by the idea that you must own every new instrument, gizmo, gadget, or accessory that comes down the pike. There is enough equipment that you *do* really need to take lots of your money without going berserk keeping up with the music-marketplace monster.

Rule to Remember:
More equipment will not necessarily make you play better.

The Bottom Line on Equipment
Here is a list of the things that every musician needs:

1. *A dependable, first-quality instrument.* You make your living with this instrument, so get the very best you can afford.

2. *Backup equipment.* Backup equipment can be older, even second-line; maybe you don't even need to own it, if you know another musician who could lend you an instrument if yours is in the shop.

3. *Extra sets of whatever is likely to break* — and you need to have them with you. Extra strings, drum heads, guitar cords, even extension cords can be important—because such things have a way of failing in performances.

4. *Whatever clothes are appropriate to your kind of performance.* If you're playing formal jobs, that means a black tux or formal dress;

if you're in a country band, then jeans and flannel shirts may be all you need. In some situations, the appropriate dress is very important and expensive.

5. *You're in business, and every businessperson knows* that it takes money to make money—sometimes you'll have to invest in nonmusical equipment to advance your career. For example, the client may not remember the notes you play, but she will notice if your tux is worn and shiny. Read the interview with Brenda Street on page 32 to get a working musician's advice on such investments in your career.

6. *A means of moving your equipment if it is bulky or heavy.* Hand trucks or dollies are among many musicians' most useful accessories, and you'll find that good quality is as important here as it is with your instruments themselves. Cheap discount-store hand trucks are much more trouble than they're worth; visit an industrial supply house before you buy. Look around and notice how many musicians have back trouble. If you play a heavy instrument, you need either a roadie or a hand truck. Either is cheaper than back surgery.

7. *Reliable transportation.* If you can't depend on your own car, then arrange to borrow or even rent one. Getting to the job on time, every time, is the starting point for success, and stories about flat tires, dead batteries, or tie-ups on the expressway don't impress bandleaders or clients.

What if you can't afford all this necessary equipment? First, decide what you *do* need, and then search for ways to reduce the cost. Can you borrow equipment from a friend or even rent it from him? Can you rent from a store—even rent used equipment? Or couldn't you buy on a manageable time-payment plan—without limiting your purchases to new, expensive equipment? Would your parents lend you money or even

buy you an instrument to help you get started in your career? They might, if you convince them that it's an investment in your future and demonstrate to them that you're taking a businesslike approach to building your career.

Getting started isn't easy, especially today when there's lots of expensive equipment to buy, but there are ways to manage. Maybe your band could pool its resources to buy the needed sound equipment, keyboards, and so on—but be careful if you try this approach. Bands sometimes have short lives, and you should decide in advance, and preferably in writing, how to divide the equipment if one of the investors leaves or if the band breaks up. It happened to the Beatles, and it can happen to you.

Office Equipment

As you progress in your career, you'll find that your one-person business is growing and that you need office equipment as well as instruments—nonmusical, to be sure, but important to your career. Though you may not need it all now, here's an overview of office equipment the fully equipped freelance musician should have.

A telephone answering machine is no longer a luxury. You must have one (or use a telephone answering service). No musician can afford to miss calls, and your machine will always be on duty. Be sure to get a model with touch-tone remote-access capability and voice actuation that lets your callers leave as long a message as necessary. Shop carefully because quality differences are significant, and be sure that local repair services are available.

A typewriter is necessary for most musicians. You'll have to send contracts and all kinds of letters to clients and prospects, and they should look professional. Handwriting, even if it's legible, isn't acceptable in business. Excellent typewriters are much less expensive today than just a few years ago, and this is an investment that will pay off quickly. If you don't know how to type, take a course at your community college or vo-tech school, or use a self-instruction course to teach yourself.

A computer is almost a necessity today, and if you don't have one you should start educating yourself about them. You can use a computer to write letters, compose sales material, keep all kinds of records, prepare your tax returns, develop mailing lists, print mailing labels — and maybe to write and print music, as well. Computers are expensive, but wise shopping can save a lot of money — and the computer will make you more efficient and competitive. More on computers in Chapter Ten.

Miscellaneous office equipment will help you get and stay organized. The best plan is to have a room or part of a room in your house that is your office used *only* for business purposes. That can save you a lot on your tax bill, and it will help keep your business running smoothly, too.

So, you need a table or desk, a filing cabinet, a postage scale, and the usual supplies. Letterheads, stationery, and other promotional materials are discussed in detail in Chapter Thirteen.

Buying Equipment

As you can see, being fully equipped means more than just having the musical instruments you need. Don't rush out and buy everything at once unless you have plenty of money, but plan your purchases carefully. Here are some options to consider:

Buying new equipment is the easiest course, but is always the most expensive. Shop around and bargain to save money. Often, "list prices" are pure fiction; ask other musicians where the best discounts are.

Mail-order outlets advertised in music magazines can offer bargains, but read the fine print carefully and be sure there is a full, money-back guarantee. If you purchase with a credit card, you'll have more protection against unethical dealers. Remember, too, that mail-order dealers won't be around to give you the advice and instructions you may need, and local dealers often won't help you understand your mail-order purchases.

Used equipment is often a good deal. In many cities there is an active market in used music and office equipment. Be sure to examine the equipment carefully, or take a knowledgeable friend shopping with you. Being thoroughly acquainted with retail prices will also guide you. Classified ads, college music department bulletin boards, or special "shopper" publications may offer terrific bargains.

Be sure you know what you're getting, however, and don't be rushed into buying used equipment just because the price is low. A used computer may be a good deal, but it may be about to become a useless, old-fashioned device, so do your research first. You won't save money if your "bargains" are shoddy or useless and have to be replaced quickly.

Take an Inventory

You'll probably be surprised at the value of your music and office equipment, and you'll need an organized list for insurance and tax purposes.

Use the work sheet on page 22 to prepare your equipment inventory. List *every piece of equipment that you use in your business*, even the second-string instruments that you rarely need and the office machines you own. Then photocopy this list and keep the copy in a safe place. When you buy or sell equipment, record the serial and model numbers immediately; in the event of a fire, theft, or tax audit, such data is invaluable.

Keep a separate list of the equipment

EQUIPMENT INVENTORY WORK SHEET

Equipment	Model #	Serial #	Purchase Price	Where bought

you'd like to have that you can't afford right now. List these things in the order you'll need them, and try to keep your priorities straight. While it might be nice to have a new seventy-five-dollar lightweight aluminum mike stand, your more pressing need may be for a typewriter, a new tux, or a hand truck.

You'll always need more equipment; that's the nature of business, and manufacturers will always have new developments and advertising campaigns to whet your spending appetite. Do you think your office is finally well equipped? Then they'll develop personal copiers and convince you that you really need one—and maybe you do. Or they'll come up with other devices—fax machines, cellular phones, high-tech beepers, and who knows what that can break your budget in a second.

Shop Smart

Always analyze your purchases by asking, and answering, these questions:

■ *Is this purchase cost effective*? That is, will it pay for itself in a month, or a year? Will this item help you *make more money*?

■ *Do I really need this equipment*—or just want it? Remember, manufacturers have spent millions of advertising dollars to make you desperately want their products. Don't be a victim of this Madison Avenue hype.

■ *Will it help my playing or business*? Remember—new equipment won't help you play better, be more productive, or make more money. Period. Practice and experience will improve your performances. A new instrument, by itself, won't; you'll make the same mistakes and play the same way before and after your purchase, though a new instrument may *inspire* you to work harder.

■ *Can I afford it*? Your goal, ultimately, is to be happy and productive, and it's almost impossible to be stress-free when you're worried about money. Much of this book is devoted to helping you find new markets for your music and to showing how a businesslike approach can help you make more money. But another way to increase your net income is to reduce your debt, and making careful equipment purchases will really help.

THREE

GETTING STARTED

You're convinced you've got what it takes to be a professional musician. You have talent, you're learning tunes, you've practiced for hours and played several small jobs with your "garage band." You're ready to move up. Now what?

LINKING UP WITH OTHERS

Maybe you aren't in a band right now, or your garage band members aren't ready to make the plunge toward professional status. What can you do? This isn't a book about forming a band, but here are some ideas to get you started.

If you want to be a working musician, and you're a "team player," say, a drummer, then you obviously can't work by yourself. There are basically three choices for you at this point: form your own band, join an existing band, or enter the freelance market.

Form your own band. If you have a good idea of what you want to do with your group, or if your plans are unique for your area, this may be the best approach. Locate the musicians you need, get together to make your marketing and musical plans, rehearse a lot, and look for jobs. You can find the players you need through your network of friends in music, bulletin boards at music stores, union "at liberty" lists, and classified ads in alternative newspapers.

Often, bands (and musicians) exist in a semiconstant state of flux and perpetually form, break up, reform, work for a while, and break up again. If you're active in the musical community in your area, you'll know people in and out of bands and they'll know you. With some phone calls and an audition or two, you'll locate the players you need.

Rule to Remember:
Since bands come and go, don't invest your life savings in mutually owned equipment until you have worked together—and maybe not even then.

Join an existing band. Even established bands change members from time to time—compare today's "Drifters" or "Platters" with the original groups and you'll see. In most areas, except the largest cities, the music community is relatively small, and everybody knows—or has heard of—everybody else. If the word gets out that you can play and are looking for work, you'll likely get calls.

Getting the word out, however, is *your* responsibility, and there is a lot of helpful information in this book that you can apply to spreading the news that you're available. For starters, stay in circulation, get out and meet musicians, sit in if you can, and pass out lots of business cards. Put your card on bulletin boards in music stores. If you're a member, call the union and get on their "at liberty" list.

Enter the freelance market. Whether you're a team player or a soloist, you'll be looking for jobs in the "hidden music marketplace" (described in Chapter Six). Often the groups that play these jobs aren't really "regular" bands. While Band X may usually be a four-piece combo, lead by the keyboard player, there may be different drummers, bass players, and singers on different jobs. If the bandleaders who play such jobs know about you, they'll be able to hire you, and this can be a good place to get valuable experience.

In practice, of course, many musicians go for whatever they can get, especially in the beginning, and play a combination of freelance jobs and regular band work. The key to both, in addition to being a competent musician, is letting people know who you are, what you do, what a fine player you are, and how easy you are to get along with. If they don't know you, they clearly can't hire you—and even if they know you they need regular reminding.

You will find that much of the professional musician's time is spent booking jobs. Chapters Five through Ten show you how to match your talent and needs to a wide variety of gigs by developing your own *Personal Music Marketing System*.

CAREER BASICS

As important as finding jobs is, there is more to being a professional musician. This chapter discusses the basics of professional music—things every professional should know. Other chapters examine some of these subjects in detail, but here's an overview of what it means to be a pro.

Knowing the Right Stuff

As mentioned in Chapter Two, you must have attained at least the threshold of professional competence before you try to enter the job market, though you certainly don't have to be a virtuoso. You'll learn quickly on the job, but you should know these things from the beginning:

Basic repertory. The "core repertoire" is the starting point for your career—you've got to know the material. A good way to learn what these "must-know" tunes are is to talk with several working musicians and ask for their ideas, then make a list. Your tune list will be different for a new-age jazz band than for a mainstream jazz combo or a traditional jazz group, so be careful whom you ask. Similarly, a traditional country band will play different songs than a country-rock, or country-pop, or country-gospel group.

Another good approach is to visit several jobs and make a list of what is played. You'll find that most commercial music jobs rely on a core of popular tunes, and while songs come and go you'll still have to know these basics. Often such tunes are called "standards," and there can be new ones as well as the older, tried-and-true songs. Many of the jobs you're after—convention dates, for example—are private, and you won't be able to hang around listening to the band and taking notes. In that case, make friends with players who are working such jobs and ask them to photocopy the band's play list. Or get a copy of their promotional material—often a tune list is part of the package. Of course, you should also ask successful players what tunes are important— "standard"—in each genre.

You can't just buy a fake book or a "Giant Hits of the Superstars" collection and learn every tune, either, because almost all books are padded with worthless tunes that you'll never play. So, compile your own list of tunes that you must know—and learn them. You can use the form on page 27 or make your own. You'll be adding to this list for years as you learn tunes, and it will remind you of how much you know—and keep you out of the "same old twenty tunes" rut. (Keep your original work sheet at home and only take photocopies to jobs with you.) You'll compile this list from records, music books, and tunes you just learn on the job. Sometimes certain songs become essential to know, against your expectations or wishes, and over the years, your repertory will expand until you know hundreds—or thousands—of useful tunes.

Of course you'll always have the chance to play tunes you like during jobs—even in the most commercial situation you can often do obscure songs that are far outside the "core." But you may need to balance such "fun" tunes with popular ones that appeal to your client and audience.

It's a strange phenomenon, but certain songs remain popular and can't be replaced. If clients request "Proud Mary" (and they will), they won't be satisfied with something else that's a lot like it, even if the substitute has exactly the same tempo and feel. If the request is for "In the Mood," you'll find that another, hipper, big band tune won't please the person who made the request. Some songs that invariably become very trite and boring to musicians remain popular with audiences.

Tune structure. This is basic, yet a surprising number of would-be musicians don't know how songs are typically put together. There are lots of variations, of course, but most pop music consists essentially of verses and a chorus. The chorus is often referred to as the "bridge" or "release," and may be called the "b" section; the verses, naturally, are the "a" sections. In many cases, if there are two verses, a bridge, and a final verse, the song structure is called "aaba." If the song is verse, bridge, verse, bridge, then it is succinctly described as "abab."

The "aaba" structure is by far the most common, but many tunes are idiosyncratic, and you'll have to learn them individually. Sometimes there is an extra bar or two. There may be a one-chord vamp or an extra turnaround, so as you work on the core repertoire, notice which tunes follow a standard pattern and which ones are unusual.

Often you'll have to fake your way through tunes you don't really know, and if you're familiar with the standard patterns you'll be surprised at how well you can get through a song you've never played before.

In jazz or improvisational settings, common practice is to play the melody (called "the head") in a straightforward way the first time, and then improvise on succeeding times through the song. You may take a solo on the entire tune, or just the verse, or the bridge, so you must always know where you are. It's really embarrassing to be in the middle of your solo when the band comes back in—in a different place.

George Plimpton is an innovative writer who puts himself in different professional situations—football player, baseball player, professional boxer, and so on—and writes books about his experiences. He says that his most frightening experience of all was when he was an apprentice percussionist with the New York Philharmonic. Plimpton says that his performance with the symphony was more terrifying than being on the field with NFL players *because once the music started there is no place to hide.* Either you know where you are in the music, or you're in big trouble. With experience, you'll automatically sense where you are or you'll carefully keep up with the score, because the consequences of being lost are embarrassing. Or worse.

Common chord progressions. You won't always have music in front of you, and in many situations you won't have music at all, so you'll need to learn the basic progressions. Of course, if you're a classical player or a

CORE REPERTORY WORK SHEET

Title	Key	In book/page	On record/tape

choral music director, you'll always have the printed page to guide you. And if you're a drummer, you'll need to know basic rhythm patterns instead of chords, though you'll still need to know song structure.

For the last fifty years or so, most popular music has been loosely based on some kind of blues pattern, so you should be very familiar with the blues. Music stores have books of blues progressions, and the play-along records listed in Appendix C are a great way to learn them, too. Of course, each tune is different, and "based on a blues pattern" doesn't mean "exactly like the blues." You'll find that many musicians are very particular about correctness and will appreciate hearing the "real" correct changes. Often, there are several ways to play a passage, and if you know the right one you're better prepared to give your own interpretation. For good players, "close" is not close enough, and getting just the right chord and just the right voicing makes the difference between approval and scorn from other musicians.

So, as you learn tunes notice the common progressions, and also notice those special variations that make certain songs memorable. If you *know* that the solo in the Beatles' "And I Love Her" is in a different key from the rest of the song, you'll be appreciated by other musicians and accepted more quickly as a professional. Of course, you could just slop through without making the key change, but the tune would lose, and so would you.

Professionalism

Being a professional musician means working at your art until you're the best you can be — and that's a lifelong task. Nevertheless, there are certain nonmusical characteristics that professional musicians share. Many of these traits are attitudes; some are skills. They are so important to your success that they are discussed at several places in this book, and related points will be covered in

the next chapter. For now, here's an overview of the key elements of "professionalism."

Your behavior will define part of your success. What is professional behavior? First of all, it's the awareness that you're providing a service and that, like any professional, your task is to provide what the client needs. That means that the customer is always right, even when she doesn't know what she's talking about.

So, politeness is required. People will be rude to you; when they're drinking, or showing off for their dates, or with their friends, your audience will sometimes get ugly. "Come on, play something *good*." Resist the temptation to actually play something good, and play what they need at that moment.

Musicians aren't the only people who have to deal with rude clients — all business-people do — so try to grin and bear it. If the situation is really a bad one, finish the job and don't come back. Remember that responding in kind to an ugly comment or request will only escalate the hostilities. You'll rarely, if ever, gain anything by being rude.

Furthermore, common politeness goes a long way. Speak to your clients, check with them during the job, and smile. A pleasant attitude will usually make any job go easier — after all, your music should help people enjoy themselves and have a good time. Most jobs, honestly, aren't life or death struggles, and if you show that you're enjoying your music, the audience will, too.

Cooperation makes everyone's life smoother. Sometimes you'll have to use the service entrance rather than the front door. Even if the back way is more difficult, remember that you're providing a service and you're working in their building, so go ahead and accommodate their wishes. A drummer I know refused to use the service elevator and ended up scratching the African Walnut veneer in the passenger elevator; and he had to pay for repairing the damage. Even worse, his band hasn't booked any more jobs for that client.

Often, at private functions there will be extravagant food and drinks, but it may not be appropriate for the musicians to eat. Every hotel staff has horror stories about musicians who descend on the hors d'oeuvres before the guests even arrive. Use your "job sense" to decide whether you should attack the food or not—a safe rule of thumb is to wait for the client to invite you to eat. Or, go back to the kitchen and find a friendly waiter.

Flexibility is important because most jobs don't run exactly on schedule. There are exceptions; if you're playing a dinner for IBM, and they're scheduled to begin the awards at 9:17, you can bet they'll begin the awards at 9:17. But most companies aren't as organized as IBM, and you'll need to be flexible when playing commercial jobs. Thus, sets may be longer than you'd like, and the breaks may come at the wrong time—but the overall success of the job is what's important.

Remember—clients aren't interested in your preferences; *they're interested in their own needs*, and you can usually accommodate them by being adaptable. If you're flexible and friendly, you can almost always work out an acceptable solution to such problems.

A positive attitude will help even a bad situation. Many professional musicians, to be honest, develop a jaded perspective toward playing commercial jobs. Their approach is to appear bored and above it all, as if to say, "I'll play this if I have to, but it's really beneath me and I hate it."

Since we're providing a service for our clients, we sometimes have to compromise. In fact, compromise is a major element in professional music because you'll always have to balance your preferences against what the customer wants. But remember that musicians aren't the only professionals who have to make such compromises. Doctors, who may prefer to work on obscure, exotic diseases will still treat the same boring common cold over and over. Accountants, who might rather work with complex corporate buyouts, will still prepare dozens of simple, boring tax returns each year. And musicians, who'd certainly prefer to play creative, meaningful music, will have to play the same old trite songs, job after job, year after year.

In music, this often means that you'll be playing tunes that you don't like; it may mean that you'll be playing tunes that you hate. If you don't think you can do it and be happy about it, perhaps you should reserve music for a hobby and do something else for a living. After all, why make yourself miserable? For most musicians, though, the pleasure of playing for pay outweighs such necessary compromises, and playing "New York, New York" for the fourth time during the evening is aggravating and irritating—but not really all that bad. It's your attitude, ultimately, that makes you successful in commercial music settings.

Here's the bottom line: if you take a client's money to perform, you should be able to do the job pleasantly, with a good attitude. If commercial music makes you unhappy, then do something else; there's no reason to torture yourself.

Respect for other musicians is basic courtesy. We're all doing the same thing—selling our music for money—and thus we're all related in a basic way. Playing, then, need not be a contest to see who's the best, fastest, most current, or most obscure. Of course, there will be a range of talent in every community from the extremely gifted to the barely capable, but each player can get immense satisfaction from performing.

The music business is competitive, and you'll be striving for jobs against other players or bands, but nothing is gained by talking badly about them. If a client tells you he's considering hiring either your group or Band X, you'll do better to respond, "Well, I don't know much about Band X, but let me tell you what we can do for you . . ." If you launch into a discussion about how bad Band X is, you'll seem defensive and mean-spirited. Don't talk other musicians down.

Gossip is wasted time. It's nonproductive at best and destructive at worst. You're going to be working with the people you know, so overlook their shortcomings if you can. Nobody's perfect.

Another aspect of professional respect is that you *never steal other musicians' jobs.* Soliciting others' jobs is against union rules, but it is also against common sense. If another band has the job you want, you'll do everyone a disservice by undercutting their price—and the same thing will probably happen to you. In most areas, the musical community is so small that everyone knows everyone else, and you don't want the reputation of being a job-stealer. Just work on your own act; if you're the best, you'll eventually get the jobs you want.

Many jobs, especially "steady engagements" such as lounge work, are performed on open-ended contracts. Never try to directly book such a job unless the current band is on notice, though it's ethical for a booking agent to approach a club manager at any time. Put yourself in the place of the musician who now has the job, and you'll know how to proceed.

Unions are important in some areas and not active at all in others. A good union should provide lots of worthwhile services for its members that they couldn't get for themselves, and you can judge the union's usefulness by the benefits it offers. For example, at the least a union should set the minimum fees for different kinds of performances ("union scale"), provide life insurance, optional health insurance, optional pension or savings plans, access to reasonably priced instrument insurance, help in finding work, and assistance when there's a problem with a client.

In addition, an active union provides a sense of belonging to a community of musicians; it provides a balance to the extreme individuality of many musicians' lives.

To join a union, often called the "local," you'll pay an initiation fee, annual dues, and a percentage of your musical income, known as "work dues." Such payments can be considerable, so do some research before you join to be sure that it will be beneficial to you.

Unfortunately, in many areas you'll find that the unions aren't really representative of the broad range of working musicians, and there may be little to gain from joining. In other areas, all musicians are active union members. You'll have to ask around and find out what the situation is in your town.

There are different unions for musicians, actors, and singers. Their addresses are in Appendix D.

Creating a Professional Image

The well-equipped musician needs a lot of collateral material, and Chapter Thirteen describes your publicity needs in detail. You'll eventually have all kinds of promotional pieces: sales letters, brochures, letterheads, demo tapes, photos, and so on.

And, to *look* professional you should have business cards, and you must have them soon. You should, in fact, have them *now.* Nothing seems as amateurish as writing your name and number on a scrap of paper. Eventually you'll devise your own logo for all your stationery, but that process might take weeks or months. Don't wait until your entire promotional package is done; go ahead and order a few hundred business cards from your local printer now.

You'll discard these "quickie cards" when you've developed your complete promotional package—but that takes lots of time, so don't wait. Visit a quick-copy center and order your temporary cards with your name, address, and phone number on them. (Don't leave a blank for your phone number to be filled in later—that's a red flag that says "amateur" and "beginner." If you move and change phone number and address, get new cards printed. They don't cost much.) You may even need a couple of cards—one for the band and one for your single performances. Possibly you'll even need a third for your teaching business. It's better to invest in several than to try to combine everything on one jumbled too-general card.

Every professional person, regardless of occupation, always carries a printed business card. It's the key to networking, and you should never be without your cards.

Now you know what's involved in being a professional musician. You've started thinking of yourself as a small businessperson, you're working on your music, and perhaps you've joined the union. There's just one more thing to consider before developing your *Personal Music Marketing System.*

As you build your career, you'll find that your "people skills" are as important as your musical ability. You'll have to manage your own feelings, mediate between members of the band, communicate with clients and other musicians, and try to find time for your own needs. Freelance musicians can't exist in a vacuum because the music business, you'll quickly find, is as involved with people as it is with rhythm, tempo, and melody. Chapter Four presents some ideas that will help you work productively with different kinds of people.

LAUNCHING A FREELANCE CAREER
INTERVIEW WITH BRENDA STREET

Brenda Street is a freelance harpist who plays for corporate events, weddings, private parties, restaurants, and hotels in Atlanta and in Europe. She is a trained librarian and did not begin to study the harp until she was an adult.

Q *How did your career in music begin?*
A I was twenty-two when I took my first harp lesson, though I had a good background in piano. I studied harp for three or four years, and at that point I was able to play a short job—maybe a wedding or an easy party like that. At that point, I started to realize that I could make money with my music and that I just needed to work on my repertory. I decided that a knowledge of pop music would be helpful because that's what most of my requests were and I knew that very few other harpists were playing many pop tunes. I even rented a piano and took some jazz piano lessons to help me with ideas, chords, and so on, because the only harp teachers were completely classically oriented.

After my first job (I sweated to come up with twenty minutes of music) I was really afraid that the client would say, "That was awful, and we won't pay you." But they were actually grateful—they didn't know that was only the second time I'd played in public in my life. After that, I quickly gained confidence.

Q *What nonmusical factors do you think are important to freelance musicians as they book and play jobs?*
A When I started my professional career, my playing was the least of my abilities—I was really pretty much still a beginner without much difficult repertoire. But I decided, "I may not be the best harpist around— there were people who could play circles

around me—but I'm going to always try to have on the nicest dress, I'll always be early to jobs, and I'll take care of all the details." I made sure that clients wouldn't be able to fault me about anything else, and I found that worked in my favor.

That's when I started hearing horror stories about some other harpists—some of them rushed in at the last minute or were often late, others couldn't get along with anybody, and so on. I took note of this, and I developed a definite idea of the "right" things that I would do. I found out that clients did remember, for example, that I was early or that I was dressed appropriately. Of course, I was working on my music, too; at that time I was practicing like crazy, but even then I knew that other, nonmusical factors were crucial.

I think it's very important, too, to give the impression that you are successful. Sometimes the image is important—if you *look* successful, people are going to say, "That's the person we want to hire because she's obviously doing things right." That's especially true with the harp, which is pretty to look at. I think that people sometimes hire harpists for the "look" as much as the music.

A lot of times, clients don't judge you on music because they really can't—they aren't musicians and don't know what makes real musical quality, so they'll judge you on the things they *do* know. That includes how your music sounds to the layman, of course, but also how you look, how you act, how you get along with people.

Q *What abilities do you think are helpful to freelance musicians?*
A Maybe more important than knowing every tune is the ability to get along with people. You have to be patient with their re-

quests and phone calls, for example, and I still have to remind myself about this—so many phone calls about the same job, and it's not always easy to reassure clients over and over and stay pleasant.

And, we are "hired hands."

For example, even though I may be dressed as nicely as the guests while playing at a sophisticated, elegant party, I'm still working—and the client may give me orders. Sometimes I think, "That's not the way you should talk to me," but again, I'm the hired help. The good side is that even an aggravating job lasts just for hours, not days, and you can be patient and pleasant for that short a time. Frequently, I've actually found that clients who were a problem the first time continue to call me, and their succeeding jobs are easy and friendly.

Q *What business techniques do you find helpful?*
A In the beginning, I did send folders to all the restaurants around that I wanted to work for, but I've found the most important publicity tools to be a good photo, a nice business card, and a repertory sheet. And I've made a few demo tapes—mostly to demonstrate appropriate music for wedding ceremonies—but I'm going into the studio soon to make two new tapes, one of wedding music and another of pop music. I hope they'll save me the trouble of constantly trying to explain what I do and what my playing is like.

Another business-related thing I do is to use an accountant for taxes and financial advice. I'm really careful about taxes because it's another big plus. Careful tax planning can help you come out well, and musicians who don't stay on top of their income tax are really losing money. In fact, you're rewarded for the money you spend on your business—every time you buy a new instrument, a new tux, or whatever, the government subsidizes you.

Q *What do you like best about freelance music?*
A At this point, I like the freedom. At first, I was a real slave to the telephone and the calendar, and sometimes I was even afraid to go away for the weekend for fear someone would call me and would never call again if I wasn't immediately available. But I've learned that if you do a good job for people they won't quit calling you; in fact, they will miss you when you're gone.

What I really like about our life, though, is that I can set my own schedule. After my first trip to Europe a few years ago, I got interested in working there—I even started taking French lessons. I decided that they must need musicians in Europe, too, and since I can't afford yearly European vacations, I decided to investigate working over there. I located an agent in Switzerland and took a one-week trip to meet him—I even rented a harp and played a job that week. With that contact, I planned a working trip—and I ended up staying in Geneva, and playing, for almost four months.

Of course, I was willing to spend money to locate agents in Europe and I was willing to take the risk, but I have the freedom to do that. I think that's one of the biggest advantages of our profession, and I always figure that if something doesn't work—for example, I didn't get any work in Europe—that I can at least come back to where I was. Of course, that requires budgeting and saving money, but again, it's an investment.

Ultimately, by doing this—by working in Europe from time to time—I'm taking advantage of the freedom that music affords me by doing what I want to, where I want to. I think that's great.

FOUR

WORKING WITH PEOPLE

Your band is in the third week of an open engagement at a local club. You'd really like to keep this job for a few months to save some money and get the band tighter. But you feel like everybody is pulling at you, wanting something from you all the time. Pressures are coming at you from several directions, and it's driving you crazy. For example:

■ The club manager pesters you to take shorter breaks, play more dance music, draw bigger crowds. If he doesn't make his weekly quota, he blames you.

■ Your booking agent wants more, newer promotional material—and she needs it *now*. But before you deliver it to her you need to have a new band photo made, and that will take at least a couple of weeks. You think the drummer might be leaving the band soon, so you don't want to invest in a picture yet anyway. But future jobs, according to the agent, depend on this photo.

■ The members of your band are beginning to get on one another's nerves, and you can sense that a confrontation—and maybe the breakup of the band—isn't far off. You feel like the referee in a free-for-all between a group of prima donnas.

■ Your nightly audience at the club makes requests that you can barely understand—"play something *good*"—and you're con-

stantly trying to translate their needs into musical terms. And when you try to play the party music you want, band members sometimes rebel at the tunes you call.

■ Taxes are due, and you've got to find an accountant.

■ You've booked a few freelance jobs for Sunday afternoons, but the clients are driving you crazy, calling you every other day to discuss the details of their parties. A couple of them want to meet with you to discuss details—details you've already discussed several times over the phone.

■ Your family wants and deserves more time from you.

■ And what you'd really like to do is go to your room, close the door, and play for hours to get away from all this pressure.

Being a professional means, above everything else, being able to do your job. In music this includes a lot more than just being able to play, and one of your most important skills will be the ability to work well with people.

"Of course I can do that," you say. "I've worked with people since I was a kid. So what's new about my professional musician status?"

The difference is that now your ability to get along with people will go a long way toward determining your success—and you no longer have teachers, parents, or a spouse telling you what to do. You have to figure it out yourself. You'll have to learn to listen, to decipher what clients and audiences want, to read between the lines and interpret for them, to understand body language, to guide discussions, to solve problems, and to keep sensitive musician-egos working together productively and, if possible, happily.

Read the interviews with Bruce Bonvissuto (on page 58) and Gary Talley (on page 96) and notice the emphasis they both place on getting along with other musicians. It's a crucial skill, but judging by typical musicians' behavior, it doesn't come naturally. You also have to deal with audiences, clients, agents, producers, club owners, and record producers—and they all want something from you. Your job, if you choose to accept it, is to learn how to deal with all these people positively, without getting stressed out, burned out, or freaked out.

WORKING WITH MUSICIANS

Any band that works together longer than two weeks usually develops personal problems. Members bicker and don't get along, and it's not just your band—it's *every* band, *every* orchestra, and *every* choral group. Eventually the band breaks up, and the process starts over again with new people.

It's not hard to understand why there is so much tension among musicians. Bands work so closely together, and music is such a personal expression, that friction is inevitable. However, you can often avoid serious problems by being aware of what is going on and taking positive steps in advance to keep things running smoothly.

Here are procedures for working together smoothly that will help any group.

Talk. Don't get in the habit of rushing to the job, playing it, and leaving. Any group needs time to discuss its status and progress, and if you have to schedule a weekly lunch together or a band meeting before Monday night's job, do it. You must communicate. Reread the interview with Dr. Morgan Worthy on pages 9-13 and notice his advice about spending *nonstressful* time together.

Deal with problems. If the drummer is playing too loud, that's a problem. Rather than griping about it behind his back, wearing earplugs, or turning up your own amp in defense, *talk* about the situation. When problems are dealt with openly they can be solved, but when they're ignored or repressed, they'll cause havoc in your band. You can count on it.

In this example, you could point out to the drummer that the overall sound of the band is important, and that he could help the group by listening more carefully. How you criticize, however, is very important because the wrong approach can be destructive to the band's morale. *Never criticize in public*, around clients, or audiences. In fact, try not to criticize when other band members are present; a private discussion will minimize embarrassment, anger, or defensiveness. Don't be judgmental, but present your ideas as being "for the good of all." Explain why changes need to be made, and accentuate group spirit and camaraderie rather than an "I'm the boss" attitude. Work *together*.

Try to separate your playing from your self-esteem. This is nearly impossible, but it is very important to try. In your career as a musician, people will often criticize your playing. Sometimes it's justified, sometimes not, but it will happen. You must realize, however, that another's analysis of your playing need not hurt your feelings.

Rule to Remember:
Criticism of your playing is not criticism of you.

Of course you put yourself into your music, and everything you play expresses how you feel, but you must be able to put distance between your work and your self. Learn not to be discouraged, depressed, or defensive when someone suggests that you play a passage differently. Read Dr. Worthy's suggestions about viewing your commercial performances as "experiments" that can be changed if they need to be without destroying your artistic integrity.

"I wish you wouldn't play that corny old-fashioned turnaround at the end of the bridge," complains the bass player. "It sounds like something left over from the thirties." Your natural reaction is probably defensive: "Well, I think it sounds great, and who are you to criticize me, anyway?" That kind of exchange leads nowhere but to anger and hurt feelings. You must learn to discuss your music without taking it personally.

Be fair about money. Sometimes bandleaders create dissension simply by their selfishness. Always pay people what you've promised, and pay them as quickly as you can. And, have a policy that everyone understands about how extra money will be divided—overtime and tips, for example. You'll find that the few dollars extra won't make up for the resentment you cause by keeping such windfall profits for yourself.

Maybe you should establish an incentive program for your group so that everybody has a chance to make more—and help the band at the same time. For example, you could pay a "finder's fee" to each band member who books a job, and that would encourage everyone to understand, and participate in, the business of running the band. (If several people are booking engagements, however, be *sure* to keep an updated central calendar to avoid double-bookings.)

Avoid cliques and gossip. Even small, four-piece bands often divide into an "us against them" mentality—and larger groups, such as symphony orchestras, are rife with "in groups" and "out groups." Sometimes it is the rhythm section against the horns, or everybody against the singer.

Keeping a sense of perspective will help. You're all in the group for the same reason—to make money with your music—and you all want success for the entire group. Unfortunately, musicians are often gossips. Talking about your friends and colleagues behind their backs is a negative force, not a positive one.

WORKING WITH CLIENTS

"She wouldn't know good music if it hit her over the head," muttered a bass player as the client walked away. The client had just requested "something good that the crowd will dance to," and left it up to the band to figure out what she had in mind.

That kind of problem is, unfortunately, very common. Clients know what they want—a good party, for example—but it's *your* job to make it happen. Here are some techniques to avoid problems and make every gig more successful.

Know what the client wants from you. Talk to everyone who hires you, and be sure that you know what you're supposed to do. Often your clients will only have a vague idea of the kind of music they'll need—they just want something "good," so the party will be a success. You should force the client to be as specific as possible.

Since most of your clients won't be musicians, they often don't know anything about music—and their ignorance can be astounding. It's up to you to figure out what they need, and be sure that they know what you can—and can't—do. A client, especially after a drink or two, may expect your violin duo to play rock and roll, or your rock band to know Viennese waltzes. This, as all musicians know, is not exaggeration, so find out exactly what the client expects from you and be sure that you can provide it. (Read the "listening" heading on page 38 for more ideas.)

Be friendly. This sounds simple, but for many musicians, dealing with nonmusician clients is like speaking a foreign language. Clients are often suspicious of musicians, and musicians don't trust businesspeople, either.

Try not to approach your boss, whether it is a club manager or the bride's mother, as if she were the enemy. She's not. She may not be a musician, but she is paying you money to perform, so treat her with respect, courtesy, and friendliness.

Put yourself in the client's place and look at things from his point of view. If you were giving a posh party in an elegant hotel, would you want the band to set up before the guests arrive? If you were producing a jingle for an ad agency, would you want the musicians to arrive at the studio on time? If you were sponsoring a street dance, would you want the music to reflect the theme of the party? Of course you would, and your clients feel the same way.

Try to realize what the client's concerns are, and you'll understand what they need from you. Since it usually isn't possible to spend your life doing exactly as you wish, you'll find that learning to get along with people will make everything much easier — and it really isn't too difficult. In fact, good communication is often the key.

Developing Communication Skills

Your client says "I really like jazz, and that's what I want you to play." You think, "Great. Finally I'll get a chance to play my Coltrane tunes."

But when the job comes, the client who "likes jazz" is really upset with your music. He thinks you're too loud, and he doesn't like what you're playing. He wants "more melody." What's wrong?

There's a basic communication problem here — that's what's wrong. You and the client used the same word — "jazz" — but you weren't communicating at all. He was thinking "Dixieland" and you were thinking "Bebop." Or maybe he was thinking "Blues" and you were thinking "Fusion."

Music is a universal language, to be sure, but the terms people use to discuss it can be vague and unclear. The first step in good communication, then, is to *define your terms.* How do you do that?

First of all, don't be afraid to ask questions. This is probably the easiest and best way to be sure you're communicating. "When you say 'jazz,' Mr. Jones, what do you mean? Can you give me some examples of what kind of jazz you like?" And then Mr. Jones can tell you whether he is thinking of the Dukes of Dixieland, Duke Ellington, Duke Pearson, or George Duke.

Often you'll know more than your client about what kind of music will be needed at a function. By asking, "What's your favorite song?" or "Is there any music you *don't* like?" or even suggesting titles, you can get a sense of what's really in his mind.

Some clients will think that Cole Porter tunes are "classical music." Others will want "fast" music when they mean current rock hits. What is an "oldie?" — a Beatles tune, a Glenn Miller tune, or last year's fast-fading number one?

These expressions are so relative that the only way you can proceed with confidence is by *defining the terms.* And in your struggles to understand what the client wants, nothing is more important.

Another way to improve your communication skills is to learn to listen. Good musicians listen as they perform; they are sensitive to what everyone else is playing. "She has good ears," is a high compliment for a musician. Interestingly, you'll find that listening skills are as important in the music business as they are on stage, and there's a big difference between *listening* and just *hearing*. When you're talking to a client or another musician, your communication will be better and you'll establish a better relationship—and avoid mistakes—if you listen closely. Here are some suggestions.

Hearing is *passive*; listening is *active*. To really listen, you must have your brain engaged and not be daydreaming or thinking about what you'll say next. Pay attention to what is said, how it is said, and even to nonverbal cues, such as facial expressions, body stance, and style of delivery.

Thus, if a client is telling you about her plans for a wedding party you're playing, you can avoid problems by listening carefully. "The guests will arrive around seven o'clock, and the band should start playing at about eight," she says. What she means is, "The band should be set up and out of sight at seven when the guests arrive," but what you may understand is, "Since the band doesn't start until eight, there's no reason to rush to the job."

Careful listening is a skill that all businesspeople need, and it isn't easy. The interview with Dr. Sheila Kessler on page 148 provides more ideas about good communication, but the following list will get you started.

Listen for repeated key words that indicate importance: "We want a *lively* party, with lots of *lively* music." Your next question should be, of course, "Can you give me some examples of what kind of lively music you like?"

Watch out for *screens* that allow you to hear only what you want or expect to hear: "We want lots of ethnic music," says the client. But you know no ethnic songs, so you just ignore him and assume that he'll forget. Don't assume that; he won't forget, and you'll wish you'd prepared polkas, horas, or whatever ethnic songs the client wanted. Don't let your own abilities or tastes become "screens" that limit communication to what you want to hear.

Don't get distracted while you're talking with the client, but pay attention: "Let's talk about the schedule for the evening," says the party's hostess—but you're thinking about where to stash your hand truck and whether you can scrounge some food from the caterer—and you miss what's being said.

Listen for the real message. Sometimes words don't tell the whole story: "Play something really fast to get this party jumping," orders your nervous client. What she really wants is for her guests to dance, but you'll know more than she does about what kind of music is needed at that particular moment. You might respond, "Well, usually in the beginning of this kind of party, a nice slow ballad will get people on the dance floor best. Why don't we try that . . . and maybe you could lead the dancing." Your experience tells you that playing something fast would be counterproductive at this point, but the client can't verbalize exactly what she wants. You have to translate her desire for a full dance floor into action.

Listen for facts and details: "We'll finish dinner at 8:30 and have a fifteen-minute break, then we'll need a fanfare and ten minutes of walking music, building up to the seventeen main awards for the evening, which will need smaller fanfares, except for the last three awards which are very important, and then . . ." the client drones on—and you quit paying attention because you think you can fake it. Even though you've done it before, try to listen to the details that the client is telling you; businesspeople tend to be more fact-oriented than many musicians, and the schedule is probably very important to him. (In fact, he may have worked on that schedule for weeks, and his job may depend on the success of this meeting.) Get a written copy and be sure you understand all those details because that's what's crucial to the client.

Watch for nonverbal cues. If you're making a sales call and the prospective client keeps looking at her watch or drumming her fingers on the desk, those are signals that you should finish quickly. Often frowns, smiles, or worried looks are as important as what is being said. "I'd like to hear more about your band," says the prospect, as she stands up from behind her desk. She really means, "Maybe I'd like to hear more about your band, and maybe not—but not right now. This interview is over." If you don't pick up on such cues, you'll lose jobs.

Respond without becoming defensive: "Your band looks like it will be too loud, and we don't like loud music," says the client—before you've even played a note. Don't get mad, even though you're being unfairly accused in advance. Just explain that amplifiers can be turned down as well as up. Remember that the client probably has little experience with music and musicians, and even the sight of a few amps may cause his blood pressure to go up dangerously. You can set his mind at ease by talking to him; or you can get into a pointless argument by being defensive—and that will raise *both* your blood pressures.

In booking and playing jobs, you'll depend on different kinds of communication. Business studies show that people often only "hear" about 25 percent of what is being said, and much more meaning is lost when information is verbally passed from person to person, perhaps as much as 75 percent. There are many times when talk is not good enough, and you'll need to write things down. More about letters and contracts is in Chapter Thirteen.

Don't trust details to your memory. Write dates, schedules, requests, and any other pertinent facts down, and you won't have to worry about remembering them. Always augment your communication skills with a notepad and pencil. No matter how carefully you listen and how friendly you are, it won't help if you forget to show up for the job.

People Who Need People

Many musicians find so much satisfaction in music that they would be happy living as hermits, playing for their own pleasure without an audience. And many of us do have a tendency to shun the world and live an isolated life.

But if you are to make money from music, you'll need people. You have to have someone to play to, play for—and someone to pay you, and in this way music is no different from other businesses. Your people skills are crucial, and you'll have to be able to get along with all kinds of folks.

Even if your natural tendency is to be aloof or a loner, you'll find that you can cultivate the kinds of social skills you need, and when you do, your career will improve. It's a cliché and pretty trite, but it's true that a smile will open more doors than an argument or sales pitch, and it's possible that a smile could do more for your career than a new horn. Try it and see.

MUSIC IS A PRODUCT

Music is the universal language of mankind," wrote Henry Wadsworth Longfellow. Friedrich Nietzsche said, "Without music, life would be a mistake." Sidney Lanier added, "Music is Love in search of a word."

Music is the most elusive, fleeting, and subtle of the arts. We would all likely agree on that. Playing music is an exhilarating experience. But when you decide to make your living from music, you may recall a famous quote from the French composer Georges Bizet. He said, "Ah Music! What a beautiful art! But what a wretched profession."

A wretched profession? Is that true? It certainly can be—but it's within your power to decide how the music profession will treat you. The goal is to survive and prosper within the craft and career of music while retaining the love of the art.

If you've won the Florida lottery, inherited a million dollars, or are content to starve in a Soho loft you can skip this chapter. Music, for you, can remain simply and purely an art and you can concern yourself with nothing beyond it. You can write atonal, arrhythmic masterpieces that nobody but you will play because you aren't playing music for a living. You can write obscure, deeply personal lyrics, too.

For the rest of us in the real world of the music marketplace, there are basic premises that must be understood. In fact, such understanding will go a long way toward keeping our profession from becoming a wretched one.

MUSIC MARKETPLACE 101

The most important idea is that *music is a product*. It's like soap or anything else that's produced, marketed, and sold to fill a need. You must understand this if you want to make money with your music.

Further, music is a *business*, and if you plan to profit from your art you have to understand this, too. This concept is as true for classical players and symphony orchestras as it is for country singers and rock bands. It even applies to religious music.

This is the reality of the music marketplace. It may not be what you'd like to believe or what your professors taught, but when you try to make money playing music you'll have to face some possibly unpleasant facts; the art has become a business and, as in most businesses, the customer is the boss.

He Who Pays the Piper Calls the Tune

The reality is that clients buy only what they need or want in music. Your clients will pay for your music only because it does something for them. Rarely or never will you be hired just to play your own music in your own way. Your music is a *service* to those who hire you, and it must satisfy them to justify its cost. Your clients usually won't be philanthropists; they aren't often interested in supporting struggling artists. That may be unfortunate, but it is true.

"But I've got a lot of terrific original material," you say. "People need to hear it. It could make me a star, and it will enlighten the audience, too."

No doubt you're right. Your original material is doubtlessly wonderful and people probably should hear it, but in commercial situations, they are not going to hire you to play original material to uplift or enlighten them. Your audience is going to insist on hearing "hits."

That is an axiom, a given, a rule, a law, the absolute truth of the music business. Almost all the time in almost every venue, people will only pay for music they like, want, and need.

Rule to Remember:
People won't buy your music unless they need it for some reason.

To compete successfully in commercial music, then, you must follow the same strategy that every successful businessperson uses. You must:

■ Develop a product—in this case, your music.

■ Locate clients for your product—do market research.

■ Bring your product to the marketplace— use sales techniques to convince potential clients to buy your music.

Why People Buy Music—A Mental Exercise
Here's an interesting mental exercise. Put yourself in a client's place, and try to think like he or she does. This is a useful practice that will help you understand how music fits into any job situation, and it will sharpen the communication skills discussed in Chapters Three and Four.

Let's say you're a well-to-do, middle-aged woman planning a wedding reception for your daughter. You're planning to invite three hundred important guests to the wedding, and you're naturally concerned with hundreds of details about this major event in your life. Among other things, you need to hire a band—something you've never done before. Here are some of the thoughts you have about music:

■ "We've got to have a good-looking band that will fit the tone of the evening. After all, at the Smiths' wedding last month the band was wonderful, and the singer was so handsome, but the band at the Joneses' reception looked like they'd slept in their clothes for a month."

■ "I don't want the music to be too loud. The grandparents won't be able to hear a thing, and loud music will make them irritable, and Lord knows they're grouchy enough anyway."

■ "On the other hand, I do want the young people to dance, so I've got to have a band that can play current songs. But what are current songs? I wouldn't know what's popular because I don't like that music!"

■ "I'm concerned about the schedule for the evening. I wonder if the band will help me run the party and make announcements? If they do, will their speaking voices sound good and be understandable, or will their announcing seem amateurish?"

■ "If the dinner starts at eight and the room is open for cocktails at seven, then the band will have to be set up and out of the room at least by seven. It just wouldn't do to have them testing their sound system during the receiving line."

■ "And what if Uncle Ervin has a couple of

drinks and wants to sing? He's so cute when he does that—I hope the band will let him sing his fabulous version of 'Danny Boy' . . . and maybe they won't laugh at him the way the musicians did at Ashley's reception."

And so on. These are the kinds of thoughts that the mother of the bride would have. Any client, for any job, would have a similar set of concerns, too—and they are all related to *their own* needs and the success of *their own* party.

For contrast, here are some typical musician-thoughts that might occur regarding the same job; notice the rather wide divergence from the client's concerns. A typical musician, preparing to play the wedding reception discussed above, might think:

■ "Gee, I hope my amp will make it through this job and not start that horrible humming it did last Saturday. I've got to get that fixed before it blows up. I wonder how much *that* will cost."

■ "What time will this party be over?"

■ "If the party starts at eight, the guests probably won't even get there till 8:15, so if I arrive about 7:50 there'll be plenty of time. I'll change from jeans to my tux in the restroom."

■ "We can do those five original tunes that Joe and I wrote. It's just a wedding, and the guests won't be paying attention to us anyway. The 7/4 blues is a neat tune, and the seventeen verses tell a good story—lots of inside, hip jokes."

■ "I wonder if I can clean my tux again with a wet cloth where I spilled the cocktail sauce on it. I've got to remember to get to the cleaners, but it'll be dark at the party, I'm sure."

■ "We need to see how loud we can sing through the PA to be sure the speaker reconing job we just paid for was done right—

because that rattle was only noticeable at high volume."

■ "I'll take my 'Real Book' so we can play lots of jazz. The crowd won't know the difference."

■ "I hope the good-looking bartender, Susie, will be working this party."

Get the picture? Musicians and clients have different concerns, but if you'll put yourself in the client's place and try to see how your music fits into the situation, you'll automatically know what to do, how to behave, and what's important. And you'll get repeat business and referrals from that client.

Balancing Beauty and the Business

Does this mean that to succeed in commercial music you'll have to "sell out"? The answer can be "yes" or "no," depending on your definition. If you're a purist who won't bend and who resents audiences who aren't up to your artistic standards, the answer is, "Yes. You'll have to sell out to make money in music."

On the other hand, if you're more flexible, you won't feel that you're selling out when you provide the music your client or audience wants. Successful musicians don't need to be hacks, and they certainly don't have to reject the art and beauty of music.

You must develop a salable product that the market needs if you're to make a living from your music. But this is only part of your art; each client only buys a little of your talent for a short time. Clients don't own your life. Play what the job requires, if you can, but remember that your musical life is broader than any specific situation.

So, if you plan to make money with your music you'll have to balance the needs of your clients against your own musical preferences. Of course you'll know more about music—you're the musician and it's your job. But they'll know what they want. And they sign the checks.

So, does success in commercial music mean playing music that you don't like, perhaps even music of dubious quality? Sometimes the answer is "yes," and there's no way around it.

Every musician, especially freelancers who work in a variety of situations, must decide where to draw the musical line. Each player must decide how "commercial" to be. Sometimes it boils down to how far you can compromise without making yourself miserable. If you simply can't bring yourself to play what the job requires then don't take it.

Competition Is Alive and Well

Next time you visit the supermarket, stop in the laundry soap aisle and think about the variety you see: brand after competing brand, all doing pretty much the same thing. Some are expensive, some are much cheaper; some are in red boxes, some in yellow jugs; some are in the giant economy size, while others come in smaller packages.

The soap companies are among the smartest marketers in the world. They know that their products are much the same and that you probably couldn't tell the difference in a shirt washed in Brand A, B, or C — yet they all prosper in this competitive market. How do they do it? Lots of market research, and lots and lots of advertising.

You'll face competition, too. There will almost always be other musicians selling the same kind of musical product that you offer, and the clients, to tell the truth, won't usually know enough about music to make an informed choice. It's up to you, then, to convince them to hire you. How do you do that?

First of all, try to *be* better. Competition forces you to work hard to do a better job than anyone else. On the other hand, every experienced marketer knows that success depends as much on image, the perceived

reality, as on the product itself. That's where advertising and publicity make a lot of difference. You have to keep your name out there in front of clients — and you have to do it all the time.

So . . . are you better than Band X? You are? Lots better? But does Band X do a superior job of promoting itself? Is their publicity material better, and do they make more sales calls and follow-up visits? Does Band X work more jobs than your group? Lots more?

"But," you complain, "Band X's vocalist sings out of tune, and they don't know a single song that was written in the last six months. Their PA is an antique, and they still use a *spring reverb* — can you believe it? — instead of a digital delay!"

You're probably right. Your band is much better. So why does Band X work so much more than your group does? First of all, remember that quality is in the ear of the client, and — to repeat — clients are rarely musicians. The client won't care about the spring reverb. The client cares about the end result, and Band X gets the crowd dancing.

Second, Band X aggressively promotes itself. One of the most popular bands in Atlanta is not one of the best, but they produce slick promotional pieces and work hard at publicizing themselves. They are on the phone *every day*. The same thing is doubtlessly true in your town, too. Bands like these realize that competition for jobs depends as much on business aspects as it does on musical quality, and they put their efforts into marketing their product. They should probably work on improving their music as well, but perhaps your band could learn a bit about marketing from them.

There will always be competition. In music, especially, anyone can call himself a "professional." There's no entrance exam, no state licensing board, and even union membership doesn't prove anything. The marketplace is the proving ground, and you'll have to work steadily to stay ahead of the new bands, the recent graduates, the new drummer who's just moved to town because he heard there was lots of work around.

Further, you have to keep working at it. You'll never be able to relax and say "I've paid my dues and I'll just lay back and relax now." All those prospective clients, audiences, album buyers, club managers, and booking agents will forget you if you don't work — and keep working — at getting noticed.

How do you do it? How do you keep your name before the right people? You create a marketing plan and work at it. You publicize your act. And, of course, you keep practicing because, in the end, quality does count.

So . . . You Have a Product

"Okay," you concede. "I'll have to think of my music as a product and be successful selling it. What's next?" The next step is to start work on your marketing plan, targeting the clients who'll be most likely to need that product — your music.

You'll be spending a lot of time on things that you may not be interested in. You'd rather practice than promote, and you'd rather sing than sell. But in the real world, you have to do both and you'll probably be surprised to find that your creativity extends beyond music. You can get satisfaction from building your career, just as you get satisfaction from building a solo. And, since no one cares as much about your career as you do, you'll have to manage that product — your music — yourself. What a challenge . . . and what an opportunity!

SIX

DEVELOPING YOUR OWN MARKETING SYSTEM

Where *is* your next job coming from? When your current engagement is over, what will you do? If your contact person at the hotel leaves, will your source of work disappear? If your friend at the booking agency finds another hot band would it be a problem for you? It's a universal dilemma—even if you've had a million-seller hit record or a sold-out Carnegie Hall concert you still have to work at booking the next engagement.

FINDING WORK—A SYSTEM

Looking for a place to play for pay is the nature of the business, but just sitting around waiting for the phone to ring is depressing. And unnecessary. Equally discouraging is the tired old habit of playing the same old jobs—including the same old songs—with the same old group of musicians.

The *Personal Music Marketing System (PMMS)* described in the next few chapters will help you deal positively with the "next job challenge." It offers every musician an easy, organized, and personalized way to find more jobs, and there's nothing complex or revolutionary about this strategy. In fact, it works *because* it's simple.

Further, this system is flexible and will grow with you. With use, it will become an automatic way of thinking, and as your com-

munity grows and the music market changes, you'll keep up because you'll be thinking like a marketing professional.

"But," you say, "I don't want to think like a marketing professional. I want to think like a musician."

Fortunately, these approaches aren't contradictory. If you're going to find work, beat the competition, and succeed in the difficult music marketplace, *somebody's got to find work for you and your band*. Unless you have a first-rate, highly experienced manager that you trust absolutely, you'll have to market yourself. Try it—you may be surprised at how much you enjoy it. You'll definitely like the results.

Why You Need a System

The job-finding plan offered in this book helps avoid the typical freelance problem of aimlessness because it gives purpose and direction to your efforts. It will help you find more jobs, true, but it will also help you *feel* successful and in control, and that's very important—especially to self-employed people.

Of course, using the *PMMS* isn't the only way to succeed, and you may devise a completely different approach that's effective for you. The point is, however, that a system is better than a hit-or-miss approach, and careful planning is better than leaving your future to chance.

Tapping the "Hidden Markets"

You can build a career or just increase your part-time work by finding gigs in the music market that are off the beaten track. Of course you'll go after the obvious jobs first—the clubs may always be your primary venue—but you'll profit much more if you build a network of clients *outside* the usual. If you go *beyond the expected*, you'll discover substantial profits in the "hidden markets."

That's where this book will help. It will show you how to locate dozens, maybe hundreds of freelance music jobs that can augment the old tried-and-true ones you're already playing. And, if you're a part-time musician, these jobs may be the only ones you play.

Here's an example of how the hidden market works. In many large cities and resort areas the convention business is very important to the local economy, and the convention business needs an enormous amount of music of every kind. However, conventions aren't open to the public, and the only people who know about them are those who plan, service, and attend these meetings, so most musicians may not even be aware of this prime market for their music.

It's not unusual for a medium-size convention to have an entertainment budget of $50,000 for an evening's show—and while much of that may be spent on a headline act, lots of local, supporting players (and bands) are also needed. Plus, there is usually a lot of convention spin-off entertainment business—from breakfast "wake-up" music to rock bands for hospitality suites—and it's all private, virtually hidden from the public.

If you don't know about this market and make a systematic effort to book some of these jobs, you certainly won't benefit from it. But if you have an aggressive marketing system in place, all the right people will know about your music—and they'll be able to book you for an array of private convention-related jobs.

The *Personal Music Marketing System* will help you target just the kinds of jobs that need you. The key to success with this system, however, is to *do it*—to make the lists and do the research. If you do, you'll have a way of finding more work than your competitors. This system depends on brainstorming, simple research, and making several lists. If you do the work and follow the suggestions, you'll discover lots of opportunities for selling your music and you'll end up with a valuable, personalized source of information that will make it easier for you to find, book, and play engagements.

To make the system work, however, you'll have to actually *do* the brainstorming exercises and, later, the research that builds your lists. *This job-finding system will not work unless you participate*. Just thinking about it won't lead to any jobs. Even though you may feel silly and awkward at first, you've got to do it.

You must *write the lists down in black and white*. It doesn't matter whether you use a pen and paper, a computer, or speak into a tape recorder for later transcription—what's important is that you *write it down*! Worksheets are provided throughout this book, or, if you prefer, use a notebook to keep all your information together. You can't trust your memory—the system won't work on thoughts alone.

"But," you say, "creating my own marketing system sure sounds like a lot of work. Is it worth the effort?" After all, for years musicians have been seeking out jobs that match their talents and building informal networks of clients. The difference is that:

- This is a *system*, an organized approach that will clearly show you who is most likely to need your music.

- The *hidden markets* will yield lots of useful leads that would likely be overlooked without this method.

■ You'll get in the *habit of thinking about marketing* and will automatically spot new leads, new clients, and new venues.

■ You'll be *taking charge of this important aspect of your life* and not passively waiting for something to happen. You'll be acting, not just reacting, and you'll appreciate the feeling that you're in control and no longer simply a helpless sideman, waiting, waiting, and waiting . . .

EVERYONE IS DIFFERENT

The spectrum of musical styles, types, and needs in the music market is incredibly broad. It's rarely possible to be a jack-of-all-trades musician today; some specialization is required. Rock players usually don't know classical music, and jazz musicians don't generally play country tunes. (This may not be as true, of course, in small towns and rural areas, where you may have to play every kind of job just to survive.)

Your *PMMS* will guide you in the effective use of your energy and time. It will direct you to clients who will be receptive because they need what you have to offer, and it will make your sales calls easier. Your *Good Prospects List* will be different from any other musician's list because it will be based on your own abilities and targeted to likely clients in *your community*. It is a precise marketing tool because it is tailored for you and you alone. You won't waste time chasing down clients who don't need your kind of music.

Brainstorming

To sell your music most effectively, you need a clearly defined target—prospective clients who'll need your kind of music. You'll use several steps and methods to locate them. One of the best ways to generate new ideas for developing your *PMMS* is called *brainstorming*.

Here's how to brainstorm. Find a good place to think where you won't be interrupted—perhaps your local library, or a park bench, or even driving along the interstate highway (in which case you'd use a tape recorder instead of a notebook). If you do these exercises at home, take the phone off the hook or let your answering machine take over. You can't brainstorm in snippets—you need extended time to let your mind roam.

Try to put your mind in "neutral." Let it coast without conscious direction, and follow wherever it goes. You'll use your memory and imagination, but you won't know where they're taking you. Don't worry—brainstorming will take you to new ideas.

Think about your subject—potential clients or possible playing venues, for example—and write down every single idea that pops into your head, no matter how unlikely, foolish, or absurd it might seem at first. Paper is cheap, and you are trying to generate new concepts, so don't hold back.

Let one idea lead to another. Let your mind roam as far as possible, and don't worry about being practical. That is exactly what brainstorming tries to overcome. Be imaginative. Be ridiculous (but don't feel ridiculous). Be as free and open as possible. For example, imagine your brass ensemble playing at the Governor's mansion, or your fifties' show entertaining on a Caribbean cruise ship. You'll edit your lists later, but at first just try to come up with new ideas.

When you are brainstorming in search of new job possibilities, make your lists as long and full as you can. No one should see these entries except you, so don't hesitate to follow your unconscious mind as it creates ideas.

Another way to expand your lists is through *association*. That is, let one idea lead naturally to a similar one. When your mind is coasting in neutral, ideas will automatically suggest others, link themselves together, and lead to even more new thoughts. If you've thought of playing upbeat music for the introduction of next year's new car models, *association* leads you to think of doing the same thing for next year's new speedboats, fur coats, computers, or swimsuits. One idea leads directly—or indirectly—to another, and the more you free your mind from its habits, the more creative it will be.

Perhaps your brainstorming leads you to a client whom you hadn't thought of before, a client who will need your musical services only once a year. That's good. If, through more brainstorming, association, and research, you can find *fifty* such once-a-year clients, you'll have discovered almost a job a week. That's significant. So don't worry if an idea seems simple, even trivial. Add it to your list anyhow. Careers can be built of many simple ideas.

One way to enlarge your brainstorming sphere is the notion of "idea spoking"—a notion taught to freelance writers by Gordon Burgett. Burgett urges brainstorming people to visualize each idea as the hub of a wheel, with many spokes leading out from it. Let each spoke lead to a related, but different idea. If you think of "fraternity parties" as a hub or topic idea, then you'll naturally think of sorority parties, then professional fraternal organizations, then social clubs, then trade associations, and so on. Each idea leads to another related concept. You could even draw a diagram of the process. (See sample diagram on p. 49.)

Always keep a pocket notebook ready for insights, names, or interesting information so that your musical employment possibilities will continue to expand. Once you start thinking in this open-minded way, you'll be constantly alert for new ideas and job possibilities. Adding to and modifying the lists that form your *PMMS* will be an ongoing process, a never-finished project that will grow with your music life and the changes in your community.

On page 50 is a sample of the brainstorming process for a beginning keyboard/piano player who's looking for places to play. Notice that the list begins with jobs she's already played, then moves on to the usual job sources and expands from there.

THE FIRST STEP: YOUR PERSONAL INVENTORY

The first component of your *Personal Music Marketing System* is a list of all the musical things you can do that might be salable. Don't think about marketing at this point; just list everything musical you can do. Thus, if you know everything Gilbert and Sullivan wrote, put light opera on your list—even if you don't know of a single job that needs this specialty. Market research comes later.

The *Personal Inventory List* has two parts: 1) a compilation of everything musical that you can do, and 2) a ranking of your abilities.

Note that this is not just a listing of the jobs you're now playing or have played. It's a list of what you *could* play now, and that you might be able to play in the future. Don't be limited by your past as you work on this list, and don't be limited by demand for this kind of music. Just add categories to your list.

This inventory will be the "raw material" from which you'll derive the target market lists that will guide your marketing plans. To give you the best chance at the most jobs, include as much as possible. And remember—don't limit yourself to the kinds of music you like.

For example, if your real love is Dixieland, but you could play piccolo trumpet for Christmas cantatas, go ahead and put

Neighborhood Pool Parties

Company Pool Parties

Company Picnics

Apt. Complex Pool Parties

Country Club Pool Parties

Neighborhood Picnics

Neighborhood Street Dance

Marathon or 10K Race Street Parties

Neighborhood Festivals

Seasonal (ie 'Harvest') Festivals – Shopping Malls

Historical Festivals

Jobs - Brainstorming Ideas

I. <u>Jobs I've played</u>

Weddings
- ceremonies
- receptions

Church services

Church choir
- rehearsals
- performances & concerts
- recording sessions

Theaters
- high school
- college - rehearsals & performances
- community

Accompanying
- recitals - college senior

Parties in homes - cocktail/dinner

II. <u>Places I could play</u>

Restaurants
Lounges
Nightclubs
Hotel lobbies - office buildings?
Office parties
Office openings, open houses, etc.
Retirement parties
Birthday parties
Bar Mitzvahs
College/Pro theatrical work
Civic club luncheons
Civic club programs
Substitute work for other musicians
Teaching - private
Teaching - school substitute?

Christmas church music on your list. And if you could teach beginning trumpet students, be sure to include teaching on your list.

To begin, use the *Personal Music Inventory Work Sheet* on page 52 and list everything musical that you can do. List *everything*. Use extra paper if you need it, but be sure to write the list down. Remember, the system won't work unless you actually put pen to paper; *you can't do it in your head*.

Rule to Remember:
No marketing system will work unless you work at it.

Don't worry yet about how good you are. Just write down everything that you have done and would like to do in music. Use your memory and your imagination.

To jog your memory and encourage you to break out of your playing habits, the work sheet is divided into the following categories:

■ *Kinds of music I can play now*. Here, you'll list everything musical that you now do at a professional, or near-pro, level. This should be easy to compile since you'll list what you already know and do.

■ *Kinds of music I'd like to play*. These are the things you could do with a little work. Also list your long-term playing goals to show where you'd like to go. If there's a style you haven't mastered or a composer whose work you don't yet know, this is the place to list it.

■ *Kinds of music I've played in the past*. Think back to your earlier playing experiences and school days. List whatever musical activities you used to do. Did you play tuba in the school band? Were you the accompanist for the men's chorus? Did you play harmonica in a blues band that only performed in your basement? Don't reject

anything because you haven't done it lately. Think back, and add to your list.

■ *Kinds of music I could play but don't enjoy*. This could be the most important category because you may find that what the market needs is not exactly your favorite kind of music. Think about the commercially useful types of music that you could do, and add them to your list. It doesn't mean that you *have* to play music you don't like, but you need a complete picture of your ability spectrum to make the system work.

Here's an example. Let's say that you're a freelance keyboard player. You have some classical piano background and can play a variety of jobs on piano, electric piano, and synthesizer; although you're mostly interested in pop and rock, you can play in other styles with some proficiency. Further, you played the trumpet in your high school band and sang in college theatrical productions. The first list in your *Personal Inventory* might look like the example on page 53. (Note that this list is in no particular order because it's the result of brainstorming.) Such a list would be a good starting point for a well-rounded pianist. *Notice that this list only notes types of music* without ranking ability or the job prospects in each field. Some pianists will compile longer lists—more specialties, more categories—while other players' lists will be much shorter.

Now Put Them in Order
Wait a few days and then read over your *Personal Inventory Lists*. Add anything that you originally forgot. You'll be surprised how many new items you think of and how your insight develops if you put the work aside for a couple of days. It gives your subconscious mind a chance to mull it over and make its own suggestions, too. Then loosely rank your entries on another sheet of paper or in your notebook. Use general categories

PERSONAL INVENTORY WORK SHEET

Kinds of music I can play now:

Kinds of music I'd like to play:

Kinds of music I've played in the past:

Kinds of music I could play but don't enjoy:

PERSONAL INVENTORY WORKSHEET

Kinds of music I can play now:

Pop, contemporary
Pop, middle of the road
Rock
Disco

Kinds of music I'd like to play:

Jazz
Recording studio work - jingles
demos, etc.
Shows
Teaching

Kinds of music I've played in the past:

Classical
Accompanying, classical instrumental
Accompanying, vocal
Church music, organ
Trumpet work, from high school band
Vocal work, from college theater
experience

Kinds of music I could play but don't enjoy:

Country
Solo work - background piano
Big-band work
Ragtime
Sing-along

such as "excellent," "fair," and "needs work."

Remember that if you are proficient at a style you don't particularly like, it should still be near the top of your list. And of course, if you enjoy another style that you don't really play very well, it should be ranked lower. Not every single item on the inventory list will deserve your time. Some styles may already be good enough, and others aren't worth the effort required to bring them up to professional quality. But you may be surprised at your own musical strengths, and you're bound to find a few areas that, with a little work, could be salable.

The illustration on page 55 shows how the pianist in our example might rank the items from her *Personal Inventory List*. Notice that her rankings do not correspond exactly with the categories on the inventory worksheet.

In the illustrated example, notice the categories toward the bottom of the list. Although trumpet playing may not be a realistic market for our keyboard player, she might decide to work on other categories to reach a salable level. Specifically, with some work, sing-along, organ playing, teaching, and vocal work could become commercially valuable.

Pay particular attention, then, to the bottom third of your list, areas that you don't particularly enjoy doing or haven't yet mastered. Here's where, with a bit of work, you might be able to double or triple your salable music skills.

Why? Because you've naturally spent most of your time working on the kind of music you like. Maybe the intricacies of contemporary jazz fascinate you and you spend hours perfecting stunning solos—and this skill will probably be at the top of your inventory. But unfortunately there will usually be more jobs available using the skills you ranked lower. Dance work, big-band engagements, even Dixieland playing will be more commercially valuable than "pure" jazz. The marketplace isn't as musically sophisticated as you are.

Think Like General Foods

One very common business practice is to survey the market to discover what is needed—or marketable—and then develop a product to meet those needs. If General Foods, through market research, discovers a market for a breakfast cereal shaped like the space shuttle and coated with artificial sweetener, you can bet that it will be in the supermarkets shortly.

You can apply the same technique to your music. If, later on, you find that there are lots of music jobs in one particular area, you may decide to become proficient in that category because you know that's what the market needs—and will support.

Here's a true example of this idea in action. A pop/rock guitarist in Atlanta wanted more work than he was getting—and he was already doing as many guitar jobs as possible. He noticed that there are lots of banjo/Dixieland gigs available, and that even poor banjo players were working a lot, so the guitarist (who doesn't especially like banjo music) bought a banjo and learned to play it fairly well. He now works several banjo jobs each month—often daytime convention work that he wouldn't have gotten without expanding his marketable abilities.

So if you discover several good possibilities in your weaker areas as you develop your market lists, it might be wise to bring them up to a marketable level. That's using the big-business approach; *develop a product for an existing market*. You don't have to be in love with a style of music to make money with it. You may find that you enjoy getting paid to play in a piano bar—even if you don't especially enjoy the music you play.

Personal Ranking

1. Rock--excellent.

2. Pop, contemporary--excellent, know current tunes, styles.

3. Disco--excellent, good synth technique, patches.

4. Solo piano--good, but don't enjoy working alone.

5. Country--fair, know more standards than newer tunes. Don't particularly
    like this style. Easy for me to improve here.

6. Big band (thirties, forties, fifties)--pretty good but know few tunes.

7. Jazz--good, fair repertory, especially older jazz standards. Weaker on
    contemporary tunes. Another area that I could easily improve.

8. Ragtime/sing-along--fair, don't enjoy these styles, know few tunes.

9. Accompanying--good with pop, only fair with classical.

10. Classical--fair, poor repertoire. Rarely play, but could be 100% better
    with just a little work.

11. Church organ playing--weak because of years of neglect. Could improve
    quickly with practice if needed.

12. Recording work--little experience, but could probably do well. Good
    reader, good ear, know lots of styles--should pursue studio work.

13. Show playing--fair with low-pressure shows; could improve with
    experience, but this has low priority now.

14. Teaching--don't know, never tried, might be a good teacher. Should look
    into this for daytime income--don't think there are many pop-oriented
    teachers around.

15. Vocal work--weak, but could improve with practice and confidence. Might
    really help commercially if I worked on my singing and confidence.
    Should learn lots of tunes.

16. Trumpet work--would take more practice time than I can allow. Not
    really commercially useful at this point.

THE SECOND STEP: CREATING YOUR "JOB POSSIBILITIES LIST"

When you've finished the *Personal Inventory List* you have a complete assessment of your musical abilities and strengths. You know all the musical things you can do, which ones you do best, and which ones need work.

The next step is to list as many possible kinds of jobs as you can—jobs that will need, could use, or might possibly benefit from your music. This *Job Possibilities List* will define the scope of your job-finding system, and its usefulness depends on how complete it is. The more possible job categories you include, the more you'll work and the more money you will make. This list will come from your experience, imagination, creative brainstorming, and a little market research.

The main idea here is to think of as many different kinds of music jobs as you can. Include jobs that you might be only remotely suited for. Don't worry about practicality at this point, and don't limit yourself to jobs that currently exist in your community.

Your task is to stay out of the ruts into which most musicians fall. There is plenty of work out there; you just have to find it—and the reward is money. It's up to you to discover the gigs and reap the reward . . . and remember, nobody else cares as much about your career as you do.

So *don't say*, "I'm a guitarist, so I can only work with top-forty lounge bands." Instead, stretch your idea of what a guitar can do to include other kinds of music. Can you play classical acoustic guitar? Couldn't you play solo jobs—background music? Do you sing? How is your improvisation, your jazz work? Do you know standard tunes? What about playing shows—how's your reading? Have you ever taught? Are you good with repairs?

Don't say, "I'm a vocalist, so all I can do is sing in a church choir." That's too limit-ing. Think instead of all the places singing could be used and expand your market thinking to include backup singing in clubs or at concerts, recording-studio work on jingle and demo sessions, singing at weddings, producing your own show (for conventions, trade shows, even cruise ships), teaching and coaching, singing in restaurants and lounges, work in dinner theaters, and roles in musicals. Can you sing in different styles? Do you read music well? Do you like people? Do you enjoy the spotlight and applause? Think big. Why not put together your own band or a group specializing in whatever kind of singing you do, whether it's barbershop quartet, English madrigals, or rock and roll. Dream creatively to expand the possible markets for your music.

When you think like this, you'll come up with other kinds of situations that could use your music. Furthermore, you might even devise jobs that neither the agents in your area nor your potential clients have thought of. Great! You'll have that new field all to yourself.

Remember the Musical Elf

One enterprising flutist I know convinced the manager of a large department store to hire her at Christmastime to walk around the store, dressed as an elf, playing Christmas carols. By thinking creatively, she had devised an unconventional job for herself—and a lucrative one. As you work on this job possibilities list, then, don't limit yourself to jobs that you've already played. Invent new ones! Make up a reason to have a party that will feature your music. Suggest celebrations of important—or whimsical—events.

Virtually every day and week of the year is special for some purpose, and Appendix E lists lots of reasons, or excuses, for celebrations. Maybe it's National Goof-off Day (in March), National Pasta Week (in October), or National Griper's Day (April 15). Perhaps a local radio station would like to sponsor a

Friday-the-thirteenth after-work party featuring your band, or an apartment complex would agree to have a midnight celebration of a lunar eclipse. Why not?

Now for the Mental Jogging

When you are sure that you've thought of every type of job that could possibly need you, go back to your *Personal Inventory List*. Think about each item on your list, play association games, and see what you can come up with. Try "idea spoking" and draw diagrams if they help your creativity. Does playing chamber music in a bank lobby make you think of playing chamber music in a shopping mall? Or at the grand opening of a new fur salon? Or in a luxury automobile dealership? Or in an elegant hotel's lobby? Good. You're associating and on your way to a longer job possibilities list.

Chapter Eight discusses many kinds of jobs for freelance musicians; each entry includes short explanatory comments. But don't read it now—wait until you've expanded your own list of job categories so the suggestions in this book won't limit your thinking. *These ideas are provided only to get you started* in expanding and diversifying your own list—the more creative you can be in discovering lots of needs for your music, the more you'll be in demand. This list will guide you as you develop your marketing plan, so work to make it as comprehensive as you can.

VERSATILITY — KEY TO SUCCESS
INTERVIEW WITH BRUCE BONVISSUTO

Bruce Bonvissuto is an active trombonist in New York City who plays a wide variety of jobs, including big bands, jazz groups, orchestras, chamber groups, recording sessions. He often does Broadway shows — he's played *Deep River*, *Dream Girls*, *Anything Goes*, *Jerome Robbins' Broadway*, *Annie*, *Most Happy Fellow*, and many others. Bruce is also an active teacher: he has a private studio at Carnegie Hall and currently teaches at Brooklyn Conservatory, Long Island University, and City College of New York. He has a Master's degree from The Juilliard School of Music.

Q *What factors do you think are important for freelance success?*
A Of course you have to start with enough talent and ability, but that's a given — that's the starting point — but if you're easily discouraged, regardless of what your musical skills are, you're not a good candidate for this lifestyle. You have to be an optimistic person and not get in a rut about things or get discouraged when business isn't good. To be a successful freelance musician I think you really have to have an innate self-confidence that things will work out.

In fact, success in this business is based on a real variety of things. Some thriving musicians may not be the best players around, but they may have a great repertoire, and that makes them valuable. Others might bring different things to the job — a pleasant personality, for example. In fact, that's a very important attribute. Contractors in New York have told me that there are so many people who play well that they look beyond musical ability to find someone who's nice to have around. That doesn't mean that you have to be a doormat kind of person, but contractors would rather hire someone who'll be pleasant on the job than

the proverbial jerk who can play. It's really that simple; especially on a steady job like a Broadway show nobody wants to hire a troublemaker. We call it the "aggravation factor."

Q *How do you market your music?*
A One thing that I've done almost unconsciously to broaden my markets is to go toward versatility. I've played orchestras, chamber music, jazz, big bands, club dates, shows, and studio work — and nothing has really been a specialized thrust. I've done so many things that there has always been enough to get me through slow times without any problem. Looking back, my attitude was, "I enjoy all these different kinds of music, so why not take the calls?" It helps keep things interesting, too, because there is a danger of boredom or burnout if you're playing a narrow, limited kind of job for a long time — say a Broadway show, or in an orchestra with a limited repertoire.

I'm playing a lot of Broadway shows now, and our contract allows us to take off 50 percent of the time. That lets me do a lot of different things, musically, and that keeps me more active than just playing the same music night after night would allow. You have to stay in touch with lots of people and remind them that you're still around.

Q *What do you especially like about being a freelance musician?*
A One of the exciting things about freelance music is that I've been able to have a lot of great experiences — playing for months in Florence, Italy, taking a month-long cruise with my wife to Acapulco, playing concerts in Africa, playing chamber music in Japan with Metropolitan Brass Quartet. These aren't like a big corporation's benefits, but they are advantages of our profession.

There is the real opportunity to have truly exciting moments in your life.

And other good things can happen. For example, once several years ago, I got a call from Freddie Green (who was an idol of mine) to do a record date, and that was a great feeling I still remember. In a real sense your dreams can come true in music. Those moments are real highs that might not happen in other professions—there's always the chance that something great will happen to you.

SEVEN

FREELANCE MUSIC JOBS— A SURVEY

Before you read this chapter be sure that your own *Job Possibilities List* is as long as you can make it. There are many suggestions for music opportunities on the following pages, and some of them may help expand your compilation, but you shouldn't depend on these ideas. This isn't a "complete" list of freelance music jobs—in fact, such a list would be impossible to make because the market is always growing and changing.

The jobs discussed here cover a wide spectrum and each one won't apply to every musician. Some will fit you exactly; a few will stimulate new ideas; others won't apply to you at all. You'll hopefully be able to add categories that aren't even discussed here—ideas for gigs you've invented.

Some of these suggestions will fit your abilities today. Others may be too difficult, demanding, or complex for you to play right now, but if they're appropriate put them on your list anyway as "goals for the future." Work on preparing yourself to play them.

Once you've developed a long list of job possibilities, the final step will be to match names, addresses, and phone numbers of potential clients with the entries on your list. This will involve some market research, which is fully explained later. Before you move ahead to making sales calls, developing promotional material, or working on a mailing list, however, spend enough

time with your *Job Possibilities List* to make it as inclusive as you possibly can, because for each entry on this list you may discover five, or ten, or fifty potential clients.

THE FREELANCE MARKETPLACE

Here, then, is a short survey, in alphabetical order, of typical freelance music jobs.

Associations link people who have similar interests and professions and give them a chance to share knowledge and ideas—and to socialize. There are well over 25,000 associations listed in the multivolume *Encyclopedia of Associations*, including 218 music-related groups. For another example, the 1989 San Francisco telephone book lists 325 associations and refers you also to Athletic, Business, Consumer, Fraternal, Political, Professional, Veteran/Military, and Youth Organization headings in the Yellow Pages.

Virtually every association sponsors state, regional, and national meetings and conventions, and many of them hold dinners, programs, dances, or fund-raisers that need music. When you begin your publicity efforts, all local associations should certainly be at the top of your prospects list. Some may be too small to need you, but you'll be surprised at the entertainment budgets of many associations.

Bar mitzvahs and bat mitzvahs are, like weddings, family affairs. The mood is often celebratory and the family and guests are intent on having a good time. If you're familiar with Jewish music and tradition, you'll find a large market here, and word-of-mouth advertising will lead to many unsolicited jobs. In some places, these events are rigidly styled and follow a strict pattern. In other communities, a bar mitzvah may be more like a large family party with a few horas thrown in.

Frequently there will be a reception before the dinner-dance that needs background music, and often the musician can make suggestions to the client. The father, for example, may never have thought of using a harp during the cocktail party or dinner, but if you suggest it, he may love the idea. Or, you might suggest a theme party—perhaps an idea based on the son or daughter's interest would be appropriate. The more creative suggestions you make (that match the client's needs, of course), the more jobs you'll book.

If you would like to work frequently in the Jewish community, you should familiarize yourself with the basic philosophy and practices of the different congregations in your area. There are many differences between reform, traditional and conservative synagogues, and regional differences as well. You'll find that some rabbis are very strict about what music can be played, while others allow whatever you and the guests would like. The best course is to talk with each rabbi in your neighborhood, both to introduce yourself and to find out what his musical requirements and preferences are. In any case, you'll need to know several "horas," and you can buy books of Jewish music at any sheet music store or order them from sources in Appendix E.

Booking jobs for your band and other musicians can add a lot of money to your weekly income, and build more job opportunities as well. What if you get several calls for a band on a busy Saturday night? Should you simply tell the callers that you're already working? Why not help them find a band—for a fee?

If you're well organized, know enough musicians, and attend properly to details, you can add "part-time booking agent" to your list of freelance opportunities. Thus, you'll line up the musicians, send the contracts, double-check with the client and the bandleader, and collect a commission. On a smaller scale, you could agree on a finder's fee or referral charge with other musicians—perhaps twenty-five dollars for every job you refer.

The full-time booking agency business is very competitive, and if you decide that you enjoy this aspect of music, you'll find it very helpful to work for one of the larger agencies before you go out on your own. Booking an occasional harpist for a wedding isn't complicated—you can do it without experience. But to book a name entertainer for a large convention is a different matter entirely—you need lots of experience before you attempt to join the big leagues.

If you enjoy selling, dealing with people, and working with lots of entertainers, you may find that the booking business offers challenges and opportunity—and lots of hard work. But you'll also discover many chances to book your own music, and that's what you're trying to do. Most large cities have several sizable booking agencies, and many of their salespeople are musicians, collecting their regular fees for playing—and a commission as well.

Businesses of all kinds are good possibilities for a great variety of music. Large companies, department stores, or professional firms will be good prospects, but don't overlook smaller ones, too. Each business-related need may apply to dozens—or hundreds—of different companies, so work at relating your music to the needs of lots of department stores, insurance agencies, car dealers, manufacturing plants, law firms, and so on. What works for one will work for another.

Business events are often booked by entertainment agents or public relations firms, though many may come direct. Here is a sampling of typical business needs for music.

■ *Ground-breaking ceremonies* for new buildings are big events, and the music often reflects the purpose of the new facility. Thus, a country band might be right for a new truck dealership, while a strolling violin duo could be appropriate for an upscale office park.

■ *Grand openings* of anything from factories to banks can be celebrated with upbeat, inspiring, exciting music. The kind of music that's needed will depend on the business—current pop tunes for a teen-oriented clothing store and Dixieland for a new dealership, for example.

■ *Seasonal sales* can call for creativity in matching the music to the event. One department store uses Mexican-style bands to introduce its Holiday Vacation Fiesta—a joint project of the travel, clothing, and camera departments. Your suggestions can help create jobs.

■ *Trade shows*, where businesspeople meet to sell products and swap ideas, frequently use music to attract a crowd to a particular display or booth. New product introductions, especially, need exciting music.

■ *Promotions and retirements* are often celebrated with elaborate parties. Legal, medical, and accounting firms relax a bit on these occasions and use background or dance music—maybe even in the office.

■ *Company milestones* such as anniversaries, mergers, corporate acquisitions, or new construction are frequently cause for celebration—with music.

■ *Christmas parties* are a staple for most musicians and offer many opportunities. Almost every company has at least one Christmas party, and large concerns may have several; one for the executives, another for the professional staff, and a third for the lower-level employees. Start planning early—May or June isn't too far in advance—for a busy December.

■ *Fashion shows* are given by department stores, boutiques, merchandise marts, restaurants, trade associations, country clubs, and civic groups. They may be held in hotel ballrooms, country clubs, theaters, restaurants, or schools. Music is a crucial element, and you should sell the organizers on using you rather than poor-quality taped music because you're flexible—and your music is excellent and appropriate.

Sometimes your task at a fashion show will be to translate the vague terms used by the organizers into specific tunes. You'll be asked for something "sophisticated," "bouncy," "urbane," "young," "chic," or "new," so it will help if your repertory is broad and you have a good imagination. Some fashion shows are little more than models walking around to background music while others are as elaborately staged as a Broadway production.

Churches and synagogues offer several employment opportunities to a wide variety of musicians. Here are a few possibilities:

■ *Church choirs*—especially the larger ones in large cities—pay their soloists for performing at regular weekly services. Freelance help is added for special holiday programs or concerts, and entire small orchestras may be contracted for special events.

■ *Instructors and conductors* are needed for orchestra and band activities at an increasing number of churches and synagogues.

These institutions offer opportunities for private or class instruction in voice, instrument, piano, and organ.

■ *Weddings and funerals* need music. Sometimes it is provided by staff musicians, but often outside freelancers are hired. Remember, too, that weddings can involve much more than organ and piano music; contemporary services use virtually any kind of music that appeals to the bride and groom.

■ *Substitute work:* organists, pianists, and choral directors may be needed by churches or synagogues on short notice. Religious services must go on even when the regular organist or choir director is sick or on vacation, so if you are available and competent to do fill-in work, let it be known.

■ *Holiday programs* often provide a yearly busy season for vocalists and instrumentalists. One freelance bassist I know regularly plays four or five *different* performances of *The Messiah* during the Christmas season— all at different churches. All of them are paid, of course, and all include paid rehearsals. Such jobs require professionalism, however, and the ability to play your part well with little rehearsal time. After all, most churches have access to plenty of amateur musicians; they hire pros to do a better job and save expensive preparation time.

■ *Staff positions* are not really in the freelance category except perhaps as part-time work; they do offer employment opportunities for the trained organist, pianist, choir director, and children's music specialist, however.

■ *Dances* may be held in church social halls on special occasions. Remember, though, that while a Catholic church may use a band for its St. Patrick's Day dance, the Baptist church down the street may not believe in dancing. Check around before making sales calls.

■ *Rehearsal pianists*, especially in larger churches, are needed for extensive choir programs. The pay may be unexciting but the work should be pleasant and regular.

Civic, social, and nonprofit organizations hold all kinds of events that need music— after-dinner shows, dances, and fund-raising functions, not to mention the ever-present banquets. Some, such as the American Legion and the Elks and Moose clubs have their own facilities with regularly scheduled dances. Others, like Optimist and Rotary clubs, may have infrequent social events, but you should stay in touch with all these organizations to be aware of their varied musical needs.

Usually, the social or entertainment committee changes each year, and the new officers may have no idea of how to book a band or locate entertainment. They'll appreciate knowing about what you have to offer.

Fund-raising events can be elaborate. Such organizations as hospital auxiliaries, committees to benefit various causes, and the Junior League sponsor extravagant shows complete with large orchestras, many rehearsals, expensive costumes, and so on—all to raise money for the group's projects.

Since the fund-raising market is a large one, you should be aware of all nearby nonprofit organizations. Don't forget civic orchestras, historical preservation societies, art museums, opera companies, theaters, health organizations, foundations, and even college athletic associations—all of which may sponsor dinners, dances, or shows to benefit a cause.

Conventions and meetings make up one of the largest, fastest growing markets in contemporary American business. Almost every fair-sized city wants to be a convention center, and every large hotel or resort has a sales staff searching for organizations to hold meetings of all sorts. Virtually every business, industry, government agency, social group, and professional association (and there are thousands of them) has, at the least, an annual meeting or convention to discuss common interests, socialize with colleagues, make useful contacts, and plan for the coming year.

This market offers an enormous opportunity to musicians, and many freelancers in major convention cities make a comfortable living from the convention trade. To get an idea of how big the convention market is, look at some of the meeting-planning magazines listed in Appendix B next time you're in the library. You'll be surprised—and you'll want to be prepared to work in this area, too.

If you are aware of what the convention industry needs, you can take steps to make your musical abilities known. Musical requirements of this industry cover the spectrum from solo background performers to forty-piece orchestras backing the biggest names in entertainment. Convention planners often try to give their members and guests the time of their lives and money may be no object. It's not uncommon for a major convention to spend more than $100,000 on a single evening's show, and the total entertainment budget may be several times that. Music may be needed from breakfast to late-night events.

Every convention is different, of course. The three hundred members of your state's Water Pollution Engineers Association may have little in common with the Association of Life Insurance Sales, but both groups will probably need some kind of music.

Here are some typical ways conventions use music.

■ *Breakfasts* use music to wake up the crowd or set a mood, particularly if a specific theme is important to the meeting. The music is often bright and cheerful—a good pos-

sibility for banjos and Dixieland combos.

■ *Daytime meetings* need music for several reasons. Marches and other exciting tunes establish an upbeat tone, particularly for a sales-oriented meeting. Walk-up music and fanfares are important for awards ceremonies, and there may be company skits or even elaborate shows that require full orchestras. Frequently, new products are introduced to the sales staff at conventions, and these events may be major multimedia productions in which music plays a central part.

■ *Lunches* need background music, of course, and again it may be related to the convention's theme. Because conventioneers often talk business during lunch, subdued music is usually preferred.

■ *Special events for families* of those attending large conventions present musical opportunities. Strolling musicians may work on tour buses or at local attractions visited by the conventioneers. Or musical programs and variety shows can entertain a spouses' luncheon. There may be an impromptu talent show by the members themselves—or a magic or puppet show for their children. Fashion shows are common and also need music.

■ *Cocktail parties and hospitality suites* are mainstays of the convention industry. Often, the real business of the convention— the wheeling and dealing—takes place in the informal atmosphere of a hospitality suite. Frequently, your client will not be the convention itself but a related business or association. Thus, at a bankers' convention you'll find hospitality suites sponsored by large banks and the companies that serve them—perhaps computer firms, software dealers, printing outfits, and office-design companies. Many of these businesses will spend enormous amounts of money to please and impress their clients, and the freelance musician can often be an important part of the hospitality suite's success.

Musical needs of hospitality suites cover the musical spectrum from single piano, violin, or guitar to a small combo that can begin the evening with background music but shift to dance tunes later on.

■ *Convention dinners* may be elaborate and often need background or dance music. As discussed above, the music may be linked to the convention's theme. Perhaps the band will need to play national anthems or state songs to salute those in attendance. Perhaps a baroque ensemble will be needed, or a barbershop quartet, or a jazz trio. Maybe the convention planners would like bluegrass music, or a performance by the local symphony orchestra, or the high school stage band. Anything goes. For example, a recent nurses' convention in Atlanta hired the Georgia Tech marching band and the college chorale just to sing "Happy Birthday" to the organization. It was an expensive rendition—and though the performance only lasted a few minutes, it helped set the celebratory tone for the meeting. Thus it was successful for both the client and the school's music department. Often, there is an awards ceremony following the dinner, and you may need to play fanfares and walk-up music. Sometimes these are carefully scripted, and sometimes you'll do it by ear and intuition. If the convention planners know that you can handle the job you'll become an important part of their plans.

■ *Dances* held in conjunction with conventions offer attendees a chance to socialize and relax—and talk a little business. Remember, then, that the music can't be too loud, at least in the early evening. And, most conventioneers want to hear music from home—even if they've only been gone a day or two—so be prepared with all the geographical tunes you know: "New York, New York," "San Francisco," and so on. Since most convention dances attract a very mixed crowd, you'll need to play a wide vari-

ety for the different ages and tastes. It may not be creatively challenging, but that's not the point in commercial jobs like these.

■ *Shows* may be the main entertainment focus of the convention, and they can be elaborate. If you're a good reader, you may be called on to back a show. Or, if you're part of a self-contained show you may be able to sing, play, and dance your way into a full-time career of convention entertaining. Such groups as The Spurlows, The Young Americans, and The Arbors command hefty fees and stay busy on the convention circuit, but they aren't widely known outside this specialized area. If you're a strong solo performer, talented, personable, and you have a good stage presence, charisma, and lots of ambition, you may want to work toward becoming a convention entertainer in your own right. Such performers as Skip DeVol, Julie Budd, and Danny Gans entertain at conventions around the world and are constantly in demand.

■ *Theme parties* at conventions may be elaborate and require specific kinds of music. By staying in touch with hotels and convention planners in your area, you'll be aware of the types of parties that are frequently given. Common ones include Hawaiian, shipwreck, M*A*S*H, disco, country/western, fifties, roaring twenties, and many others.

If you play in a steel band, say, you may not work every wedding reception that comes along, but your availability might make an "islander" theme party possible. And if the convention planners know of your availability, they may even plan entire parties around your music.

Whatever your specialty, from old-time rock and roll to old-time big-band music, be sure to let the party planners know so that your music can be a central part of their events. And use your brainstorming sessions to come up with new uses for your music that these clients may not have thought of. It's up to you to tell them.

Convention work, then, covers a broad spectrum and includes virtually every kind of music. The convention planners who put these meetings together, and the booking agents who work with them, are looking for entertainment—sometimes desperately. If your suggestions, backed by a good reputation and professional appearance, can help them avoid the "same old thing," you'll be appreciated and in demand.

Country clubs—and other types of clubs— need lots of music for an astounding variety of occasions. Obviously, country and athletic clubs with their own imposing facilities have regular dinners, dances, and parties— and you should pursue them if they match your musical specialty. These clubs also host:

■ *Special events* for occasions like Valentine's Day, New Year's Eve, Mother's Day, and so on.

■ *Seasonal and holiday activities* which can be as varied as the social director's (and your) imagination will allow. Typical functions include summertime pool parties, Labor Day cookouts, Oktoberfest, Halloween costume parties, Christmas and other holiday events, and special functions that you may concoct (see Appendix E for a list of holidays and annual happenings).

■ *Elaborate theme parties* where musical requirements may be quite specific. Perhaps the club's members will be involved in a fifties dance, a roaring-twenties extravaganza, or a Hawaiian/tropical-theme pool party. If your specialty is ethnic, geographic, or unusual music be sure your abilities are known. (Theme parties are discussed in more detail later.)

■ *Athletic events*, such as golf and tennis

tournaments, will often begin or end with dances and parties.

■ *Shows* are often presented by larger clubs, and famous entertainers often appear at private clubs. Sometimes they'll need local backup musicians; this is a good market for players who can read a show well. And, if you have a show of your own, stay in touch with club managers and social directors.

■ *Children's parties* are a good country-club market. If you can team up with a magician, juggler, mime, puppet show, or similar act, many clubs will welcome you. Social committees may be looking desperately for some activity to involve young people, and your suggestions can generate jobs.

■ *Special events* held by private groups in club facilities are another part of the "hidden music market." Wedding receptions, office parties, retirement dinners, birthday parties, class reunions, and other such events use music for entertainment and dancing, but you'll never know about them unless your network of contacts includes the right people.

When you think of "clubs," however, don't limit yourself to just the big country clubs. Include every organized group you can think of, and you'll expand your market to include all kinds of nonpublic but well-paying possibilities.

Other clubs may not have their own facilities but still need music for the same kinds of functions listed above. Groups of tennis players, marathon runners, sports-car enthusiasts—any group that is organized for a specific purpose—may have at least one social event each year that needs music. For example, the Atlanta Ski Club holds frequent dances and parties and is one of the largest social clubs in the city (even though it rarely snows in Atlanta). Don't limit your job possibilities to the obvious.

Another club source for freelance music

opportunities is the almost endless variety of organized hobby groups—philatelists, photography buffs, model railroad clubs, amateur radio operators, big-game hunters, tall-peoples' clubs, square dancers, or experimental aircraft builders. Almost all such groups will have dances, banquets, award ceremonies, cocktail parties, barbecues, picnics, or other annual events. They need your music.

Gospel and contemporary Christian music allows many musicians to practice their religion through music—and make money as well. Today, this is a very active and expanding market, and both instrumental and vocal groups find ample opportunity to perform.

Many contemporary performers have adopted their secular competition's style and show-business glitter but see themselves primarily as religious entertainers. Amy Grant, for example, has a collection of gold and platinum records, and *Newsweek* called her "the first evangelical superstar." Special concerts in churches, civic auditoriums, schools and colleges, public parks, and even huge tents feature gospel and other religious musical groups—sometimes six or eight different groups per performance. There are national magazines for the religious music market (see Appendix A), and most cities have at least one "Christian music" radio station.

Despite the religious aspects, performing contemporary Christian music requires the same quality and attention to show-business details as any other kind of entertainment. Your musical and business skills, not your religious fervor, will assure your success in this increasingly competitive area.

Government-sponsored work gives you a chance to get some of your taxes back, and though governments aren't usually thought of as music buyers, you may be surprised at the opportunities they offer. Here are a few examples.

■ *Park programs* abound, and governmental or quasi-governmental agencies are often in control. In Atlanta, for instance, the Cultural Affairs Bureau sponsors large and small music festivals around the city, and there is even a "Jazzmobile" that goes from park to park during the summer. Usually, local talent is used.

■ *Inner-city festivals, grand openings of newly renovated areas, and parties* to celebrate special days are commonly produced by governing boards. When it's the anniversary of your town's founding, why not suggest a concert in the park or a street dance? The city may sponsor and organize the event or work with a private-sector sponsor.

■ *Cultural enrichment programs and historical musical services* are widespread, and government-sponsored music at national parks and historic sites offers interesting opportunities. If you perform Native American or early American music, you may find a government-owned place to perform. (Don't overlook foundation-sponsored historical centers, too, such as Old Salem, Williamsburg, and Sturbridge Village.)

■ *Foreign tours* to entertain our troops overseas provide lots of work for musicians and entertainers. Many bands have spent enjoyable (though hardworking) summers doing USO tours of European, Asian, and other military bases. Navy pilots stationed in Greenland need entertainment, too.

■ *Bands* are maintained by each branch of the armed forces, and these provide secure employment, travel, and excellent musical experiences for musicians who are interested in full-time playing jobs—and who join the armed services. Many of these bands are of excellent quality, and they offer stage, jazz, and dance work in addition to traditional ceremonial playing. Often, too, armed-forces band members can accept outside freelance work to augment their incomes.

■ *Officer's and NCO clubs* on most military bases need bands for regularly scheduled dances and for special occasions. Sometimes units from the base's band supply music, but usually outside groups are hired. If you live near a large military installation it could provide you with a substantial amount of work.

■ *Grants, scholarships, internships, stipends, and student loans* are offered by governmental agencies as well as by private foundations or organizations. Each grant or scholarship will have specific requirements and be for a specific purpose, but if you have a musically worthwhile project that needs funding, you should research such sources of money. (See Appendix B for further reading.) Some states offer college scholarships to students who agree to teach in the state for a specified time, and there are many other sources of government-sponsored education money and student loans.

Hotels are a primary market for musicians for several reasons.

■ *Music in the lounge* is a mainstay for many musicians and bands, and some hotel chains maintain a circuit for musicians among their properties.

■ *Music in the lobby* is increasingly popular in finer hotels. A grand piano, or string quartet, or jazz combo may show the guests that the hotel wants them to have a memorable visit.

■ *Hotel-sponsored parties* for clients and employees. If you have a good relationship with the catering or sales staff, you'll get these jobs.

■ *Conventions, trade shows, and business events* are mainstays of the hotel business. Each of these areas is discussed in this chapter.

Music-related jobs may not require perform-

ing, but shouldn't be overlooked; your knowledge of music may allow you to profit from your talent in nonplaying ways.

■ *Radio and TV jobs* requiring music knowledge include program planning and on-the-air work. If you're a real bluegrass buff, for example, you might produce a weekly bluegrass show for a local FM station or a jazz, folk, or chamber-music hour if that's your specialty. Many colleges now have radio stations that offer valuable experience to their students, and while listener-supported and college stations may pay poorly or not at all, you'll gain valuable experience.

■ *Music libraries* are specialized centers requiring trained librarians. A degree in library science or media-center administration combined with your musical knowledge could start a new career. Currently, there are about six hundred music libraries in this country, and your reference librarian can help you find a directory of them (see Appendix B).

■ *Music therapy* requires special schooling and certification, but a college degree combined with your performing background might lead to a satisfying career helping people through music (see Appendix D for more information).

■ *Music criticism* may be satisfying for musicians who also like to write. Local newspapers, magazines, and broadcasting stations all need music critics. If you understand music, the qualities of a good performance, and the essentials of writing clearly, part-time music criticism may get you free tickets, free records, *and* a paycheck.

Nightclubs and cabarets offer an abundance of work to the freelance musician. This is the most obvious venue for most bands, but it offers possibilities beyond the steady, six-night-a-week engagements that you may be already playing. Other nightclub opportunities include:

■ *Special events* that need extra musicians or groups.

■ *Fill-in work* if the regular band or individual musicians are gone for a day or a week.

■ *Daytime work*—music for luncheons, fashion shows, wedding receptions, business meetings. Such events offer extra opportunities in many clubs.

Nightclub work can be difficult; long hours, poor working conditions, and unsympathetic management are common. Nevertheless, clubs offer great opportunities to thousands of musicians and may provide a base of operations and a steady income while you pursue other—perhaps more lucrative—freelance music jobs.

Novelty uses of music can be as creative, unusual, or even silly, as your imagination allows—and probably more entertaining than musical. Nevertheless, these can be lucrative outlets for your music—and, again, you'll sometimes find these jobs where you make them. Use your imagination.

■ *The "singing (or playing) telegram"* is a new, growing market offered by such companies as Eastern Onion and Balloons and Tunes. If you are outgoing and funny, are blessed with creative flair, and have, perhaps, a touch of the bizarre, you could do well here.

■ *Street musicians* working in many large cities make an art of creating their own jobs on the spot. These contemporary minstrels strive for direct communication between player and audience: if the crowd likes your music, you make money and if they don't, you starve.

Some street musicians reportedly make up to four hundred dollars a day, and certain San Francisco street players are said to make more than $30,000 a year. This can't be verified, but if it's true you can be sure that the musicians earned every cent the hard way.

Some cities issue performance permits for street musicians, and others arrest them. "On the street," one player commented to *People* magazine, "the police are the ultimate critics." If you're adventurous and something of a showperson, you might consider this kind of performance; some people thrive on putting their talent on the line every day, and it's hard to imagine a job with more freedom—and risk.

So, don't be limited by the same old traditional jobs. Be as creative as possible with novelties in music. Remember the flutist in Chapter Six who created a job as a "Musical Elf." You can do the same thing if you brainstorm to think of unusual jobs to match your talents—and then sell those ideas.

Orchestras frequently use supplementary musicians for special concerts, adding extras as the music demands. Good freelance players with appropriate backgrounds should be alert to this possible source of employment.

Classical players can often work with community and professional orchestras in smaller cities or on college campuses. Often such symphony orchestras or chamber groups will draw first-chair players and soloists from larger cities for their concerts, so expand your job-search area to include smaller cities and towns within driving distance. Every large city helps support the arts in smaller surrounding communities this way, and a willingness to make a few hours' drive can improve your market outlook—particularly if you play a relatively obscure instrument, such as the oboe or bassoon.

Parades, fairs, carnivals, street dances, and

many other events also raise money and create publicity for civic organizations. You may be asked to donate your services to a worthy cause, and if you do you can often take a tax deduction for the value of your contribution. But many fund-raising organizations will pay for your music, just as they pay for the food they serve, and raise their money from the public. A few benefit gigs may be helpful and you certainly want to support good causes, but in most communities there are so many worthwhile charities that you could bankrupt yourself by donating too much. Try for a good balance. Remember that "exposure," though valuable, won't pay your rent, and such exposure is usually not worth much to your career unless the audience includes lots of potential clients.

Parties in homes are another specialized but excellent market. Most home parties employing musicians are given by well-to-do people, so it's important that you be able to relate socially as well as musically. Perhaps an elegant dinner will require sophisticated piano background, a wedding reception will need a string quartet, or a garden party could use a dance band. People at such intimate parties often like to stand around the piano and sing. That's good for you if you are a pianist, your repertory is extensive, and you get along well with people. The word will spread, and you'll be in demand. You may even be able to "train" the wealthy party-givers in your area to expect your music at all the "best" parties, and in doing this you may create not just a few jobs, but a whole career. If you remember names, faces, and favorite tunes of your clients and their friends, they'll think you're terrific (sometimes regardless of your musical skills), and they'll want you at all their parties. (See Appendix B for books to help improve your memory.)

Private teaching is a good way to share your own proficiency and knowledge with others and offers a stable way to augment your income. It could even become your main occupation. But teaching isn't easy—it requires patience, organization, and the ability to demonstrate and explain difficult concepts. For some kinds of teaching, college preparation is required, but for other musical styles, playing ability and professional experience is more important. If you want to teach advanced classical piano, for instance, you'll most likely need at least an undergraduate degree. If, however, you want to teach improvisation—a skill not always taught in college—you'll need to be an excellent jazz/pop player yourself.

Teaching can sometimes be an alternative to "selling out"; it allows you to make a living from music without playing jobs you may dislike. One prominent Atlanta pianist, for example, is more interested in jazz and his own compositions than in pleasing commercial clients. He finds that teaching jazz, improvisation, and theory offers him a sizable income without the pressures of performing music he doesn't enjoy. He has fifty students, charges fifteen dollars per half-hour lesson, and enjoys teaching, so he doesn't mind working in the same studio all day. To prepare yourself for teaching you'll need to organize your approach, determine what you have to offer, and attract students. Often you can work with public-school music teachers and music stores to find pupils. Word-of-mouth advertising is the best kind. One satisfied student will quickly lead to another.

How much can you make? How much should you charge? Teaching fees vary widely depending on where you are, how much education and experience you have, what you teach, and how much competition you have, but most musicians can add significantly to their income by taking at least a few students. Find out what other teachers offer and charge, and price your services accordingly. Read books and magazine articles on music teaching to get more ideas on this important aspect of professional music. (See Appendixes A and B for suggestions for further reading.)

Public relations firms and advertising agencies can be good music clients because they are involved in creating and staging all kinds of events. Whatever your musical specialty, you should let all the advertising and PR firms in your area know, so when they need your type of music they'll know about you. Some of these jobs will be booked directly, while others may come through entertainment agencies. Regardless of how you get them, however, you can look to advertising and PR people for lots of performing opportunities.

■ *Political campaign events, fund-raisers, and victory celebrations* are enlivened by Dixieland, country, or rock bands. Usually, political events are planned by the advertising or PR firm that's handling a politician's campaign. (Here's a helpful hint: make *sure* that you have a firm contract and know who will pay you when you book political events; sometimes collecting from defeated candidates isn't easy.)

■ *Ground-breaking ceremonies* for new buildings often need music to mark the celebration. The music can be exciting and lively or sedate and sophisticated. For example, a large bank in Atlanta recently hired (through its PR agency) a string quartet to play for a black-tie cocktail party at the ground-breaking festivities at the site of a new headquarters—in the middle of a suburban woods.

■ *New product introductions* can be staged with true show-business extravagance. Trumpeters with herald trumpets, for example, lend a special air to such events with colorful costumes, banners—and fanfares. A car show might feature a sophisticated jazz quartet for the introduction of a new line of luxury passenger cars.

■ *Grand openings* for all kinds of new buildings are often celebrated with lavish parties. Whether it's a skyscraper, parking garage, or airplane hangar, the developer's PR firm will handle the party plans, including music.

■ *Office parties* are important business functions for many professionals. Stockbrokers, attorneys, accountants, and many others need a chance to socialize with current and potential clients. Their parties can be lavishly produced and often enlivened with music. Again, PR firms may plan the events and hire the musicians.

If your music can be used to draw attention to a product, service, or even a building, the PR and advertising firms in your area should know about you. Public relations and advertising people thrive on innovation and often are open to suggestions for new or unusual uses of music. When you talk with these firms, then, be as creative as you can. Make suggestions that are too unusual to present to other clients, and you'll be treated as a kindred spirit.

Or, if your band is currently the "hot" party band in town, the ad and PR people will want to know about that, too, because they're very interested in trends and in being on top with what's popular. The bottom line: tell them about your music—and don't let them forget about you.

Recording implies record albums, hit songs, the quest for gold or platinum records, and the fast-lane world of the pop celebrity. The record industry, to be sure, is a very visible part of the music world, but recording means much more than trying for a hit record.

In the recording industry, rapidly developing technology is having a big impact. Sophisticated digital recording equipment has made it possible for smaller cities to have excellent recording facilities and to produce better sound and a better product. No longer do New York, Los Angeles, and Nashville have a monopoly on recording. Today, excellent work can come from virtually any city in the country—and more recording studios mean more work for musicians. Several kinds of recording sessions should interest you.

■ *Jingles* are musical commercials, and the time, money, and energy spent on thirty- or sixty-second commercials may astound you. Payment for jingle sessions ranges from fairly low for local, limited-use spots to extravagant for union players and singers who receive residuals for long-running national commercials. Be aware that this is a *very competitive* field.

■ *Demo sessions* produce demonstration tapes of some sort—perhaps for a songwriter, a singer, a band, or even an advertising agency working on a speculative project. Since these tapes are often financed by one person (a songwriter, for example) the pay may be quite low. Demo sessions, however, provide a lot of work for studios and musicians and can lead to more important, higher-paying studio jobs.

■ *Record sessions* once were limited to established recording centers, but today, albums, cassettes, and CDs are produced in studios throughout the country. Usually, at least in metropolitan areas, the pay is set by union scale (American Federation of Musicians or the American Federation of Television and Radio Artists). Studio players in major cities are among the most competent, accomplished, and best-paid musicians anywhere. Consequently, this area is among the most difficult markets for many musicians to enter. However, even if you never play a record session in Los Angeles, you may be needed locally by entertainers and groups who are making their own albums or videos.

■ *Miscellaneous recording work* includes production of audiovisual and film scores, recordings for sales meetings, and music for television shows. For example, a large company may decide to record the upbeat music for a series of sales meetings rather than depend on local musicians at each location. Or a comedian may want to record backup music because his budget won't always support a live band. Such recording sessions are typical of a local studio's work, and the variety can be as stimulating as if a platinum album were the goal.

If you are a capable musician and a good reader and you can play different styles, you should stay in touch with nearby studios regardless of your instrument. There may be few calls for a French horn player, but when a French horn is needed, nothing else will do.

Remember that tape is unforgiving, and mistakes and approximations that work in live performances may become big problems in the studio. To succeed in this field you must have mastered your instrument and be a precise, exact player. Most sessions allow little rehearsal time—maybe once or twice through the part—so excellent sight-reading is essential. Nothing is so embarrassing as making the mistake that requires another "take," causing more work for everyone and costing the client more money in studio time.

Recording work, despite these requirements, is fun and challenging, and you may enjoy playing on a sixty-second commercial that becomes part of popular culture, or helping a songwriter hear her composition professionally performed, or playing on a local celebrity's album. Sometimes the players who do sessions form a tightly knit clique, and you may have to constantly remind the studios of your existence and ability—but persistence and talent can pay off in the long run.

Repair services are another opportunity for technically minded musicians. Many musicians learn the specialized fields of band-instrument repair and piano tuning and are able to augment their incomes substantially with these skills. Further, musicians who are interested in electronics may find that technical schools in their areas need instructors for their low-cost or free training in electronics, thus opening a new career for daytime work.

Restaurants, especially larger, elegant ones, offer a lot of work to musicians. Typically they need:

■ *Background or dinner music* to set the mood for quiet, elegant dining. Often piano, violin, harp, or acoustic guitar are appropriate.

■ *Music for special events,* such as wedding receptions, club dances, private cocktail parties, and business functions. These events are good examples of the "hidden market." There is a great need for music of all kinds, but unless you develop a network of useful contacts, you'll never know about them.

■ *Dance music*—provided by dance orchestras, top-forty groups, or show bands—may be popular in a restaurant's lounge, and if you're able to handle both background music for dinner and dance music later, why not collect payment for both?

■ *Ethnic music* to create the appropriate atmosphere. As the American melting pot expands, there are more and more ethnic restaurants even in smaller towns and music can be important to their success. No longer are French and Italian bistros the only foreign ones; now your town probably has Ethiopian, Vietnamese, Thai, Middle Eastern, and Caribbean restaurants. Music helps create the ambience. If you play the balalaika, for example, there is probably a Russian restaurant looking for you.

■ *Special events* such as St. Patrick's day or the Fourth of July often need extra musicians or an unusual kind of music. If you're aware of special promotions, you can profit from them.

Sales is important to all musicians; selling your music is, after all, what this book is about. But have you thought of selling musical equipment? If you enjoy working with people this might be an excellent opportunity for you to make money while keeping up with the music market.

■ *Working in a music store* is natural for many musicians because knowledgeable salespeople are needed to sell today's complex instruments. It would be extremely difficult for a nonmusician to explain and sell a synthesizer, for example, so music stores offer a profitable way to broaden your experience with music. And, you'll get a discount on equipment you buy if you're a salesperson.

■ *Selling in record stores and sheet-music shops* offers the same advantages. Your specialized knowledge of the field will make you especially valuable to the store manager.

■ *Selling in a booking agency* can be competitive but offers you a chance to make an excellent income while expanding your contacts with music. Many musicians work in booking agencies, primarily to book themselves at first, and they become such successful salespeople that they may abandon playing in favor of selling. While you may not want to go that far, working in a booking agency may offer worthwhile advantages.

You've never sold anything and don't think you could? Don't worry. If you're interested in this field you can develop sales skills, and your knowledge of music gives you a decided advantage. Many excellent and inspirational books teach sales techniques (see Appendix B for suggestions).

Sales meetings are similar to conventions but are usually smaller and are produced by individual companies. Music is often used to motivate employees and excite others in the audience about the company's plans and products, and can be needed for skits, sales awards, sports awards, and walk-ons and walk-offs. Sometimes there are company songs, and these can be taken very seriously by the company—though their musical value may be questionable. These events provide useful daytime income and usually require upbeat, lively, inspiring music. Since trips are often awarded as incentives, you may need to play music from particular destinations—Hawaii, Spain, or the Bahamas, for example.

Schools offer a broad market for all kinds of music.

■ *Substitute teaching* offers an excellent opportunity for the freelancer who has a teaching certificate. Check with the school districts in your area, including private and church institutions, for policies and needs. A few days of substitute teaching each month can make a sizable difference in your income without interfering with your evening jobs.

■ *Part-time teaching* may be needed by nursery schools, private schools, or smaller districts. Depending on your education and their requirements, you may be able to arrange a part-time job teaching music, leading singing, or directing the band. Or you might team up with jugglers, puppeteers, clowns, or actors to produce simple shows for nursery and elementary school audiences. Schools often have money budgeted for such special arts-related events.

■ *College theatrical and musical groups* frequently need professional soloists or musicians. Watch for announcements, casting calls, and tryouts, and stay in touch with the school's music department.

■ *Accompanying for recitals* can be a good market for pianists who live near colleges and universities. Voice and instrumental music students often have to give recitals, and their accompanists are usually paid.

■ *Concerts for the student body* may be sponsored by the student association or the college's activity fund and may feature famous entertainers or locally known groups that may need backup players. Or, if you have a packaged show that would appeal to college audiences, such as a "History of Rock and Roll" show, why not try to book your own act? Many colleges have regularly scheduled concerts and performances, sometimes featuring student or local bands.

■ *Fraternities and sororities* are a steady market for rock, pop, soul, and country bands, shows, and soloists. These Greek organizations hold parties and dances as often as deans will allow. Rush week at the beginning of the school year is particularly active.

■ *Student parties* of every description have always been a staple of college life. Party sponsors may include the student center, activities fund, alumni association, and many special-interest groups and clubs. College students love dances, parties, reunions, street fairs, and carnivals, and for many students such events are as important as classroom work.

■ *College-sponsored fund-raising and social activities* may require music. Cocktail parties, for example, are typically given for wealthy alumni and contributors, often before or after athletic events. Fairs, carnivals, pageants, or dances may be staged to raise money.

■ *Thousands of class reunions* are held every year—frequently in the summer months—for alumni of high schools, vo-tech schools, and colleges. Almost all these functions need music, especially music related to the class' graduation year. This is an excellent market for many musicians regardless of age or musical preference because somewhere there is a reunion looking for your kind of music. The Class of '44 will want big-band music, while the Class of '94 will want whatever is popular that year. The range is enormous, and if you specialize in a particular era, you should market your music to the classes that match it.

■ *Grants and special funds* are available for presenting educational programs in schools. The Music Performance Trust Fund (MPTF) of the American Federation of Musicians is an example of a program that promotes live music productions, often in the schools. Government, school, and foundation sources also fund this kind of activity. If you're interested in educational performance, your librarian can direct you to excellent books on grantsmanship (see Appendix B), and the musicians' union can give you details on the MPTF program.

Shopping malls are everywhere, and many of them are like small towns in themselves. Often the mall is actually the center of community life and thus hosts lots of events, many of which need music. Here are examples.

■ *Seasonal events* sponsored by the mall itself attract crowds and shoppers. Festivals at Christmas, band concerts for the Fourth of July, and German oompah bands for Oktoberfest are only samples of what enterprising mall promotion directors will do to create excitement.

■ *Special sales* sponsored by individual stores use a wide range of music depending on the store—from a harpist in an elegant fur salon to a country band at the western-wear outlet store. Use your imagination and make suggestions. Remember, the cost of your band may be only a fraction of the store's promotional budget, so don't hesitate to tell store managers how music will

create excitement and attract shoppers. (Remember what the store owner is interested in, and you'll know what to say.)

■ *Weeklong festivals* sponsored by larger malls attract huge crowds. "Heritage Week," "Local Artists' Week," or "Visit England" week all need appropriate music. Large malls always have something special going on. Don't hesitate to make suggestions—perhaps the mall could sponsor a battle of local jazz bands or even a local composers' concert series. Or you could link your suggestions to the calendar and suggest a back-to-school sock hop in the mall or a beach music evening at the beginning of spring break. Think about seasonal sales as you develop ideas to present to the mall's managers, and don't forget that merchandisers plan far ahead—fall and back-to-school fashions appear as early as June. You could also suggest regular ongoing events—a tea dance on Friday afternoons or a Sunday morning Dixieland brunch. How about single acts to circulate through the mall entertaining shoppers? The spontaneity of such "street musicians" always adds zest and life for the mall's crowds.

Substitute work can be an important area for freelance music income. Musicians who work all those steady engagements get sick or need occasional vacations, and enterprising freelance players will stay in touch and make their availability known. Remember, many musicians are justifiably afraid of losing steady jobs; often they are only "two-weeks' notice" away from unemployment, so if you're interested in doing sub work make it clear that you are not after the job permanently. Other players will be more likely to hire you to fill in if they trust you and know that you won't try to take their jobs. In large cities, subs can work frequently—perhaps as much as they'd like—simply by staying in touch with the six-night musicians in the area.

Technical assistance is increasingly important each year as sound reinforcement, electronics, and computers become more and more important to performers. Musicians who are technically inclined and trained and who understand electronics will find many jobs waiting for them.

■ *Sound reinforcement* is crucial to many performers—it's not the sound that leaves the stage that's important, but the sound the audience hears, and that's the sound engineer's responsibility. This is true for classical ensembles as well as rock performers, and even beginning local bands often depend on a sound person to keep the sound "right" in the house. Sound work includes both the set-up of mikes, speakers, monitors, and amps, and the very important job of mixing—or controlling—the sound at the board.

■ *Teaching electronic music techniques* is a new opportunity for those who understand changing technologies. Synthesists, for example, may find work teaching other keyboard players how to program their new instruments, use MIDI, and interface with personal computers. Since many traditional pianists are confused and frightened by electronics, enterprising synthesists and computer experts will find many students if they can share their knowledge.

■ *Synthesizer programmers* can also find work at recording studios or special promotions in music stores and trade shows. Some experts create and sell programs on computer disks or cartridges—ready to be loaded into the synthesizer's memory—and they advertise this service in music magazines. This is a perfect example of enterprising musicians taking advantage of changing technology.

Theaters and shows, both amateur and professional, need music. Musicals must have accompaniment from rehearsal pianists to pit orchestras. If you are an instrumentalist and a good reader, playing shows as they come through your area may provide a considerable part of your freelance income. And if you're a singer, you should be aware of the chorus or backup vocal needs of all the shows that come to town, including theatrical productions, concerts, and nightclub acts. In many places, theater companies aspire to professional status but constantly battle to survive. These community, semi-professional theaters may not offer much money, but there should be some compensation—and this is a good way to meet people, gain experience, and build your network of contacts in the field.

■ *Shows featuring famous entertainers* usually pick up local musicians for the orchestra. Well-known acts often travel with a conductor/pianist and hire all other players locally. Since the theater season can last several months, this can be a lucrative market for those players who enjoy it and can cut it.

■ *Dinner theaters*—although an endangered species—offer work to both players and singers, including small backup bands. If you are just starting your career, you may find such a theater provides excellent training. If you are an established singer, you may land a lead role. At dinner theaters where actors and actresses may also wait on tables, the work is hard but the experience can be rewarding.

■ *Your own show* can be booked for civic groups, conventions, fairs, festivals, and even cruise ships, and if you are an entertainer—a singer, for example, who enjoys close interaction with the audience—you may want to investigate creating your own show. Remember, though, that a show must be *entertaining* to the audience, so you'll have to slant it that way. Writing and producing top-quality, salable entertainment isn't easy, however, because elaborate and expensive TV productions set the quality standard for today's audiences. However, if you do produce an entertaining show, you'll have a very salable product that can be booked "as is" for years. Many successful performers for convention dates—singers, comics, and instrumentalists—develop a format that works well and rarely change it. The market for shows is huge and expanding, and fast-paced entertainment is what show business is all about. If your show is consistently entertaining and of high quality, you'll have plenty of venues and agents will fill your mailbox with offers of work. The hard part is developing the product and maintaining it at a high level, but if entertaining is in your blood, go for it. You may be able to join such successful groups as The Arbors, The Spurlows, Main Street, and Showboat and develop a fast-paced, well-paying career.

Tourist-related jobs may be plentiful and lucrative in your area, but you may need to use your imagination to find or create them. Obvious employers that use lots of music include large theme parks such as Six Flags, Disney World, and Carowinds, but there are others.

■ *Riverboats* evoke another era, and use banjos and Dixieland bands.

■ *Historical sites* suggest many musical applications. Think about period music at such restorations as Williamsburg, Old Salem, and Sturbridge Village—and you'll double your opportunity if you also can make, for example, lutes or recorders. By combining this craft with the appropriate music, you could make yourself a featured part of the tourist attraction.

■ *Sightseeing tours* sponsored by local companies for conventioneers may need special music at various destinations or even on the tour bus, boat, or train itself.

■ *Cruise ships* take thousands of tourists yearly on elaborate vacations and use dance bands, show groups, and single performers.

■ *A restored opera house or theater* in your area may provide another opportunity for producing a show from the building's heyday. If you find the appropriate venue and create the right music for it, you'll have a corner on this market.

■ *Seasonal festivals or neighborhood celebrations* attract many visitors and need music. Why couldn't your chamber music group work with the botanical gardens activities committee to cosponsor a concert in the gardens? (It regularly happens exactly this way in Atlanta.) Or how about a recital in a restored mansion during a candlelight tour of homes?

■ *Special programs.* A famous composer or performer from your community need not be alive to help you. A program of his or her music might be just the thing to perform at the birthplace or memorial center, or as an after-dinner show for civic or convention groups. The opportunities for tourist-related music are nearly endless, and if you match your imagination and musical ability with creative marketing, you may find jobs where none had existed before.

Traveling shows, the circus, and sports music offer miscellaneous opportunities to many instrumentalists. The work, particularly playing circus shows, can be very demanding, but the pay is good and the shows often come to town every year—resulting in a regular week or two of dependable work. These road shows—rodeos, ice shows, and so on—use local musicians, so you should stay in touch with the local contractors and agents who book these jobs. Ball parks and sports stadiums also use music, and not just an organist for baseball games, either. Pep bands, halftime entertainment, and other excitement-producing music go well with professional sports, and this market includes minor league and college levels as well as big-league opportunities.

Weddings offer lots of opportunities to all kinds of musicians.

■ *Music for ceremonies* ranges from traditional organ processionals to almost anything imaginable. If you can suggest an interesting musical combination to wedding planners and brides you can create jobs for yourself. Common instrumentation includes harp, piano, woodwind or string ensembles, lute, acoustic guitar, harpsichord. But there's no reason to be limited by the usual—one wedding in Atlanta recently used only a string bass for music.

■ *Rehearsal dinners* also need music, and these occasions are often more lively than the reception itself and may need a more contemporary band. In fact, rehearsal dinners can be more like a fraternity party than a staid reception.

■ *Reception music* following the ceremony ranges from strictly background performances, such as solo piano, harp, or strolling guitar, to large dance orchestras or pop bands. A large wedding reception can be a major production with a consultant to direct everything, so you should get to know all the wedding consultants in your area. Brides and their families want their weddings to be memorable and happy occasions, and enterprising musicians who make practical suggestions about instrumentation and repertory will often be able to create more work for themselves.

Writing, arranging, and copying can be a lucrative sideline for many freelance musicians. Depending on your talent and skill, there are several kinds of writing that you may do.

■ *Writing lead sheets* for soloists, vocalists, bands, or shows is a much-needed talent.

(Lead sheets are simple transcriptions of individual songs, with only the melody line and supporting chords indicated—a bare minimum that leaves interpretation up to the performer.) This may involve simply transcribing melodies and chords from records, or it may require working with "composers" who don't read music. Singers, particularly, need lead sheets in their keys, and this is an area where a bit of expertise will be lucrative. There is a steady supply of new bands and vocalists who need lead sheets of current tunes, and this market can provide a dependable part of your income.

■ *Writing full arrangements*, scores, and shows is a much more challenging field and usually requires special schooling and study. Good arranging skills are rare, and a freelancer who is a gifted composer/arranger may have as much work as she or he can handle. Typical jobs include writing shows for vocalists and bands, creating special arrangements or scores for audiovisual productions and movies, and composing advertising jingles. It is not uncommon for a player who writes a little to evolve into a writer who plays a little. Good writers and arrangers in such a specialized field as advertising jingle writing may make much more money than the players who record their music.

■ *Copying music* requires a meticulous mind, close attention to detail, and an artistic flair with pen and ink. Good copyists, particularly in large cities, can make substantial incomes. Synthesizer/computer music-writing programs are becoming more practical, though, and many copyists will have to become computer-oriented to survive. There will probably always be a need for beautifully hand-copied charts, however, so if you enjoy calligraphy, don't mind detailed work, and know music well, you can augment your income through copying. Certainly, every musician who plays a clear, well-written part will thank you.

■ *Songwriting* is not—at least for the beginner—a dependable way to make money, but it's alluring because it offers at least a chance to write hit songs and collect royalties for years. That possibility, however, is fairly remote because of the enormous number of people diligently writing and submitting songs. Don't quit your job and move to Nashville to become a songwriter, but if you like to compose music or write lyrics, be persistent. It's hard to get started, but once your name is known you'll be able to get your work heard. Some excellent books and magazines for songwriters are suggested in Appendixes A and B, and many songwriters' clubs offer support, suggestions, and recognition.

TAKE TIME OUT TO REVIEW YOUR LIST

You should now have many entries on your list of job possibilities, and your own compilation is probably quite different from the jobs discussed in this chapter.

Now is *not* the time to be exactingly critical of your list. It is the time, however, to review the list to see if you have followed the guidelines described earlier. Here are a few questions to keep in mind as you look back over your ideas for jobs that need your music:

■ Have you written down every job idea you yourself might possibly handle—no matter how apparently outlandish or far-fetched or even silly it seems?

■ Have you brainstormed for new uses for your music, or have you restricted yourself to ideas listed in this book? Have you gone beyond the same old jobs you've always played?

■ Have you practiced your association techniques to expand your list? Always look for similar but new uses for your music.

■ Are the entries relevant to your own instrument(s), musical tastes, and ability?

■ Have you, in essence, used this list as an opportunity to branch out and search for new horizons?

The *Job Possibilities List* you have made and are about to review is yours and yours alone. You are going to use it later as a work sheet for planning exactly how to market your musical wares. The list you finally end up with will be the one you use to find work, create jobs, and earn more money for yourself. Better that your list is too long than too short, for the idea you discard today might appeal to you tomorrow.

EIGHT

COMPLETING YOUR MARKETING SYSTEM

Now you should have completed a long list of possible jobs that could use your music. Think for a while about the *Job Possibilities List* you've been working on. There's no rush to complete it right now, and you'll probably do better if you mull it over for several days before you move on. If other possibilities pop into your mind, add them to the list. Remember that the *PMMS* isn't a one-time thing. As you progress your career expands, and as your community changes, new jobs will appear, new venues will develop, and other possibilities may disappear. Keeping the lists should become automatic for your marketing efforts to stay organized and on target. Don't think, then, of a marketing system as a one-shot effort; General Motors and Ford do marketing research, product development, and advertising every day of every year, and you should, too.

WORK SMARTER, NOT HARDER

Your completed *PMMS* will be a ranking of top prospects, complete with their names and addresses, and you'll probably be surprised at the number of potential clients you discover. For each job category you may have eight or ten—or as many as forty or fifty—names of people who need to know about your music.

Don't let this good news overwhelm you, though; you don't want to be swamped by all those prospects who need to be contacted. Thus, you'll need to work smarter, and to do that you'll start with the most likely clients, those whose needs most closely match your musical offerings. Don't discard the talent-to-job match-ups that aren't at the top of your list. You may eventually end up contacting every single prospective client (especially if you live in a small town), but you'll save energy if you target your efforts to a select group of people—those you've identified as the best bets. The reality is that you won't have the time or energy to call on everybody, so you must be selective; if you start with the best prospects, you won't be overwhelmed with the sheer number of sales calls that should be made, and your success ratio will be higher.

Start by reading over your *Personal Inventory* of musical skills and review your strengths and weaknesses. Then check your longer *Job Possibilities List* to see which ones make best use of your strong points, and underline or highlight those entries. Some jobs will match your abilities precisely, others will be close, and a few would be more trouble than they're worth—at this point, anyway.

What you're doing now is ranking the possibilities according to your ability and your musical preferences. If you could play dance-band music but you hate it, then put country clubs lower on your list. If you love to teach, put that at the top. As you do this ranking, use another sheet of paper and try to put the jobs in order, from best and most likely to the least likely prospects. You may find, of course, that there are lots of job possibilities in areas of music that you don't really enjoy, and only you can decide whether to book such jobs or concentrate only on the ones you like.

Ranking the Possibilities

If you're a trumpet player and sight-reading is one of your best-developed skills, your best job possibilities would include playing shows, working at recording studios, freelancing with local symphonies, and church concerts. These job possibilities should go at the top of your list because they match your abilities. If your speciality is playing Polish music but there isn't a Polish community nearby, you'd be foolish to put Polish weddings at the top of your list. If Hawaiian music is your main interest and you live in rural Kansas, you'll have to temper what you like with what your local market needs.

While you go through your *Job Possibilities List* to pick out the best bets, keep these points in mind.

Pay is important, but it need not be the primary factor in your rankings. If, however, two possibilities are equally appealing to you, why not rank the better-paying job higher on your list? Thus, playing for a share of the gate at a tiny folk club will probably pay very little, but playing folk music in a school arts program would probably mean much more money—and both jobs involve playing the same kind of music. Money isn't everything, but it does pay the rent.

Ease of booking varies from job to job. Some are as easy as answering the phone and mailing a contract, while others require immense sales effort and hand-holding of cli-

ents. If you know that some categories, such as booking convention shows, would require lots of effort, correspondence, and salesmanship while other kinds of jobs are much easier to book, rank the easier ones higher. You'll go after the difficult-to-get jobs, of course, but start with the easy ones. You'll build confidence by tackling the sure bets first.

Year-round jobs should rank higher on your list than seasonal ones. Sure, Christmas parties are important to most bands and the Fourth of July is crucial to community orchestras, but weekly and monthly jobs are better.

Jobs you're already working, even if they aren't your ultimate goal, should be at the top of your list because they provide a base of operations that requires little energy to book. Those clients already know you and what you can do and you won't have to work as hard to convince them—thus, they belong higher in your ranking.

The self-discipline that Dr. Worthy discusses in Chapter One comes into play here. Not only is it work to devise the marketing system, but you must be honest in deciding how to structure your lists. The easy approach is to just continue what you're doing now or to go after only the jobs that you'd really enjoy playing. A better approach for the professional, however, is to honestly survey the market, decide where the jobs are, match your talents to them, and then go after them. That's the way to build a career.

FINALLY . . . THE GOOD PROSPECTS LIST

The final step in developing your *Personal Music Marketing System* is adding names to each category. Here, you'll find the prospect's name, telephone number and address, and each category listing may yield dozens of entries.

This final list is the most crucial one. It will require a good bit of research, and it will take more time to complete than the other lists did. But, the time you spend finding names and numbers will be very worthwhile because this list will be your blueprint for a successful career in music. As you work on your marketing plan, remember that the prospects have to be told, and retold about your availability.

Rule to Remember:
If they don't know about you, they can't hire you—and if you don't tell them, who will?

You'll be using this *Good Prospects List* for years, and it should become an automatic part of your marketing efforts—seeking out and contacting the people who may need your music. So, establish an organized and neat system for keeping up with this information. It won't help if you acquire lots of names and addresses but can't find them when you need them, or if you can't remember what material you've sent or to whom. A system is essential, and here are three good alternatives:

■ *Use a loose-leaf binder* for this information with dividers for each category and a separate page for each client. You'll keep information about your sales calls, promo material sent, phone calls, and job results, and you'll need space for names, addresses, telephone numbers, and personal notes. Remember, paper is cheap, so set up a neat system that can grow and that will be useful.

■ *Use file cards*, one for each client, with dividers for each job category. Keep the same information mentioned above on each card. You'll find that four-by-six or even five-by-seven cards are big enough to do the job.

■ *Use a computer* if you have one. You can use either a word-processing or a database program to keep up with your records and print mailing labels for different categories of clients automatically. Computer expertise, however, doesn't come quickly, so go slowly in buying hardware and software; if you're not computer literate, work with a friend or even hire a consultant to help you set up your system. You'll find more advice on computers in Chapter Ten.

Since you'll use your own previous lists as guides, this one will be particularly useful since it's tailored to *your* music, *your* abilities, and *your* community. The names on this final list will be the people you'll call on to sell your music, so the more good prospects you have, the more you'll be able to sell. The sources for names on this list will be:

■ The Yellow Pages of the phone book

■ Your experience

■ Your network of contacts

■ Newspapers

■ City and regional magazines

■ Chambers of commerce, convention and visitors' bureaus

■ The *Encyclopedia of Associations* in your library

Categories for All Freelancers
To start the *Good Prospects List* there are three general categories that should be on almost all musicians' lists:

■ Booking agents, producers, and music brokers

■ Established bandleaders, contractors, and conductors

■ Recording studios, if you read well or have mastered a unique style

These three categories are important to all freelance players. Even if you think booking agents wouldn't be interested in your Early Music Consort, you may be surprised. Agents want to have *everything* available for their clients, and they'll welcome your promotional material for their files. Of course, your early music group won't work as much as a top-forty band, but when a client needs your kind of music or a viola da gamba or recorder player, you'll get the call. And if you only get one call a year from each agency, that's still a call you wouldn't have otherwise had.

Let Your Fingers Do the Walking

You already own one of the main resources that you'll use to locate clients: the Yellow Pages. This annual compilation of businesses listed by category will be invaluable. You couldn't afford to buy the information that is available free in this very useful book.

There is a skill to using the Yellow Pages most effectively, particularly in large cities with huge books. Fees for listings and ads in these pages are very high; consequently, many businesses aren't listed in multiple categories and you may have to dig a bit to find all the relevant entries. For example, booking agents may be listed under "Entertainment Agencies," "Musicians," "Convention Services," "Party Planning Services," or "Booking Agents." Be sure, then, to look under each applicable category while you're compiling this list.

Go through the Yellow Pages and find all the booking agents, music producers, and bandleaders you can. Write down their phone numbers and addresses. You'll likely find that all the local bandleaders won't be in the Yellow Pages, and you'll have to use your union contacts, networking skills, and word of mouth to add to that list—but several of the more established leaders will probably be listed. It doesn't matter how you get the names and addresses, of course. What's important is that you get them.

Remember, too, that you should get in the habit of checking each year's edition of the Yellow Pages for new entries and new prospects as well as for those that faded away during the year. You have to keep up with the changes in your town, and this is an easy, almost automatic way to start.

Define Your Markets

If you live in a small town, or within a megapolis, or near a resort area, you'll also want to consult the Yellow Pages for communities near your own. Include all the potential clients within easy driving distance, and remember that it may sometimes be worth your while to drive a few hundred miles for an exceptionally profitable job. Your primary market should include all cities and towns within, say, a hundred miles, and your secondary market area could extend to two or three hundred miles—even further in some cases. (Remember that travel involves extra time and expense, so adjust your rates to cover this and more. You might charge by the mile or by the time involved to get to and from the job, or just double your in-town rates. Each situation will be different, but don't underestimate the costs of going out of town.)

If you play an unusual instrument or have an uncommon act, enlarge your market area so that anyone who needs your rather rare skill will know of your availability. Thus, double-reed players, operatic tenors, and harpsichordists will probably define their primary market more broadly than, say, guitarists or drummers. A bassoonist can certainly count on less freelance music work than a sax player, but the bassoonist will also face less competition—perhaps none. When a recording studio, a symphony orchestra, church music director, or theater group within a hundred miles needs a bassoon, there may be only one choice.

So depending on your area and instrument, find Yellow Pages for all your target markets. You can find phone books for other cities at the phone company or public library, or you can buy Yellow Pages for any city in the country through the phone company's business office. Currently, prices range from thirty-three dollars for the San Francisco Yellow Pages to eleven dollars for Hilton Head Island, South Carolina's entire phone book—not a great expense if such resources help you book more jobs.

WATCH WHAT HAPPENS

Once your *Good Prospects List* contains names of people and groups from the general categories (that is, agents, producers, recording studios, and bandleaders), you are ready to start personalizing it. Now, refer to your ranked compilation of the *Job Possibilities List* for types of jobs relevant to your music. Still using the Yellow Pages as your primary research tool, go through this refined list and find applicable names, addresses, and phone numbers for each type of job you are considering. You may not find many names of individuals, but company names and numbers will do. Later we'll discuss how to find the appropriate contact person at a company.

For example, let's say that you are a classical guitarist and that one promising job category in your list is weddings and receptions. You think that sophisticated solo guitar music could be effectively and profitably used in wedding ceremonies and receptions, and you need to match specific names with this idea. You have the Yellow Pages in hand. Where do you look? In this case you start with the wedding category and expand from there. You'll probably find:

■ *Wedding chapels.* Some towns have nonsectarian halls devoted exclusively to weddings. Obviously, the owners and operators of these chapels should know what you could do for their clients, so add them to your prospect list.

■ *Wedding consultants.* These are wedding planners, and they should be at the top of your list. Many will be women operating freelance businesses from their homes, some will be florists, others may be photographers, and a few will work for large department stores. You can be sure that they are very much into the wedding business, and they should certainly learn of what you can offer their clients.

■ *Wedding receptions.* This listing in the Yellow Pages may refer you to "Caterers" and "Banquet Rooms." Both categories should be added to your list. Anyone connected to the wedding business must be informed of your availability to play classical guitar music at weddings and receptions.

■ *Wedding supplies and services.* This category includes rental companies, photographers, card shops, printers, and any other kind of business that could be important to a prospective bride and groom, and you'll want them to know of your musical availability. Some businesses keep card files or bulletin boards on which you might display your card or promotional literature. In return, offer to recommend *their* services when possible and ask for their cards. You might even want to work out a reciprocal referral or finder's fee arrangement with other businesspeople in the field. You could send them twenty-five dollars or even 10 percent of every job you book from their referrals.

Now, follow up by looking under the cross-referenced suggestions for "Caterers" and "Banquet Rooms."

■ *Caterers.* Here you'll have to filter through all the listings to find those that specialize in weddings and similar functions. Obviously you shouldn't spend time calling on the local barbecue spot or a fast-food restaurant that lists itself as a caterer; concentrate on those listings that could be good wedding prospects—perhaps those listings that mention weddings in their ads or the larger, more established caterers in your area.

■ *Banquet rooms*. Large restaurants, hotels, and meeting halls are listed here. Most hotels will insist on providing the food for affairs held in their facilities, so adding them will not duplicate your "caterers" list. Use your discretion and don't list so many places that you'll be dumbfounded by the number of sales calls to make: you may have to do some research and ask other musicians to determine which are the most promising prospects.

■ *Florists and photographers*. You noticed many listings for these businesses in the "Wedding Supplies and Service" classification, so check these two categories separately in the Yellow Pages and you'll find more businesses specializing in weddings that weren't listed elsewhere. Add them to your list.

You still aren't finished using the Yellow Pages to locate possible clients for your classical guitar performances at weddings and receptions. Next look at the listings for:

■ *Churches and synagogues*. You should contact ministers, rabbis, organists, directors of music, and social activities directors, especially if you live in a smaller town with fewer caterers and wedding consultants. Since you play classical guitar, you won't be viewed as inappropriate or as competition to the staff organist. You may not get many jobs from these contacts, but you should receive enough referrals to make at least an introductory visit or call worthwhile.

■ *Tents*. Many wealthy people rent large, expensive tents for wedding receptions on the lawn. If they can afford to have a party under an expensive tent, they certainly can afford you, so contact the rental companies that provide for these parties. If you are on good terms with them, they'll give you promising leads.

■ *Formalwear and other rental services*. This category includes companies that rent tuxedos, as well as those that provide party supplies. Get to know these businesspeople, and you'll expand your sources of wedding leads and tips. Leave a few of your cards with these companies.

This example should show you how useful the Yellow Pages can be. You'll probably find even more listings for the job categories that interest you, especially if you live in a large city. In searching for names and numbers to call on, the Yellow Pages will be a continuing resource. In fact, it might be better to call the Yellow Pages the "Gold Pages" because they offer so much valuable information.

You, the classical guitarist in our example, now have lots of specific names on your list, all from the Yellow Pages. At this point, you have listed names and numbers for these referral sources and potential clients:

Booking agents	Caterers
Musical producers	Banquet rooms
Production companies	Florists
Recording studios	Photographers
Bandleaders	Churches
Wedding chapels	Synagogues
Wedding consultants	Tents
Wedding supplies	Rental services

You've now researched only one category, weddings and receptions, from your *Job Possibilities List*, but you've found sixteen different kinds of job contacts within that single classification—probably over a hundred names of individual prospects—just from using the Yellow Pages.

When you see all these prospects listed

with several names and numbers for each category, you may feel overwhelmed by all the potential buyers you've found; but don't worry—you don't have to contact them all at once, and one good contact will often lead to another. In fact, you'll find that the network of referral sources you've discovered is more important than any specific wedding lead.

This, then, is the way to find jobs. Do your market research, and you will be astounded at the number of prospects for your music. All it takes is a little work—and you know that many of your competitors are still in bed asleep.

Let Your Fingers Do the Walking, Continued

From the example above, you see that the Yellow Pages can really be a gold mine of job prospects for you. Continue working with this list, the *Good Prospects* compilation, matching the job types on it with all the listings you can find in the Yellow Pages. If you are interested in substitute teaching, look under "Schools and Colleges," "Private Schools," and "Music Stores." If electronic instrument repair is an interest, check all the listings under "Music Stores,"

"Music Instrument Repair," "Electronics," and so on. Be sure to use any cross-references that are given and look in all possible categories for company names and numbers.

With more general categories, such as "businesses," you may have to be quite selective in how many names you add to your *Good Prospects List*. In major cities with large business communities, you'll want to limit your efforts to excellent prospects—the largest, or the most prosperous, or the best known, or the most specialized companies in any given field. On the other hand, if you live in a small town or rural area, or if your music is unusual or esoteric, you may have to list every single job possibility you can locate.

In any case, the Yellow Pages will be a continuing and valuable source of job prospects, and you should start your market research with this easy-to-use, always available, and up-to-date source. When you have exhausted the information in the Yellow Pages, you'll probably have more names of potential clients than you could possibly use.

And just think—you've still only used *one* of your sources for information!

GOOD PROSPECTS WORK SHEET

	Company	Address	Phone
Booking Agents:			
Music Producers:			
Recording Studios:			
Bandleaders:			
(add your own headings)			

NETWORKING AND MORE MARKET RESEARCH

You're now adding names and numbers to the *Good Prospects List,* and you've discovered the gold mine of the Yellow Pages. But there are many more ways to add to your list. Some require visits to the library or a newsstand because there are lots of books and periodicals that you'll find useful.

Perhaps most important, though, is the network of contacts that you develop during your professional life. You've already started building such a network, even if you weren't aware of it, because everybody you know, and everybody who knows you, can be part of your marketing plan. All your present and former clients, all the musicians you know, and all the professional people who are acquaintances may be important to your success. So, as you go through your *Job Possibilities List* adding names and numbers, be sure to remember all your former clients and others who know you. One principle of salesmanship is that it's easier to sell to a former customer than to a stranger.

Former Clients Equal Future Clients

Since former clients know your work and appreciate what a great job you do, they should be among your best prospects and their names should be scattered throughout your *Good Prospects List.* Of course you don't want to be limited to the same old jobs by depending too much on your past, but

you can use it as a springboard to find new jobs. Use past clients in the following ways:

1. *As a core group of people who have used your music in the past and are likely to need it again.* Companies, agents, party planners, and wedding consultants, for example, have continuing need for music, so keep them up-to-date on what you have to offer.

2. *As a starting point for idea expansion.* Use the association and brainstorming techniques you've learned to expand your list. Thus, if you've played a Christmas party for the First National Bank, you can assume that the First Savings and Loan (if it's still solvent) will have a similar party.

3. *As a source of recommendations.* When you have played an exceptionally good engagement, it is appropriate for you to ask for a letter of recommendation from the client for your files. Later, as you prepare publicity material, a few quotes (or even entire letters) will be very effective. You'll be surprised by how glad most clients are to write such letters; they're flattered that you value their opinions. (Of course, the job has to go well for you to make such a request!)

BUILDING YOUR OWN NETWORK

"Networking" is simply a fashionable term for using personal or business contacts to further a cause or a career. Whether you call it networking or just "being friendly," you'll find that one good contact leads to another. People, not new equipment or the ability to play pentatonic scales sideways, are the life-blood of our profession.

Consider the biggest law firms in your community for a moment. There may be two hundred attorneys and many more support people working every day, and their clients pay premium prices for legal services. Where does the law firm get those clients? Most large, successful firms, even today, don't advertise.

The answer, in a word, is "networking"—talking to people and using contacts and established business relationships to develop new ones. That's how most professionals build their businesses, and you'll do the same thing.

Where do successful attorneys find new clients? Everywhere they go. They find them on the golf course, having a drink at the club, doing community service, at a Rotary luncheon, even at church. Wherever they meet people, they're always alert for someone who might be a potential client, and you should be just as aware. You may not develop new clients on the golf course of your club like many attorneys and accountants do—in fact, like most musicians, you probably don't belong to such a club. But you'll do the same thing and use the same techniques to meet and cultivate prospects.

Let's face it: the music business, like almost everything else, revolves around who you know. Your network of contacts, acquaintances, friends, friends of friends, and former clients is crucial to your success. You need to know as many musicians, agents, and possible clients as you can—not to mention secretaries and office-staff members. Potentially, almost everybody you meet is important to your musical life, so you should always keep your business cards handy and be alert for possible clients wherever you go.

Since music is such a "people business," cultivate your social skills. You'll be dealing with top people in business and society, and if you don't have good manners and conversational skills, you won't fit in. Is that important? Absolutely. In business and social situations how you look and behave can be more important to the client than how you play.

So, as Mom would say, mind your manners. If you're making a sales call and your prospective client invites you to lunch at a fancy restaurant, will you be comfortable and know which fork to use? You don't have to memorize an etiquette book, but you should be certain of expected business and social manners. Check into one of the books listed in Appendix B, and you'll know how to act in every situation. *Believe it or not, this may be the most important advice in this book.* High-end, successful, socially aware people simply won't accept you if your talk, dress, or behavior is sub-par. Reread the interview with Brenda Street on page 32, and notice her emphasis on these nonmusical aspects of a successful freelance career.

Rule to Remember:
In social situations, manners are very, very important.

Marketplace Mnemonics
Want to get ahead faster? Then work on improving your memory. If you can remember clients' names and faces, they'll be impressed—and they'll remember you. Read a book on memory (such as *Stop Forgetting* by Bruno Furst—see Appendix B), and use the recommended techniques. People are flattered when you remember their names and may be offended when you don't. Many successful piano-bar entertainers, for example, have prodigious memories for regular customers' names and favorite songs.

Sometimes remembering is simply a matter of paying attention to what is going on. If you're introduced to a client's partner and you can't remember her name thirty seconds later, you probably weren't really concentrating. The simplest technique here is to repeat the person's name as you're being introduced. "I'm glad to meet you, Ms. Franks," will help you establish and remember the partner's name. Again, it's not a musical skill, but it's important.

To supplement your memory, buy a business card file at an office-supply store. Ask for cards from possible clients, musicians you meet, and other contacts. Jot down pertinent information on the back of each card such as where and when you met and what you talked about. File business cards alphabetically by name or subject—that is, under "agents," "drummers," "prospects," "regular clients," and so on.

Establish a networking file and keep information here about people who are important to your business. This expanded version of the business-card file will contain entries like "Janice Traylor, catering manager at new Marriott. Met 9/17/90 at Smith wedding. Recommends bands frequently, sometimes bills for music through hotel. Has new baby. Secretary's name: Sandra Underwood." Next time you call on Janice Traylor, you'll be able to recall these personal items and keep your relationship moving—and the secretary will be flattered to be called by name. (Never underestimate the power of secretaries, either.) Update this file—which could simply be a sheet of notebook paper for each client kept in alphabetical order—each time you talk with this client, because babies grow up fast and secretaries move on. Notice that Dr. Sheila Kessler, in the interview on page 148, emphasizes the importance of such notes for all businesspeople. (See sample notes next page.)

Expanding Your Network

An excellent way to build a really useful network of contacts is to ask for referrals. If you've ever bought insurance, you'll remember that, as he was leaving, the salesperson asked, "Do you have any friends who might need insurance?" Insurance salespeople are always among the best-trained sales experts, and we can learn from their techniques. Asking for referrals works, and it's a terrific way to get more names of prospects. Every bride will have friends who have just gotten engaged or are about to, and many of them will need bands. So ask for those names and make them part of your network of prospects.

Will clients mind making referrals? If you've done a good job, they'll be happy to, and they'll often be flattered that you asked. Sometimes, a businessperson will even volunteer to call a colleague in another company to recommend you—and you can't do better than that. But you have to let them know that you're interested in building a network and reaching out for new clients.

Another way to expand your personal network is to become active in unions and professional organizations. That way, you'll know lots of your colleagues and competitors, and they'll refer work to you. If you teach piano, for instance, then you should certainly join the local Piano Teacher's Guild, both to improve you skills through workshops and seminars and to let them know what you do. Remember, other teachers can't refer students to you if they don't know you.

Also consider becoming active in other community affairs. You don't want to join churches or community organizations just to make contacts, of course, because such organizations do a lot of good for the community, and you'll want to join in those efforts. But you'll meet people from many professions and walks of life, and you may be the only real, live musician that many of

> The Cato Agency
> 1663 12th Ave., St. Louis
> 767-1243
> St. Louis office mgr: Joe Sisk
>   receptionist/sec.: Nancy Jones
> 9/17/90 — mailed brochure
> 9/17 — called, talked to Mr. Sisk – set up
>   appointment – mostly interested
>   in 'society bands'
> 9/23 — sales call to Mr. Sisk. Took demo.
>   photos, etc. Seems interested. Might
>   have possibilities for Oct 26 and
>   Nov. 4. — Will check
> 9/25 — Booked Oct. 26 by Joe Sisk —
>   details will be handled by
>   'Account Exec' Susan Cox.
> 9/25 - Called to introduce the band to
>   Susan Cox. She has music degree
>   from NorthWestern State, and

them have ever met. Naturally, they'll call on you when they need music or advice about it.

Another reason to join different organizations is to counteract the natural tendency of many musicians to lead a solitary, almost antisocial life. Your interests and values are probably different from most members of the Optimist club, true, but it will be good for you to meet lots of different people. It will broaden your knowledge and enlarge your perspective — and keep you from becoming a hermit.

If you're really gung ho, there are actually "networking clubs" that get together for breakfast or lunch. Each member describes his or her service to the group, business cards are swapped and, hopefully, useful contacts are made. You might not want to go that far, though it would be interesting to see if such a club would be beneficial to your career.

Or why not have your own networking party? Many musicians throw an occasional party — often on a Sunday afternoon — and invite other musicians, bandleaders, agents, party planners, and as many potential clients as possible. You'll have a chance to meet people in your field, expand your network of contacts, and maybe make a little music. You could work with a hotel or caterer to combine forces for such an event: they provide the place or the food and you supply the music, and both of you invite guests. Such parties when planned for business purposes are tax deductible, too.

MARKET RESEARCH

To keep up with current activities in your community, read the local papers and city or regional magazines. These provide up-to-date information that will be valuable in your search for more clients.

Newspapers

The newspaper keeps you informed about events that use music, and you should read it every day. The only disadvantage to using the paper for research is that the lead time may be too short; the music for an event may have already been arranged by the time the newspaper publishes its story. If it is a recurring event such as an annual dance, clip the article and put it in your tickler file (see Chapter Ten) for the following year. Then make your first contact eight or nine months before the job. It's better to act too soon than too late.

The most useful newspapers are the local ones. Local papers concentrate on what's going on in your community—new businesses, neighborhood events, school and college schedules, and weddings. That's what you need to know.

Here are some specific ideas for finding leads in the paper.

Society or lifestyle sections cover weddings, parties, and social events. You'll get lots of leads for weddings and receptions, for example, from the engagement announcements. And people who are frequently mentioned in the "Who's News" columns as party givers certainly need to know who you are. Club news is also covered here. Notice which clubs are about to expand, are most active, or are planning special events. There is usually a "Social Calendar" that will tell you about dances and parties, society balls, and charity extravaganzas. Again, while the music may already be booked when the newspaper story appears, you should clip the article, put it in your tickler file, and contact the client early next year.

The business section alerts you to conventions, trade association meetings, grand openings, new-product introductions, retirements, mergers, and so on. Many of these events use music, often booked through the company's public relations firm, and you may have to move fast. Often, however, last-minute decisions are made, and if you make a creative suggestion, you'll get

the job. In many business situations, the cost of your music (while significant to you) is almost negligible to the company.

Pay special attention to the "Who's News" columns that cover business personalities in your area. You'll find important contact names, such as the public-relations firm handling a political campaign, or a newly hired catering director at a major hotel, or a developer planning a new resort at a nearby lake. Be alert, and you'll find leads everywhere you look.

The business section will also inform you of new restaurants coming to town, clubs going bankrupt, new ad agencies, or even new recording studios being formed. These pages offer much more than just the stock market reports.

The arts and leisure section yields news of upcoming concerts, newly formed chamber music groups, auditions or tryouts for community orchestras and theatrical productions, recitals, and nightclub appearances. Your music could be needed in many of these situations, and this section of the paper helps you keep up with who's doing what and what's going on in the local music community.

As you read, gather ideas to use in your own marketing. Thus, if you notice that the symphony is presenting educational concerts in elementary schools, you could apply that to your kind of music, whether it's bluegrass, jazz, or medieval church music, and explore the possibility of getting a grant for the same kind of school concert programs. The paper will give you lots of ideas that can be applied to your own situation.

The religion or church section announces special music events and programs, many of which need professional musical help. Holiday seasons are especially active, and if you miss this year's performances, make a note to check on these jobs earlier next year. Also note which churches sponsor dances.

Other sections give the alert reader lots of ideas. Sports stories about major golf tournaments should make you think of the parties that go with such events—kick-off parties, awards banquets, and so on. Education stories can be important; did your community just pass a bond issue to expand the music program? Are the schools planning special weeks to celebrate ethnic cultures? Is the community college sponsoring a music festival?

General trends and fads are also covered in the paper. Feature stories help you keep up with what's hot, what's coming in, and what's fading from the picture. You may be able to profit from a new interest in ethnic history, acoustic jazz, or folk music. You may learn about new ways to apply computers to teaching improvisation, keeping up with tax deductions. You might read about noontime concerts in a downtown park and work to book your own group for a similar concert series in a suburban park.

In short, a close reading of the newspaper will prove directly beneficial to most musicians. Read with a pair of scissors handy, keep a tickler file of clippings, a more general file of interesting, relevant articles, and add important names to your *Good Prospects List.* A thorough reading of the paper will pay for the subscription many times over.

Magazines

An interesting development in American publishing today is the success of city and regional magazines. (The Atlanta area, for example, currently has over ten such periodicals.) Some are published by chambers of commerce; others are strictly independent. Some concentrate on business; others are interested in a region's special style of living. You'll find that both types are interesting and useful.

Use these magazines much as you would a local newspaper, but remember that magazines have a much longer lead time and rarely have any really fresh news. However, most of these magazines are filled with feature stories and personality profiles, and you can use both kinds of articles to generate job ideas. For example, let's say you are reading an article in the winter issue of *Santa Barbara* magazine. You notice an article titled "Casa Palmilla, Hacienda by the Sea," describing an elegant oceanfront home. The style is Spanish, and your specialty, let's suppose, is classic Spanish guitar music. Obviously you'll need to let the homeowners know that their next party would not be complete without your appropriate music.

Or, for another example, you're reading *Business Atlanta,* and you notice a column called "Meeting Facility Review" that discusses a different hotel or resort each month. The information and names given in this article go straight to your *Good Prospects List,* and since the hotel being reviewed is a new one, you should be able to make a good contact for booking convention work.

The ads in a magazine are the most expensive pages; great care and lots of expense go into preparing an ad, and you can often get good ideas from them. When businesses are spending big bucks promoting their products and services, let them know how your music can help. (Be very careful, however, about placing your own ad in such a magazine—the costs almost always outweigh the benefits for a space ad, though you might get value from an inexpensive classified. Read a book on advertising from Appendix B before you commit any money to a newspaper or magazine ad. Don't depend on the magazine's ad salespeople, either. Research is crucial before you place an ad or you can kiss hundreds of dollars goodbye in a flash.)

When you think like a businessperson, you'll realize that music can be very useful in creating a mood, generating excitement, or attracting a crowd, and you'll begin to notice all the kinds of events that your music could enhance. Newspapers and magazines will provide a continuing source of these ideas for your *Good Prospects List,* and you'll find that reading current periodicals can be just as important to your career as reading music.

Chambers of Commerce and Convention Bureaus

These organizations can be very important to freelance musicians because they promote business in your area and are at the leading edge of community development and activities. The convention bureau's most valuable help is a listing of all the conventions and meetings that are coming to your town. Understandably, these listings are worth money to vendors and service people (like you), and policies vary concerning who can use them. Many convention bureaus won't give nonmembers access to this information, and membership may cost a lot (from a few hundred to thousands of dollars) but it's worth a try. If you can't pay the price, try to find a friendly member in another service area, perhaps a florist, photographer, or caterer who will share this information with you.

If you live in a major convention center that attracts hundreds of annual conventions, you obviously won't have time to contact each convention director to sell your music. In that case, you should work with a booking agency that specializes in convention services because they have the resources to go after this competitive business. If, however, you live in a small town that hosts only a few meetings and conventions, you should probably contact the meeting planners yourself—and they'll welcome your suggestions.

Chambers of commerce try to promote all kinds of business activity, and they can provide helpful information about what's happening in your area—expansions, new industries, community celebrations, and events. Often they publish schedules and brochures that you'll find helpful, and you may even want to join the chamber if it's not too expensive.

Using the Library for Fun and Profit

As you continue to find good prospects to match the entries on your *Job Possibilities List,* you may be surprised at the aid your local library can give. Reference librarians have access to unbelievable amounts of information; you'll find them to be very helpful as you do your market research. And reference librarians are trained researchers who enjoy helping you find the data you need.

Even if you weren't a good student in school and never darkened the library's door, you should start spending time there now because your marketing plan will profit if you do. Here are a few resources to look into when you visit the library.

References. Get to know *The Encyclopedia of Associations,* which will be in the reference department. This is a valuable and up-to-date set of books that lists all the associations and organizations in the United States—there are over 20,000 of them. The reference book gives their addresses, short descriptions, and often tells where the next annual meetings will be held. You'll find the geographic volume especially useful. It lists all the associations in each state by city, so you can find the names of those in your area. Remember that associations have frequent meetings and social events, and many of them use music.

Another interesting feature is the astounding number of music associations. Currently, more than 150 music-related organizations are listed, from the "Country Music Association" to the "Lute Society of America." All musicians will find this a way of keeping up with activity in their areas of musical interest.

The reference department also has out-of-town telephone books from nearby cities. You'll find these useful, especially the Yellow Pages. Countless other references from directories of music schools to listings of hit tunes are available as well. Ask the librarian to direct you, then browse through the shelves.

Trade and regional magazines. Your library may subscribe to magazines such as *World Convention Dates* or *Meetings and Conventions* that list upcoming conventions around the country. Ask the librarian. If your local convention bureau is too expensive for you to join, look through these magazines to obtain some of the same information. Regional magazines from nearby cities can also help you locate potential clients, and the library will have other periodicals that you'll find interesting, including music magazines.

Clip files. Most libraries maintain clip files which contain news stories, press releases, annual reports, and assorted brochures pertaining to leading companies and citizens. If you are producing a show with local or historical interest, or if you are looking for information to use in preparing a sales call, these files could be a gold mine. Always ask the librarians for help because they know exactly where to look.

How-to books. Don't forget how helpful books can be. For example, before you start making sales calls you'll probably want to read one of the many excellent books on sales techniques. Also, to keep up with changes in the tax laws, you can find a current handbook on tax preparation for the self-employed. (Several helpful books in

these fields are listed in Appendix B, but your library will have a larger assortment.)

If your public library is too small to be much help, don't forget about college and university libraries nearby; they'll almost always be available, but don't do your research during the busy week of final exams. And libraries can borrow material from other institutions through the Interlibrary Loan program, so you can probably locate all the information you need at your local branch library.

Your Personal Marketing System Is Shaping Up

Your *Good Prospects List* should be quite substantial now that you've researched the information sources discussed in this chapter. Devise reminders to consult these sources routinely: newspapers every day, magazines each issue, the Yellow Pages at least every new edition, convention bureaus and chambers of commerce every few months, and the local library depending on how fast it acquires new publications.

You may already have so many names on your *Good Prospects List* that you can't call on all the people included, but what a problem to have! At least you've proved that you don't have to limit yourself to the same old jobs for the same old clients—there are new jobs out there if you'll just discover them.

You know that finding work is probably your most important task as a freelance musician. You can proceed in a hit-or-miss fashion, as most of your competitors will, and be satisfied with mediocre results. Or you can use your *Personal Music Marketing System* to locate jobs that are matched to your talents—*jobs that need your music.* It takes a little work, but it's worth it.

THE ADVANTAGES (AND DRAWBACKS) OF A FREELANCE MUSIC CAREER

INTERVIEW WITH GARY TALLEY

Gary Talley has played the guitar since before high school—in fact, one of his first bands, The Boxtops, had two million-sellers, "The Letter" and "Cry Like a Baby." Gary now lives in Nashville, where he has played on albums by Jerry Butler, Ace Cannon, Tammy Wynette, Willie Nelson, Waylon Jennings, Billie Joe Royal, and others. He has toured with stars like Louise Mandrell, Johnny Lee, Charlie McClain, Shelly West, and Tracy Nelson.

Q *How did you get started in the music business?*
A I've been a professional player since 1966. My very first jobs were just playing gigs around Memphis—sock hops, skating rinks, community centers, fraternity parties. That was my first summer out of high school.

When I was in college I started playing music and making money at it, but I wanted to be a psychologist, so that was my major—at the same time I was playing in a band called The Boxtops. We had a big hit record, "The Letter," so I never went back to college.

Q *What do you like most—and least—about the freelance lifestyle?*
A I like the lack of sameness in the freelance music life compared to an office job where you'd go into the very same place every day at the same time and do the same things. I enjoy the flexibility, the variety.

I also like the fact that in music you can never do your job perfectly—you can always learn to do better, broaden your "hireability" and your horizons. Sometimes, just for your own enjoyment you can try a different kind of music, a different approach, even a different instrument. There are so many aspects of music you can work on that it's always a challenge.

Once I got fed up with some aspects of the music business and I did other things for about six months—didn't play music at all—and I was miserable. When I went back to music, I felt that, "Yeah, this is what I should be doing."

The worst thing about freelancing is the lack of security, I think, and sometimes that's harder for a spouse to deal with than yourself. If you have a relationship with someone who can't handle the freelance lifestyle that can be very hard. In fact, there aren't a lot of people who can deal with these aspects of freelancing—the unpredictability, the hype, the empty promises, and that sort of thing.

Another thing that bothers me is that a lot of people still look at musicians as being drug-oriented, irresponsible, not punctual, and I don't like that stereotype. It's sometimes true, but certainly not in all cases, especially among successful people, and it bothers me to be grouped with those people.

Another difficult part of making a living in music is staying current and being able to do a variety of things instead of being completely into one style. Of course there are lots of players who take the opposite approach and specialize so strongly in one area that they're absolutely the best in that area—and that can be a good approach, too—doing something no one else can do.

The other approach, the one that I follow, is to be very versatile and keep up with current trends in music, and that requires a lot of time.

Q *What nonmusical factors do you consider especially important?*

A Of course it's very important to be punctual, likable, and be able to get along with people. I'd even say the social aspects, in my experience, account for more than half of your success. Just being able to play your instrument well isn't enough. Assuming you can play, which is the bottom line, I'd say that the other factors might even account for 75 percent of your success.

Somebody for example, who locks himself up in his room and is a technical wizard but can't be on time and can't get along with people, just isn't going to get any work. There are people in Nashville like that, but they never reach the level of really doing well. They won't be the players who get a lot of sessions or the better gigs because they develop the reputation of being unreliable. And, it goes without saying that there's no time for people with drug problems that keep them from being able to concentrate. I've known people who came to town, who were great players, but who didn't last long because of problems like those, and that's really a waste.

Q *What about career advancement?*
A In a place like Nashville, there are always so many new people coming to town from all across the country that you never get to the point where "everybody knows you" without working to make sure that they do. Any kind of publicity that you can get is good. One thing I've done is to go hear other bands, introduce myself, and sit in — that really helps enlarge your circle of acquaintances.

Now that I'm spending lots of time writing songs, I've found that meeting songwriters is a great way to get on demo sessions. And the more songwriters I meet and know, the more demo sessions I play on, which helps expand the number of studio players, engineers, producers, songwriters, and so on, that I know.

I'm not a real aggressive self-promoter — my personality doesn't really lend itself to that — so I don't go out to offices and introduce myself very often, though if I did I'd undoubtedly get more work. Since I'm not that type personality I try to put myself in positions to meet other people without being too obvious about it. In Nashville, for example, lots of music business people go to lunch at two or three restaurants on Music Row, and that's a good place to meet people. Sessions are often at ten, two, or six o'clock, and just before those times these restaurants are full of music-business people. That way you can meet lots of people, and it's a lot more pleasant for me than trying to get past an unfriendly receptionist in somebody's office. But Nashville is probably unique in this regard because so much music activity takes place in a four- or five-block area.

Q *How do you stay motivated?*
A Staying motivated is another very difficult thing for musicians to do. It's sort of a personality trait; some people are highly motivated, and others are more passive "go-with-the-flow" types, which I am. So I sometimes have to just *make* myself get out and make a new demo tape or update my résumé. What motivates me, at least partially, is fear — there are lots of new, talented people coming to town all the time and you have to compete on a high level, and you can't quit doing that either.

A lot of what motivates me is just sitting down and evaluating my life and asking, "Where do I want to go from here?" You can't expect to be discovered . . . you can't expect people to come after you. You've got to let them know you're there first. And they've got to like you as well as knowing that you can play, write songs, sing, or whatever. For example, I've got to have a new promo picture made and update my demo tape — those are my current projects. There's always something you need to do. In fact, doing these tasks, like freelance music in general, can be either a task or an opportunity, depending on your attitude.

Q *What advice do you have for younger, newer players?*
A I think that younger players a lot of times are caught up in one kind of a bag—maybe they're great at rock and roll playing, for in-stance, which is good as long as they want to play that and nothing else—but if they get called to play another kind of gig, it becomes painfully obvious that they can't fit into an-other kind of style. There are a lot of good schools where young musicians can learn to play a wide variety of styles, and I think that's a very important idea.

TEN

SETTING UP YOUR BUSINESS

You're ready for serious business now. The central part of your business plan—the *PMMS*—is finished, and you're ready to use it. To implement the plan and make it work for you, you'll need to:

■ Publicize your music to make the best prospects aware of what you have to offer.

■ Make sales calls to tell them in person how your music will help them achieve their goals.

■ Follow up by sending contracts or continuing your sales calls and mailings.

■ Play the jobs you've booked, making sure everything goes well. Your goal is for each job to be successful and to lead to several others.

That's a lot to do, and you'll find that if you follow certain businesslike principles you'll save time and energy. Remember, it's not "anti-art" to be organized and efficient; it actually frees you to have more time and money for your music.

Dr. Michael Mescon, dean of the business school at Georgia State University, wrote a best-selling book called *Showing Up for Work and Other Keys to Business Success* that answers the question, "How do you succeed in a business venture?" Dr. Mescon, who is a consultant to many large corporations, says, "The effective manager-leader-entrepreneur works wonders by working, and creates miracles by showing up, showing up on time, and showing up on time dressed to play."

That message is important for anyone who is in business. It is: concentrate on the basics and be sure you're doing them right. Figure out what your task really is and do it. You're in music, so you're providing entertainment as a service to your clients. That's your bottom line. That's what you do, and whether you entertain and uplift through chamber music, or entertain and excite through neo-destructo-rock, the basics of the business are the same.

■ *Show up for work and be on time*. Literally. Your client will never remember your guitar solo, or whether your intonation was perfect, or whether your guitar was a Stratocaster, a Jackson, or a Les Paul. But he'll remember if you're late. *Get the little things right, and the big things will usually take care of themselves.*

■ *Be appropriate*. If you're playing a late-night demimonde club where outrage is the norm, you'll have to be outrageous. If you're playing for a country-club dinner where the loudest sound is the tinkle of ice water being poured, you'll be quiet and sophisticated. Remember, *you'll know what's appropriate* if you reverse roles and think like a client.

■ *Manage your people* — the members of your band — so that you do the job you're hired to do. "That's too obvious to mention," you say. Actually, doing the job you're hired to do often isn't easy, and managing people is usually complicated, frustrating, and difficult. Convincing any group of musicians to work together may call for skills that would daunt the Chairman of General Motors. You've not only got to find out what the client really wants; you also must see to it that the job gets done, and that your people do it.

MANAGING MUSICIANS — IS IT POSSIBLE?

Here's an example of why doing a good job is difficult. Let's say that you're the leader of a nine-piece combo playing for a convention dinner/dance. You've talked with the client, but none of your musicians have, of course, so you're the only one who has a personal stake in pleasing him. You're the one who will have to sit down with him after the job to get the check, and you're the one who will catch any complaints if things don't go well. And, since you're the leader, you're probably more "job-oriented" than your sidemen; you're more aware of what's involved in doing a good job.

But the musicians in your band don't have that pressure or awareness; in fact, what they expect from the evening is probably very different from what you want them to do. You know the kind of commercial tunes the client wants and he's made it very clear to you that he wants the music *very soft* during dinner, but your alto player hates commercial tunes and will probably rebel at playing them. In fact, if you insist on doing the tunes he dislikes, he'll instantly develop a bad attitude, talk about how you've "sold out," and he'll play either very obscurely or exaggeratedly commercially. Worse, all the horn players will unconsciously move in his direction, each striving to be more hip than

the other — with nobody paying attention to what the jobs needs to succeed.

The drummer is only interested in finding a groove, and if that means changing a quiet bossa nova to a driving jazz samba, then that's what he'll do — and he really doesn't care if what he's doing is inappropriate for dinner music. To tell the truth, he really has no sense of what's appropriate, and after all, he's not the one whose reputation is on the line, he's just the anonymous drummer. Dinner music to him is just another chance to play.

And the singer, who has a case of prima donna–itis, can't think of a single appropriate song to do, but she really wants to do some hip new pop tunes that the piano player probably doesn't know and that the client would hate. If you call a nonhip tune, perhaps a standard ballad, she'll make it clear that she's only singing it because she has to, and the bad attitude spreads throughout the band.

At every break, the members of your band gather around the bar talking about how bad the job is and how nobody wants to play *those* terrible tunes, and how if you — the leader — would just relax and quit worrying about the client, everybody could have fun playing.

Your job, like any businessperson's, is to manage your employees and see that the product is the right one for the occasion. This task is made more difficult by the fact that all the musicians you've hired are your friends, and you really don't want them to think badly of you or that you've become a hack or an unreasonable boss. So you are caught between doing what you should do to please the client and doing what you could do to please your friends in the band.

Sound familiar? It will take all your management skills to keep your musicians happy while doing what the job requires. Taking care of business isn't easy, and there will be times when you'll have to be a firm, strong-willed boss. Remember, the musicians who're working for you don't have the responsibility that you've assumed, and they certainly aren't as interested in your career as you are. Many of them, in fact, will happily remain poorly paid sidemen all their lives; there's nothing wrong with that as long as you realize that their attitudes won't necessarily match what's needed. You may have to do some active managing to make each job successful.

Work Together

You know how much you enjoy playing music with other people—when it's right, there's nothing else like it. You rehearse for hours to achieve that goal, but it's not automatic; really playing together and "getting a groove" doesn't happen every time, no matter how hard you work toward it.

Building your career is similar and is just as difficult. True teamwork is as rare in music as it is in basketball, but it's just as important. Here are some ideas that will help.

Work to develop "job awareness" among your musicians. Let everyone in your group know how you view your job. Let them know that you're providing a service to your clients—this notion will come as a shock to many players. Explain to them what you want to achieve on each job, and be sure they understand. Lots of players develop poor attitudes, a disrespectful manner, or even an active dislike of clients and audiences.

To counteract this tendency, explain what the client wants and let everyone make suggestions about how to achieve that goal. Find ways to share responsibility and encourage your players to understand that successful jobs don't just happen, that lots of work goes into booking and preparing for each job. Suggest a bit of role playing to the drummer who insists on playing too loud: "Joe, what if you were the singer out front

who can't hear anything but drums? She can't hear the keyboard, and she can't find the pitch. Put yourself in her place—what would you do?"

Talk about what's good for the entire group. Have band meetings now and then to assess your progress, and plan the next steps. Work to create a team spirit in your group by sharing responsibilities—and money. In many areas it's traditional for the leader to make twice as much as the sidemen but you may find that a different distribution of money is very effective. However you do it, try to have everyone in the group working together for the same goal.

Change personnel if necessary. There are in most cities terrific musicians with lousy attitudes. You know who they are—and they can poison a job very quickly. If there are other competent players available, hire them, because the last thing you need in the middle of a difficult job is a trombone player who says loudly, "Are you *really* going to play that (expletive deleted) "In the Mood"? I hate that (expletive deleted) song." There is a point in commercial jobs where phenomenal playing ability and a bad attitude is worth less than good playing ability and a great attitude.

BEING BUSINESSLIKE

Once you have a firm idea of the kind of service you're providing and how to go about it, you need to look at the business side of your musical activities. You don't have to think like an MBA to succeed, but certain practices and procedures are essential. They'll save time, help you make more money, and keep you out of tax trouble. Here's an overview.

Be prompt and follow through. Know what you need to do, *and do it*. If a prospect calls about booking your band and you promise to send her a demo tape, then send the tape today. Do it now, and you won't feel guilty about putting it off, your prospect will receive it while she's still interested, and you won't forget it. *One secret of business success is to always follow through on every lead.*

When you've been out of town for the weekend and you come home to find fifteen messages on your answering machine, be sure that you return those calls on Monday morning. If you put them off, you're throwing effort and money down the drain. After all, why bother to promote your music half-heartedly?

Don't promise what you can't deliver. If you get a call to play a middle-of-the-road background-music job, and you're really a hard rock player—but you really need the money—should you take the job? If a client wants only classical music at her reception, and your classical repertory consists of half of "Moonlight Sonata"—but you really need the money—should you take the job?

Sometimes the music business seems to run on hype and exaggeration; the truth is often buried and forgotten, and it's easy to assume that everything and everyone operates on the same level. But, in dealing with people outside the music world, you'll find that most of them mean what they say and expect you to be honest and straightforward, too. For example, a client hires your band to play for a country-music theme party. You don't really know many country tunes, and, to tell the truth, you hate country music—but you really need the money—so you take the job. You assume from your experience in the music market that the client probably knows little about music. You're sure that you can just slide by with the help of a fake book, and when the client's had a couple of drinks he won't care anyway, will he?

When you promise what you can't deliver, you're setting yourself up for an un-

pleasant confrontation. Maybe *this* client really does know country music, and you won't do your reputation any good by attempting to slide by. In fact, you might not even get paid for the job if you don't deliver what you've promised.

Be reliable. This means that you have to be organized and mature enough to deliver on your promises. And that means that clients and other musicians must be able to trust you. In building your freelance music business you'll face a common dilemma. Let's say you've taken a job for Saturday night that pays a hundred dollars. A few days later, you get a call for another job on that same Saturday night that pays *two* hundred dollars. What should you do? After all, you need the money.

Stop and think. *What you need most of all is the reputation for reliability.* If you're building a career, it is more important that people can depend on you than that you make an extra hundred dollars Saturday night. There is a terrific guitarist/vocalist in Atlanta who has practically destroyed a great music career because he can't be depended on to show up if he gets a better offer—and he always seems to get a better offer. It didn't take long for all the leaders and contractors in town to quit calling him because they couldn't depend on him, and this very talented musician is now driving a delivery truck. His career, which was flourishing, self-destructed because he wasn't reliable.

Organized for Business

Artists aren't supposed to be organized, right? A clean desk, a neat filing cabinet, or the ability to write a concise business letter—these things are anti-art, right? Aren't creative people supposed to be scatterbrained, impractical, unable to find important papers, and generally above the day-to-day humdrum of the business world?

That's a popular notion, but it's wrong.

In fact, the opposite is true—it's the organized person who has time to be truly creative, and it is the successful musician who has enough money to enjoy the benefits of a career in music. Starving artists don't have much energy to devote to art. If you lose a contract and forget to show up for the job, or don't write down telephone messages and forget to return the calls, your career won't get off the ground. And it won't help your creativity, either. Time spent looking for a lost sheet of music or a missing tax form is time down the drain.

But you don't have to be a sterile, obsessive-compulsive, Type-A person to get yourself organized for business. To get started, you'll just need the following basics.

A place to work. Even if you don't have a spare room that can be used as an office, you'll need a place to keep your business material organized and do your work uninterrupted. That may mean a desk in the corner of the room or a couple of shelves in the closet. Your "office" could even be a cardboard box stored under the bed, but what's important is that you have all your music-related items together where you can find them when they're needed.

The idea of an office at home is popular now, and if you have a room that you can devote strictly to your music-career business, you can save a lot of money on your tax bill. The area must be used only for business, however, and must be your primary place of business. Tax regulations change almost yearly, so get up-to-date advice before you invest heavily in an expensive home office.

Office equipment, though it need not be elaborate. To set up a workable office, you'll need a desk or table, filing cabinet (or cardboard box), shelves, a telephone and an answering machine, a typewriter and, if possible, a computer. You don't have to have all this equipment at once, and you certainly don't need to buy a seven-hundred-dollar executive desk and a plush chair. Used furniture stores and yard sales are great sources for inexpensive but very serviceable office furnishings.

One key to working smarter is to take advantage of new technologies as they develop and become affordable. Just a few years ago the idea of having your own computer was outrageous, but today it's virtually a necessity. The same thing is happening with personal photocopy machines, telephone technology, beepers/pagers, and fax machines. You don't have to buy every new gadget or gimmick that's touted as an office automation breakthrough, of course, but you'll find that today's luxury is tomorrow's necessity—and that many new technologies really do help your business run smoother and more efficiently.

So as your business grows, keep up with what's new in office equipment. You may be able to increase your productivity and your income by investing in high-tech devices, but don't go overboard. Remember the "music-store trap." It applies to office equipment, too.

Office supplies and stationery. As you develop your promotional material, you'll have stacks of printed brochures, business cards, invoices, tune lists, photographs, and demo tapes to send out. In addition, you'll have letterhead, typing paper, stamps, pens, paper clips, and all the little things that every office needs—and you'll need a place to keep them organized. If you have to dig through boxes that are inconveniently stored under your bed, you'll probably procrastinate about sending out promotional material; but, if everything is neatly stored on shelves or in drawers in your office, you'll be more likely to keep up with your promotional schedule. Stay organized and stay ahead.

Getting Organized

Certain tools will help you get and remain organized as your client list expands. The following list provides an outline of the bare necessities.

■ *A filing system.* It doesn't matter if it is a file cabinet or a cardboard box; what's important is that you file contracts and client information so you can find it. Use a separate file folder for each client, and within each file, add material with the most recent things on top. If you keep your files updated you won't waste time searching for missing papers.

■ *A datebook.* Get the kind that allows lots of room for making notes, perhaps a loose-leaf version that can be refilled each year. Many datebooks concentrate on weekdays and cram weekends into one page, so if your kind of music is mostly weekend-oriented, be sure your datebook allows a full page for every day. One popular brand is the *Week-at-a-Glance* series that most office-supply stores have; another, available by mail order (see Appendix C) is the *Daytimer* line. This will be your nerve center and will tell you where to go, when to be there, and what dates are booked. Don't lose it.

■ *A pocket notebook.* You'll have great ideas, hear terrific new songs on the radio, and want to write notes to yourself. A simple pocket notebook will keep you from forgetting important but fleeting thoughts.

■ *An expense-record book.* As a businessperson, you must keep up with where your money goes and be able to document all those important tax deductions. (You can increase your real income by being smart about taxes as well as by working more jobs, so every single deduction is important.) The *Dome 700* record book (about three dollars) is a good one and widely available. Don't use a loose-leaf binder for expense records; the IRS is suspicious of them and may not accept the entries in case of an audit.

■ *A tickler file.* You can't rely on memory alone to direct the complicated details of the freelance music business. Will you remember to write that follow-up letter or call that prospect next May about her upcoming Christmas party? You'll have lots of appointments to keep, tasks to perform, and important details to follow up and, like every small businessperson, you need a system to schedule activities, often far in advance. The solution is a *tickler file* to augment your datebook.

Office-supply stores sell elaborate tickler-file systems, but you can devise your own inexpensive one. Set up a file folder for each month and enter chronologically the details of things to be done. Cue the entries in your datebook. Thus, your datebook for June 6 might read, "Letter to Acme Co." Referring to your June tickler file, you would find: "early June—sales material to Acme Co. re Christmas party. To Bill Smith, Ass't VP. Had 7-piece band last year. Budget around $1200. Lots of top-40." The address and other pertinent notes follow.

You'll also keep newspaper and magazine clippings about upcoming or recurring events in your tickler folders to remind you to act on them at the appropriate time. In short, anything concerning a future event or date should be in your tickler file if it's too far in the future to enter in your datebook.

After you mail that letter to Mr. Smith at Acme, note in your datebook and tickler file that one or two weeks later—say June 15 or so—you should follow up this letter with a sales call.

Another simple tickler system uses index cards with monthly dividers, again filed chronologically. Whichever system you use, make it as foolproof as you can *and use it.* That means you'll have to look at both your datebook and monthly tickler file every day to be sure you're not forgetting something.

This is a great system for freeing your mind from annoying details — but, like the *PMMS*, it won't work unless you do it.

JOINING THE COMPUTER AGE

As you develop promotional material, lists of clients, reams of names and addresses, personal contract forms, and so on you may feel overwhelmed by this growing mass of important data. You can't let all these business needs overwhelm you — after all, your primary interest is music, not business. How do you cope?

One answer is, of course, to buy and use a computer. You may already be computerized, and if you are you know how much it helps — in fact, you probably can't imagine living without your computer. If, however, you aren't yet computer literate, here are some reasons that you should begin to think, at least, about becoming a computer owner and user. (Remember, you don't have to know *how* it works to use a computer. Today all you have to do is flip a switch and follow the directions on the screen.)

■ The computer reduces repetitive tasks or eliminates them. Rather than typing the same letter over and over, simply press a key, and the printer produces a perfect copy every time.

■ The computer is a great help for writing, figuring taxes, devising new sounds for your synthesizer, making mailing lists, producing publicity material — and playing arcade-style games.

■ The computer offers new chances to be creative. Perhaps you'll use a simple desktop publishing program to design your logo and all your publicity material. You can easily produce a newsletter, complete with masthead and different type sizes, and you can update lists of all kinds with just a few keystrokes.

Remember: *the computer field changes almost daily, so do research before you buy anything.* Balance what you think you need against what you can afford. Books are helpful and so are friends, but magazines do the best job of keeping up with the rapid changes. There are very helpful, specialized computer magazines on every newsstand, and some are listed in Appendix A.

Software and the Freelance Musician

To use a computer to your full advantage, you'll need several software programs that tell the computer what to do. Here are three suggestions for helpful software.

A word-processing program will be the most useful software you own, so shop around before you buy. You can spend from thirty to four hundred dollars, and while it's probably not necessary to buy the most expensive program available, the higher-priced programs are often the easiest to use. Look for an established (but not brand new), easy-to-use program that allows you to write and edit all kinds of documents, includes tutorials, includes a large, clearly written handbook (called "documentation"), and offers good customer support. The better programs supply free "800" telephone answer lines to help with problems.

Among the best and most expensive programs are WordPerfect and MultiMate, and they're often heavily discounted by mail-order firms. Other less expensive but very good programs are available, but try them out before you buy. Look carefully at the manual. Is it clear? Easy to read? Understandable? Has this program gotten good reviews in magazines? Do you have computer-oriented friends who use it and like it?

A good word-processing program allows you to write personalized form letters, produce mailing labels, keep lists of clients subdivided by any category you like, and update your printed material easily. For example, tune lists have always been an irritating problem for bands because new songs are constantly added. If you keep the list on a computer, you can add and delete songs easily and print out neat, professional-looking lists as you need them.

When you put your *PMMS* into action, you'll be sending mailings to new clients, past clients, and frequent updates to your best prospects. Your computer will change this task from an overwhelming drudgery to a very simple process, and your mailings will look as professional as those sent out by big businesses.

Desktop publishing programs allow you to create all kinds of printed material, including contracts, postcards, newsletters, flyers, and brochures. The better word-processing programs, such as WordPerfect, include many desktop publishing features, but there are several inexpensive programs that will give you the ability to produce great-looking material.

A desktop publishing program, however, will only produce output that's as good as your printer. Your city probably has laser-printer centers, where you can take your disk and print out your material on their high-quality printers for a few dollars a page. That way, you can have the advantage of beautiful, typeset-quality output without investing in an expensive laser printer. A good dot-matrix printer, though, will be good enough for most of your needs. You'll be amazed at how good your publicity material can look doing it all yourself.

Financial programs allow you to figure your own taxes (and sometimes to even print out IRS-acceptable forms) and do all kinds of accounting chores from writing payroll checks to computing your net worth. You simply enter all the appropriate figures prompted by instructions from the screen, and the program figures out the answers for you. These programs, such as *Managing Your Money*, *Swifttax*, and many others, range widely in price and offer lots of options. The tax programs change yearly to keep up with IRS developments, so be sure any program you buy offers inexpensive annual upgrades.

Some of these programs also allow easy bookkeeping; you set up categories such as "travel expenses," "subcontractors," "equipment repairs," and others, and enter expenditures as they occur. At the end of the year, the program will print out an up-to-date list of each category and even complete financial statements if you need them.

There are many other programs that you may find useful, interesting, or just fun. You may need a database to keep up with lots of lists or tabular information, or a mailing-label program, or one of the many music composition or recording programs. MIDI-able synthesizers and computers offer unlimited opportunity for composing, arranging, sound creation, and digital recording, and, again, magazines are the best way to keep up with this developing field. See Appendix A for electronic music publications.

Buying a Computer

What brands should you buy? There are dozens of machines and many competing systems; you can spend from a few hundred to a few thousand dollars to achieve the same results. To decide what to buy, look at competing systems, ask lots of questions, read reviews in magazines, talk to your friends, try out the machines in stores, and be sure that whatever you choose will do what you need—now and in the future. It's true that you can find very inexpensive used computers, but sometimes these are so outmoded and outclassed that you'll soon regret spending money on them. Whatever you buy will eventually become obsolete, but don't compound the problem by buying something that is already out of date.

Wherever you buy, get as much information as you can, look for guidebooks, find knowledgeable friends to help you—and you'll soon be a computer expert yourself.

(Some stores offer a guarantee of "technical support," which means they'll answer your questions and help you get your system up and running. That can be a very valuable addition, so ask if such assistance is included before you buy anything. You'll always have questions.)

Computers are easier to use than ever, and all good programs are "self-teaching." The most popular programs have lots of available support, too—dozens of books on how to use them, low-cost programs offered by community colleges on learning them, and very helpful "800" numbers to answer your specific questions when using them. Don't worry that you'll be overwhelmed by the task of learning how to use a computer; the truth is that if you don't get computerized, you'll be overwhelmed by doing things the old way.

Once you're used to your word-processing program, you won't know how you got along without it; and if you occasionally curse the machine for doing something you don't understand, you'll still find it the most useful partner you could have in developing your business.

TAKING CARE OF BUSINESS

If you're working six nights a week in a club, you'll have to sleep late to stay healthy, and your daily schedule won't match the nine-to-five of the business world. So how and when do you promote your business?

It will help to have a regular time each day, even if it's only an hour or two, to spend on your music career. If you can manage it, set up a regular schedule that's devoted to nothing else, and spend it making and returning calls, sending out promotional material, setting up sales calls, and typing and filing contracts. If you group all this activity together you'll be much more efficient, and the tasks won't fill up your entire day.

Many musicians rely on an answering machine to help control work time. The telephone can easily become a tyrant, constantly interrupting, frustrating all your plans, and keeping you from getting anything done—but, of course, every call is important. One answer is to let the machine take all your calls; just pretend that you're not at home. Later, after the contracts are typed and the promo material has been mailed, you can get those messages and return calls when it suits your schedule.

Time management is important for all businesspeople because they realize that there is never enough time and that it is an easily wasted resource. Books on time management offer good ideas on organizing your life, but common sense and a clear idea of what you need to do each day are often enough to guide you. One easy, useful technique is to make daily lists of what needs to be done. Many experts find that this practice itself reduces stress and helps you stay organized because once a task is on the "to-do" list you don't have to worry about it any more. You just check it off the list when it's done—and, like the *PMMS* lists you've worked on, you'll find that *actually writing out a list* is the key. Just thinking about it won't do.

As your music career grows, and you start booking and playing more and more jobs, you'll find that a businesslike approach is not only helpful—it's necessary. You're going to have lots to do—that's inevitable, and it's what you're working for—but you don't want to be overwhelmed by all those nonmusical tasks that are so important.

So, if you get organized in the beginning and establish the habit of keeping up with paperwork as it develops, you'll be in control. If you stay organized, work efficiently, and make use of the available technology, you'll be taking care of business rather than letting it take care of you.

ELEVEN

MONEY MATTERS

Money really does matter, and if you're smart with it you'll be happier. Having enough money is one of the prerequisites for comfort; if you're worrying about the rent, you won't be able to concentrate on music or anything else.

As you work to locate clients who will pay you to perform, it's essential that you know how much your music is worth—to them, and to you. It's crucial to make your pricing right because if you don't charge enough, clients won't respect you. Clients know that you get what you pay for, and they know that good music doesn't come cheap. Another obvious drawback is that you won't make as much money as you could, and you want to maximize your profits. Also, if you undercut the going rate for your area, other musicians will resent it and you'll become unpopular with your colleagues. On the other hand, if you charge too much, you won't book many jobs because you're too expensive.

Correct pricing is a function of the quality of your music, your marketing ability, and community standards. A four-piece band that charges a thousand dollars in New York may only be able to charge six hundred in Montgomery, Alabama. So, how do you establish a realistic price? The following guidelines should help.

Find out what your competitors charge by calling them or having a friend do it. If you're on good terms with other musicians they'll probably tell you their rates, and ask about yours, but you may have to ask a friend to make the inquiry for you by pretending to be a prospective client. That is not really deceitful or underhanded—all businesses "comparison shop" to see what the competition is charging. Keep a comprehensive and up-to-date list of what other musicians in your category charge, and try to price yourself just above the average or even at the top if you're good enough and there's plenty of work. Every shopkeeper knows exactly what other stores charge for each item, and you should, too.

Know what it's worth to you to play a particular kind of job. As a bottom line, have *minimum* prices firmly in mind so that if you have to bargain, you'll know your lower limits. If your standard charge for a three-hour solo gig is $200, would you play it for $150? For $100? Even for $75? If you took it for less than $200, would you resent it and be angry with yourself for lowering your standards, or would you decide that half a loaf is better than none? Decide on your pricing before making sales calls.

Join a union if one is active in your area. In many parts of the country the American

Federation of Musicians is involved in all aspects of professional music, and membership should offer several advantages. One is *union scale*, which should be your *minimum* charge. Usually, scale is a complex system of charges based on the kind of job, number of hours played, and other factors. Sometimes, scale is too low for your talent and the market; if that's the case, raise your price. Other times, scale will keep the price up, and you'll be glad you're affiliated with the union.

You'll find that different kinds of music—recording, for example—involve different unions, and they're listed in Appendix D. Certain kinds of engagements, such as six-night nightclub work, may not normally be covered by any union in your area, and the players on these jobs may be nonmembers. If a union is active in your area, find out if most of your colleagues belong and use scale as a guide in setting your own prices.

Remember that agency commissions must be added to your fees; you may decide a cut in pay is worthwhile when booking through an agency. In return, however, you should expect the agency to take care of such business details as contracts and billing. On the other hand, when you book direct, your price should be competitive with what the agency charges so you don't inadvertently undercut agency prices. Many bands establish a "wholesale" and "retail" price structure to account for the agencies' need to add a commission to your fees.

Never perform free of charge unless it's for a very good cause and you are philanthropically contributing your time and talent. *Only amateurs play for "exposure,"* and such "exposure" is almost always nonexistent and thus worthless. If you play without a fee, you are likely to be taken advantage of.

Think carefully before you donate your music to even a worthwhile charity. It's

likely that other participants are being paid—the caterer, florist, and photographer, for example—and you should be no different. Often legitimate fund-raising events have considerable production budgets, and their money is raised from those who pay to attend, not from those who perform. If you do perform gratis, you should get a letter from the sponsor thanking you for your specific donation so that you can at least claim a tax deduction.

This is a practical, not an unfeeling, cold attitude. There are so many good causes that you could give your music away every week. Unfortunately, that won't pay the rent. Ask: "Would I contribute money to this organization? If so, how much would I give?"

Make a chart listing all your prices for various-size groups, times, and different kinds of jobs. Then you'll be able to quote prices promptly when talking to different clients. Devising such a chart isn't easy because you need to be consistent and fair to yourself at the same time. Should a three-hour job cost the client three times as much as a one-hour job? Should overtime simply be prorated, or should your overtime rate be higher to compensate for unexpected changes in your schedule? You must *know* what you'll charge for every kind of job so you'll be confident when prospects call you. Indecision isn't professional.

Don't forget to include any extras that the union or "local custom" adds. There probably is a standard extra fee for rehearsal time and for shows. But what about cartage for such instruments as pianos, drum sets, and harps? What about "doubling fees" for players who provide more than one instrument? Such fees can add a lot to your quote, and if you're involved in planning for shows and large orchestras, you'll have to be very careful to include all these charges. Sometimes inexperienced leaders are surprised, for ex-

Price List--Joe's Band

Band prices (not negotiable on weekends)

Hours	Price
2	$ 800
3	$1,000
4	$1,300

Overtime is prorated up to 4 hours.

Early setup fee--$100.

Deposit required--50%. Not refundable unless we book another job during the same time slot.

Single piano prices (not available with the band).

Hours	Price
1	$100
2	$200
3	$275
4	$350

Cartage fee for providing electric keyboard--$50.

Overtime is prorated.

50% deposit required.

This is a sample of a price list made for Joe's own use. Often, musicians don't send price lists to clients, because it limits their flexibility. If Joe were a union member, he would figure into his price such variables as pension fees and dues, and he would probably use 'union scale' as a basis, at least, for his prices.

ample, when the alto sax players in a big band want to be paid "doubling fees" for also playing clarinet, flute, or tenor, baritone, or soprano sax. Knowing what's considered to be normal in your area can save you lots of hassle and money.

Television and videotaping have other, usually higher, scales and sometimes present pitfalls to unwary musicians. More than one band (usually in large, active-union cities) has walked out when the client started videotaping a stage show or business meeting without paying the union's "video production scale." Be sure you and your musicians will be paid for your music if the client decides to make a training film or videotape of your performance. And be sure that this is understood in advance—it's *your* responsibility and not the client's to discuss such possibilities in your preliminary meetings.

Charge what the market will bear. As you work more and are more and more in demand, you'll probably want to follow the basic free-market pricing strategy and charge what you can get. One Atlanta four-piece group specializing in Jewish music recently raised its price from $750 to $1,050 per three-hour job without losing any clients. If you are the best or only show in town, you may be able to raise your price accordingly. Be careful, however, not to disregard your community's norms, or you may price yourself out of the market. And obviously, when you charge more, you should provide better music and entertainment for the client's dollar by being willing to go the extra mile. Maybe that means playing for an extra ten minutes or so, or not taking a break when you'd like, or meeting with the client two times in advance of the job. If you charge top prices you should provide top service.

Interestingly, you'll probably discover that the more you charge, the more you are respected. The opposite is usually true, too. The less you charge, the poorer your repu-

tation—not to mention your pocketbook.

GET IT IN WRITING

If your town has a talk-radio station with a legal-advice progam, listen to it. You'll hear the attorney giving the same advice over and over and over. "Get it in writing. Oral promises don't mean anything in court. Always have a signed contract."

That advice applies to music, too. Of course your client is friendly and you're on good terms. And you're going to work diligently to maintain that relationship, but you should still get everything in writing because it reduces the chances of a misunderstanding. Spell out the day, the date, the place, and the time. There is always room for error, but if you have a signed contract hiring you for seven o'clock on Tuesday, May 12, your client can't claim that you should have been there at six o'clock on Monday, May 11. This is not a far-fetched example; such mistakes happen every day. Or if the worst should happen and your client won't pay, a signed contract will be crucial when you go to the union or to court to claim your money.

Rule to Remember:
Get it in writing. Always. Every time.

What form should your contract take? What points should it cover? This book does not offer legal advice; if you need an ironclad legal document you should have a lawyer read your contract form over and make suggestions for changes in wording or additions. Of course, you may never have to go to court—you'll work hard to develop good client relations—so your aim in devising a contract will be *clarity* rather than legal wordiness, but get your lawyer's opinion on your contract before depending on it.

If you are in a musician's union, usually the American Federation of Musicians, use its standard contract form. It is widely recognized, covers the important points clearly, and protects you as much as possible. Before you lock yourself into the union contract, however, check, with your union secretary to find out what the union will do if a client doesn't pay. If the union suggests putting him on the "International Defaulter's List" rather than going to court, you should know that you can't depend on the union for real help. An active union will offer prompt legal assistance, but unfortunately, many locals aren't nearly as helpful as they should be. Find out in advance what assistance, if any, the union will give you.

If you aren't a union member, or if you'd prefer to devise your own contract or confirmation form, be sure that it includes all the necessary information. Standard practice is to send two signed copies to the client—one for him or her, and one to be returned, signed, to you. Sometimes a third copy is required for the union.

Creating Your Own Contract

One good idea is to have your own contract form printed on your letterhead and include clauses pertinent to you. This personalizes the contract, makes you seem more professional, and saves lots of time. If you decide to create your own standard form, be sure to include:

- Today's date

- Date of engagement

- Time of engagement

- Place of engagement

- Definition of band or group—number of musicians

- Compensation agreed on and when payment will be made

- Overtime charges, if necessary

- Deposit required, if any, and conditions for refunding it

- Appropriate dress for the job

- Special requirements or requests

- Client's name, signature, address, phone number, and title

- Your signature, address, and phone number

You may also want to include preprinted "conditions" clauses that will be applicable to all your jobs. Unexpected circumstances can cause real problems, and you'll avoid confusion if you decide *in advance* what to do.

For example, what if the affair is canceled? The wedding is called off, there's a death in the family, or the couple starts divorce proceedings a week before the anniversary party. Will you return the deposit, or is it (as it usually is) nonrefundable?

What if bad weather causes a last-minute change? Snowstorms, ice storms, tornadoes, and hurricanes can play havoc with plans. If extremely bad weather is remotely possible in your area, make provisions for it in your contract. (Remember that the weather could force *you* to miss a job as easily as it could change a client's plans.) You might use school closings or another "outside" authority as criteria for determining when the weather is bad enough to present a problem.

What if a sudden rainstorm forces the pool party you're playing at an apartment complex to move inside with only one hour remaining? You may wish to add a clause to your contract specifying additional setup fees or cartage charges to compensate for the unpleasant task of moving unexpectedly during a job. Or perhaps the client just forgot to tell you that the cocktail hour would be out by the pool, the dinner would be up two flights of stairs on the deck, and the dance would be in the ballroom. If you've written in an extra fee for location changes, you'll feel better as you drag your amp up and down all those steps.

If the client is providing an instrument for you—usually a piano—specify that it be in reasonable tune and in good working order. Or require that it be tuned prior to your performance. Specify the cartage fee that applies if you have to bring your own equipment in the event that theirs isn't playable when you arrive. Remember, clients often don't understand that pianos must be maintained, and they won't bother to fix nonplaying keys or inoperable pedals unless you insist.

You may wish to add an extra fee for an early setup time or a consulting fee for extra meetings with the clients. What if the host of a house party wants you to drive forty miles out to "look over" the room where you'll be playing? Will you charge for the extra trip? What if the bride and groom want to have a two-hour meeting to discuss the music for their two-hour reception? Will you charge for your time? Or what if you have to buy special music and spend time transposing and learning it for a wedding ceremony? You may have to buy a fifteen-dollar book you'll never use again to get one obscure tune. Will you pass this charge on to the client?

These aren't easy questions because your music business, after all, is a service to your clients. It's difficult to decide where your expected efforts end and charges should begin, but with experience you'll know how to structure these fees. It's best to be flexible, and you may rarely charge a "consulting fee," but sometimes a client will take up so much of your time that you'll have to charge for it.

If you simply spell out these items as stipulations in your standard contract form and note that they apply to all jobs, you'll save many headaches and much confusion. Usually, just deciding in advance what to do

will ensure that the engagement goes smoothly.

Write a Letter

Maybe your kind of music doesn't require so much detail, or maybe you don't work that many jobs. In these cases, a simple letter to your client will probably suffice, but be sure to include any pertinent details mentioned above. Use your letterhead and be simple and direct. (See the sample letter, next page.)

You'll save time with a standard contract form where you can just fill in the blanks, rather than having to compose a new letter for each job, and most of the time you'll use a standard form. Also, a contract will keep you from overlooking any important details.

In any case, whether you have an attorney help you devise a "boilerplate" contract or just write a simple confirmation letter, be sure you get a written agreement. Everything will go better if you do, and you may be sorry if you don't.

Make Provisions for Swift Payment

Emphasize that you expect to be paid after playing a job. The only normal exception might be large corporations that have a rigid "accounts payable" procedure, but even with such corporate clients you should try to be paid when the job is played. Make this condition very clear in your contract, letters, and conversations with clients. If an occasional client is slow to pay (or worse, won't pay), you should act quickly. Follow these steps:

1. Send another invoice with a note thanking the client for the job and asking, politely, for payment.

2. Call the client, tell them you expected to be paid at the job, and ask when you can expect a check.

3. Send a *registered letter, return receipt re-*

THE MELLOTONES
59 Main Street
Lake Success, NY 11040

September 17, 1992

Mr. John Class, Manager
Proper Country Club
Lake Success, New York 11040

Dear Mr. Class:

This letter will confirm our engagement to provide music for your special "Autumn Days" party to be held on Saturday, October 12, 1992, from nine o'clock until midnight in your club's main ballroom. My group, "The Mellotones," consists of five pieces plus a female vocalist, and we will be dressed formally.

As we discussed on the phone, we will provide our own sound system but will use the house piano. You have assured me that the piano will be tuned on Friday before the job and will be on the stage by seven o'clock Saturday evening.

Our fee for this engagement is $1,100, to be paid to me at the end of the evening. If overtime is required, the rate is $200 per <u>half hour</u>.

We will begin the evening by playing the club's theme song, "Give Me The Simple Life." If there are other special requests, please let me know in advance if possible.

One copy of this letter is for your file, and the second copy should be signed and returned to me.

Thanks again for all your help. We are looking forward to another fine engagement at the Proper Country Club.

Sincerely,

Nancy Betts

Nancy Betts
Bandleader

Accepted by _____

Address_____

Phone_____

quested to the client, enclosing an invoice, and asking for prompt payment.

4. Ask your union to intervene. Many times unions are slow, ineffective, and of little use in such situations, but they *should* give you legal assistance, assuming you're a member in good standing and have filed a union contract. But, if the union seems to be moving slowly to help you, don't wait on them.

5. Have your lawyer write a stiff letter requesting payment.

6. Take the nonpaying client to Magistrate's Court, often called "Small Claims Court." You don't need a lawyer to sue in these courts, and they are usually set up to be helpful and accessible to all citizens. There is, however, a top dollar limit for such courts—often a thousand dollars or so.

7. Have your lawyer sue the nonpaying client. This will cost you a percentage of the money that's recovered—but it's better than nothing.

Trying to get paid by deadbeat clients is depressing and difficult, but if you devise a clear contract, do a good job, and maintain good relations with the client you'll rarely—or never—have such unpleasant experiences. Use your common sense, too, in deciding whether to take a job; be wary, for example, of a nightclub that's doing very poor business, or a political candidate who seems destined to lose. If any job seems likely to present payment problems, don't take it. It's not worth the hassle.

HOLDING ON TO WHAT YOU'VE GOT

Most freelance musicians with a business-like approach and a good marketing plan are able to earn a significant income. The next question is, "What do you do with all that money once you've made it?"

Rule to Remember:
The important thing isn't just how much you make, but how much you keep of what you make.

Financial awareness is very important, and it can be very complex. But, it can also be very simple: if you make forty thousand dollars a year, save none of it, and spend forty-two thousand, you're in trouble. But if you make fourteen thousand and manage to save a thousand, you're heading in a positive direction.

Freelancing vs. Stability
A freelance career can be exhilarating and exciting. You don't have to trudge to the same old office every day and you have the challenges of new clients, new venues, and new associations on every job. But everything has a tradeoff, and ours is that freelancing does not offer the stability found in regular "day jobs." We don't have company-sponsored retirement plans, insurance plans, vacation plans; in fact, many musicians don't have any plans at all, and that can be a big problem.

Marketing your music aggressively will bring in more money, true, but there will be slow periods when there isn't as much work as you'd like. Perhaps the summer doldrums aren't busy, or there's a recession in your state. Or, perhaps you are unlucky enough to break your arm or come down with mononucleosis, and your income stops while you recover.

Coping with unforeseen situations is *your own responsibility* as a freelance musician. You won't have the paternal arm of a corporation looking out for you, so you'll have to do it yourself. Achieving financial security isn't impossible, but it takes self-discipline and planning. In planning for the future, there are basic financial steps that every self-employed person should take that will help compensate for the uncertainties of the freelance lifestyle. If you satisfy these needs, you won't have to worry about all the "what if's" that can come up because you'll be protected. *But if you don't do it, no one else will.*

As a self-employed freelance musician, you should be saving for that inevitable rainy day. Saving part of your income takes real self-discipline, but you have to do it. Force yourself to live on less than your total income, and "pay yourself first" by putting part of each check into a savings account. Set a percentage—say, 10 percent—or a specific amount, and put it into a savings account that doesn't pay for everyday living expenses. *Then forget about it.* Don't consider this savings money to be a source for new equipment, clothes, or cars. Everybody needs a permanent nest egg that will grow as the years go by.

One good way to build this savings account is to save all the extra, unexpected income from last-minute jobs. All freelancers sometimes get such calls, and since you weren't counting on that money for the rent, why not save it?

Many self-employed people actually have more than one savings account: one for long-term, permanent savings, and another for the big-ticket items that you want—new equipment, for example. The important thing about financial planning, like other aspects of your career, is to do it. *Planning* to save money isn't the same thing as saving money, and good intentions don't count.

Where should you keep your savings? Bank or savings and loan accounts are convenient, but they pay very poor interest, and an important principle of financial management is that *little things mean a lot over time.* Search out sources of higher interest rates, investigate their safety, and go for the highest safe return you can get. A passbook account may pay about 5 percent, a money-market fund could yield 7 or 8 percent, and

a certificate of deposit might pay you even more for your money, but each plan has drawbacks that you should consider. Money market funds are great but usually require a sizable minimum deposit; certificates of deposit are safe and secure but lock up your funds for long periods of time. Consider the options, and pick a plan that you know you'll stick with.

You might try an automatic deduction from your checking account and have the bank put fifty or a hundred dollars into a savings account for you each month. Some people set up loan payments that add a few dollars a month to savings accounts; in effect, you overpay the loan each month and the extra dollars go automatically into a savings account so you never miss the money. The form you use isn't important, but your financial stability and your ultimate happiness depend on having enough money saved to weather the inevitable storms. If you don't do anything else this book recommends, do this—set up a savings plan and stick with it.

Cover Yourself—with Insurance

Every time you mail a premium payment to an insurance company, you'll resent it because insurance payments seem wasted if you don't have a claim. But when you do have a claim—and eventually you will—you'll be glad you're covered.

Insurance is a complex subject, and most advice you'll get will come from insurance agents who are usually superb salespeople trained to *sell you as much insurance as possible.* Maybe they'll always sell you only what you need, but maybe they're looking out for their own commissions more than your welfare. The best, and only, protection against spending too much on insurance is to prepare yourself by researching what you need, what the options are, and what you can afford. Read magazines like *Money, Changing Times,* and others to become an educated insurance consumer. The following list provides a quick outline of the different kinds of insurance self-employed people may need.

Health insurance pays doctor and hospital bills. Typically you'll pay a *deductible* amount—probably the first few hundred dollars a year of medical expenses—and the insurance company pays most of the rest. Health care is incredibly expensive today, and a few trips to the doctor or one trip to the hospital will justify all your health insurance costs. Maybe you're young and healthy now, but anything can happen even to you, believe it or not.

By far the best way to buy health insurance is by being part of a *group plan*, but freelance musicians aren't usually covered. If your spouse has a steady job, you can probably be covered there, but you may have to search for other group options. Group insurance should be offered by every musicians' union, but unfortunately it isn't; it varies with each local. If your union doesn't have such a plan, work to have one made available or threaten to quit the union. It's that important. If your musical abilities make you eligible for membership in more than one union—both the AFM and AFTRA, for example—shop around for the best insurance coverage because every plan is different.

If you can't join a group plan and must buy individual health coverage, you'll find that it's very expensive. Shop and compare widely; a higher deductible amount usually means that premium payments are lower, and your savings account should cover any deductible costs if necessary.

Nobody plans to be in accidents or to get sick, but bad things happen to good, unsuspecting people. Be prepared.

Life insurance is available in several forms that are beyond the scope of this book. If you have a family, life insurance—and probably a substantial amount—is essential. But if you're single, you may have very little need for lots of life insurance.

The two basic kinds are *term insurance*, which is relatively inexpensive and only provides payment if you die, and *whole life*, which combines insurance coverage, an automatic savings plan, and a borrowing-back option. Many experts contend that term insurance is best, but if you have trouble saving money you may do well with a whole-life policy that builds "cash value" through the years.

Do your own planning before talking with insurance people, and have a clear idea of what you need. It won't help you at all to sign up for a program that's too expensive to maintain, but good coverage is available at reasonable rates if you shop around carefully.

Automobile insurance is familiar because most states require it before issuing a license plate. Be sure that your liability limits are very high because that's important coverage if you're in an accident. As a musician, you'll probably be driving a lot at night, and that's prime accident time.

Does your car insurance cover theft from the car? Would it cover *professional equipment*? Don't assume that it does, because many policies don't. Ask your agent and read your policy.

Apartment or homeowner's insurance is important coverage since it protects against fire and theft. Many policies, however, specifically *exclude* coverage of professional equipment, so talk to your agent and *read all the fine print on your policy*. Never, never depend on what the agent tells you unless it is also clearly written into your policy; the agent may not know, or he may just be trying to sell you the insurance. *Always get coverage specifications in writing*. Is your home office equipment covered? Your tuxedo? Your home recording studio?

Use the equipment inventory sheet you

made in Chapter Two as a guide; you may be surprised at how much you own, and a theft could literally wipe you out. Musical instruments are hot items among thieves, and you must protect yourself. Sometimes, good coverage for instruments is available as a "floater" attached to your homeowner's or renter's policy, listing each piece of equipment separately by serial number and value. Such coverage may be a good deal, but it can be prohibitively expensive. Compare it with other available types of coverage.

Instrument insurance is offered through many unions or musical organizations and is often an excellent bargain. Such coverage may be hundreds of dollars cheaper than similar insurance bought through a general agent, so read professional publications, check with your union, and compare the available options.

Many musicians don't buy instrument coverage, preferring to "self-insure" through savings; but, if you have a valuable collection of instruments, and most of us do, you'll really come out ahead by buying inexpensive coverage.

Of course, all musicians should try to avoid unnecessary losses by being security-conscious. Most instruments can easily be stolen, so don't flaunt your equipment by storing it exposed in your car. If you leave equipment in clubs, try to get the club to agree, in writing, to cover any losses, and take expensive, small items, such as microphones, ram cards, and so on, with you each night. Be alert to security risks, and you can avoid many problems and keep insurance rates down, too.

There are other kinds of insurance that you might consider, such as disability coverage or extra liability policies. Each person's situation is different, and your needs may be small or very large. You won't like paying lots of money for insurance coverage that you may not need, but remember that you're planning for the possibility that everything may go wrong. If that rainy day gets here, you'll be prepared.

Planning to Take It Easy . . . Someday.

One of the few ways the government allows self-employed people to get ahead is through *Individual Retirement Accounts*, known as IRAs. Through this plan and other similar ones, you can save two thousand dollars each year in a special account that won't be taxed as it grows, and your initial contribution may reduce your tax payment, too. You can set up such an account at any bank, savings and loan, or brokerage firm, and make contributions each year or just now and then, as your situation allows. You can't get to the money, however, without paying substantial penalties, so this should be considered to be your "longest-term savings." (If you can afford to save more than two thousand dollars a year for retirement, consult your accountant about other plans such as Keogh or 401 (K) programs that provide good options for self-employed people.)

What's the big advantage of an IRA? Simply that as time goes on, the *miracle of compounding* increases your savings almost magically. Interest payments increase the amount of your savings, which result in larger interest payments, which increase the amount of your savings. Here's an example. If you contribute a thousand dollars a year to an IRA in a bank that pays only 5¼ percent (which is probably the *lowest* rate you could find), here's how your totals would add up:

Year	Total amount contributed	Amount available
1	$ 1,000	$ 1,056
10	$10,000	$ 13,671
20	$20,000	$ 37,278
30	$30,000	$ 78,042
40	$40,000	$148,433

The benefits of compounding start slowly and increase rapidly as time goes on, and this example is based on a very low rate of return. If your IRA accrues at 8 percent, or 12 percent, or even more, depending on the market, your money grows *much* faster. The advantage of an IRA is that you don't pay taxes on the earnings until you retire.

Thus, in this example, if you put just a thousand dollars a year into a passbook IRA when you're twenty-five, you'd have nearly a hundred and fifty thousand dollars in this one account by the time you're sixty-five. (In reality you'd seek out a higher return and hopefully contribute more than a thousand a year, so your totals would be much higher.)

Your IRA can be set up in any way you'd like — stocks, bonds, mutual funds, bank certificates — but since this is your pension, you'll want to be careful with it. If you start early, and you really should, you can work with a financial advisor to diversify your investments, with part of them safe and secure and part in a more adventurous vehicle. Time passes quickly, and you'll be planning for retirement sooner than you may think. When you're sixty-five, you'll still be playing music, of course, but you may not want to work as hard as you did when you were younger, so don't let this year pass without starting an IRA.

Rule to Remember:
Set up an IRA as soon as possible, add to it regularly, and watch it grow.

SUCCESS IS TAXING

Another difference between being a self-employed freelancer and working a nine-to-five job comes when it's time to pay taxes. In most jobs your taxes are deducted and you don't even miss that money because you never see it; take-home pay is what you're accustomed to. But, self-employed people have to pay the IRS directly, and that's always painful. You'll notice and probably moan over every cent that's due as you write those quarterly checks to the government.

That's why you must learn to play the tax game wisely. Learn about deductions, and keep careful records. Buy a tax handbook each year and find out what's different. Most important, locate an accountant (see Chapter Twelve) for professional advice. Tax regulations change yearly and get more complex, regardless of what Congress says. Unless you're good with numbers and enjoy working with depreciation tables, amortization, capital gains and losses, and lots of other complicated notions, find professional help. The bottom line is that you can often make more money by careful tax planning than you could by working a job for the same amount of time.

Before you visit an accountant, read a current tax book and educate yourself to some extent. You'll save time and money by knowing what you need, being familiar with basic tax terms, and having your records organized. This book won't take the place of an annual tax guide, but here are some useful ideas about taxes.

Don't try to fool the IRS. You can't do it, and penalties today are severe. Ignorance isn't acceptable as an excuse, either. You are responsible for paying taxes on all the money you make, and that includes those rare payments in cash. Just because you read about millionaires who don't pay taxes (and most of those stories are incorrect) doesn't mean you can avoid them.

Make quarterly payments. If you play only part-time and your music income is less than five hundred dollars, you may not have to pay quarterly; you can raise the deductions on the W-4 form at your "day job" to pay the extra amount due. But if you're self-employed, you must estimate your tax liability in advance and pay part of it every three months. If you don't, the fine is substantial.

To pay quarterly, you must estimate your income for the year and pay a fourth of it each quarter using form 1040-ES. An accurate estimate may, in fact, be impossible, but using last year's return as a guide, you should be able to come close. You can use your final quarterly payment to bring your estimated payments to within 90 percent of your total tax bill (to avoid a penalty). Again, seek an accountant's help to be sure you're doing it right.

Know what's deductible and keep careful records because legitimate business expenses lower your tax bill. Allowable deductions change from year to year, but the need to keep clear, detailed proof of such deductions doesn't change. Buy a tax-record book at the office-supply store and get in the habit of recording deductions in ink. Write checks or use charge cards rather than cash so you'll have proof of payment, and, of course, save your bank statements and charge bills. (In fact, you should save those along with receipts for deductions for seven years to be on the safe side. Keep old tax returns forever.)

An easy way to keep receipts is in a nine-by-twelve envelope, starting a new envelope each year. Write the amount of each business expense down in your record book or record it on a computer program if you're using one because it's easier to add up your deductions from a neat record book than an envelope stuffed with receipt forms.

Allowable deductions can change, so consult an up-to-date tax guidebook (see Appendix B for suggestions) each year. In general, though, if you're reporting self-employment income you'll use Schedule C, "Profit or (Loss) from Business or Profession," and list your allowable deductions on this form. Some typical deductions for freelance musicians are listed on page 121. Keeping an accurate account of allowable, legitimate, deductible business expenses is very important, and listing deductible expenditures *as they occur* should become a habit. You'll save a lot of money this way.

Be sure your business isn't just a hobby because the IRS limits the expenses that can be deducted for hobbies. The sure way to prove that you're a legitimate business is to make a profit for three out of five years; otherwise, you can't claim business expenses as deductions. So, don't buy office and musical equipment that exceeds your income for three years running. Your goal, of course, is to make a profit anyway. There are exceptions and ways to prove that you're *trying* to make a profit, but such arguments can be complex. Consult your accountant if you have a question about whether your deductions are truly business-related.

Deducting automobile expenses is complicated and you'll need your accountant's advice, but there are essentially two methods for recovering business-related transportation costs. You can either deduct the actual cost of the car through depreciation (including purchase price, repairs, and upkeep), or you can claim a mileage allowance (which may change yearly). Discuss which method to use with your accountant because you must compute your automobile deductions the same way each year.

You'll probably use your car partly for business and partly for personal reasons, and you'll have to be able to prove the percentage of business use you claim. Thus, if you claim that 60 percent of your car expenses are work-related, you should have mileage records to back you up. Get in the habit, especially on long trips, of keeping a logbook in the car listing date, mileage, and reason for each trip. It's a hassle, but it's worth it.

Other musicians who work for you are your "subcontractors." Keep track of how much you pay them and, at the end of the year, send each one a 1099 form showing how much they received from you. Actually, you don't have to send a 1099 to anyone paid less than six hundred dollars, but you might want to send all subcontractors such a form to prove to the IRS that all the money that passed through your checking account really wasn't yours. These forms must be sent out by the end of January.

Don't forget state and city taxes. Often they parallel federal requirements, but not always. Follow your accountant's advice.

Typical Deductions for Freelance Musicians

If you file a "Schedule C" to report your business profits (or losses), you can claim legitimate business expenses. This is not a definitive list, and you should consult a current book and an accountant to be sure your expenses are allowable; but, in general, these are the expenses you can deduct — and these are the receipts you should record and save.

■ Home office expenses — including a percentage of your mortgage or rent, utility payments, property taxes, and insurance — *if your office is used only for business and is your primary place of business.*

■ Automobile expenses

■ Union dues

■ Professional publications

■ Books

■ Uniforms that are required for work and not suitable for other wear.

■ Payments to subcontractors

■ Advertising costs (including postage, printing, typesetting, photography)

■ Rent (for example, you may store your instruments in a mini-warehouse facility)

■ Music and records, if required for your work

■ Travel expenses, when job-related

■ Business entertainment expenses (now limited to 80 percent of the total)

■ Accounting fees

■ Commissions you pay to agents

■ Repairs

■ Business telephone expenses (including long-distance calls)

■ Office supplies

■ Equipment purchases. Large items such as instruments, computers, automobiles are "depreciated." That is, you can deduct a portion of the item's cost each year for a specified number of years. Smaller items are "expensed" and deducted in the year of the purchase.

■ Flowers and gifts sent for business reasons

You can reduce the burden of taxes by staying up-to-date on current laws, keeping good records, and using professional help. There's no need to give the government more than your fair share, and while figuring out that fair share isn't easy, it is a very worthwhile task.

If you plan wisely and don't overspend, you'll be able to avoid those money-worry ulcers that plague so many freelance people. Remember to avoid the music-store trap discussed in Chapter Two, and set up a savings program described in this chapter. If you do, you'll be money ahead and you'll look forward to each month's bank statements that show your net worth growing faster and faster. Keep it up and you might be able to retire to your garage to once again play only the music you love.

GOAL-SETTING FOR MUSICIANS

INTERVIEW WITH LEE J. HOWARD

Lee J. Howard is a freelance pianist who now lives and works in Atlanta. He comes from a musical background (both parents are music teachers) but was about to attend graduate school in business when he decided he'd rather do what he loved to do—play the piano. He approaches music in a very businesslike way and has built an impressive list of clients in just three years. Lee J. plays a variety of solo and band jobs, concerts, and has produced two tapes of solo piano music. His purpose in music and in life is to "inspire and uplift people."

Q *You've built a thriving music business in a short time. How have you done it?*
A Setting goals is very important for anyone's success, I think. My first goal, a really broad one, was to become a full-time, committed musician. At that point I decided that I would no longer take outside daytime jobs to support my original music and the concerts that I wanted to do. I decided that I needed to put my efforts into music, so I did.

Then, three years ago I sat down with my wife and made financial goals, and she asked, "Well, what would you like to be making in four years?" I said, "A hundred thousand dollars a year." But I'd only made twelve thousand dollars the year before, so I thought that goal was totally insane. A couple of months later, though, I set an intermediate goal of doubling the previous year's income, and I made it. In fact, it seemed relatively easy. The next year, I set a goal of increasing my income fifty percent—and did that. When setting goals, I usually don't have an exact idea how I will reach them, but by having a goal to work toward, I often will be inspired to come up with new ideas.

Q *What happens if you don't meet a goal?*
A Actually, a goal is like a game to me, be-

cause if you don't reach your goals, you can be miserable. An important thing to me, then, is to stop when the period of time is over and say, "If don't reach the goal, it's okay. Now I'm going on to next week's efforts. For example, if I typically made five hundred dollars a week last year and this year's goal is fifteen hundred dollars a week—but I only made one thousand dollars this week—I'm still ahead of last year and I'm still moving in a positive direction. Last year I would have been very happy with the thousand, and if I hadn't set a higher goal for this year, I probably wouldn't have even made the thousand.

As important as goals are (and I think they're very important), it's important to be able to let go of the goals you set, too—at the end of the week, or month, let it go so you're not carrying over the unhappiness of any failure to meet that week's goals. It's important to meet your goals, of course, but you can't have them hanging over you, causing you to feel guilty or depressed.

Q *What kind of business techniques or ideas do you use to build your career?*
A Something that I've found really helpful in focusing on my goals is to clear up any leftover business before I start my day. If my office is a mess, I'll usually clear it up first—go through everything and file it or throw it away. It helps to clear your mind to start with a clear desk every day; don't have anything hanging over you or troubling you first thing in the morning, or you can have that problem on your mind all day. And always do the most important, difficult, or troubling thing first.

Lately I've started getting up in the morning, getting dressed up, and going to my office even though the office is in my house, and the difference is amazing. That really helps, because now that I'm setting a series of financial goals—weekly, monthly, and yearly—I have to really work at it. Now, I sit down in my office at 9:30, and make a list of activities that I should do each day. For example, I could call musicians I don't know and introduce myself. Or I could call a country club or a prospective client and try to set up a meeting or an audition.

Q *How do you market your music?*
A I try to *meet* new clients and not just send them cards or information because a meeting gives me a chance to make a stronger impression. There are many musicians who'll send their cards—and I want to stand out. When I meet new clients, they can, I hope, see that my presentation is sharp, that I dress neatly—in short, that I'd look good in their club. And, if possible, I try to play for them, too.

On a sales call, especially to businesses where time is important, I try to be more businesslike. I want to tell them what I do, the qualities that make my quartet special, for instance—the punctuality, professionalism, and good references from other corporations and country clubs—in short, that I'd fit in with what they're planning. But I still try to meet them to establish a personal rapport.

And I keep trying. I'm not obnoxious, but I'll be fairly persistent because I know that if prospects—say, agents or meeting planners—are really committed to their jobs and they're trying to fit wonderful music with the right client, then they're better off knowing what I do. They *need* to know what I do so they can call me when I'm appropriate.

For example, yesterday I called the new catering manager at a small restaurant where I've done a lot of work in the past. I said, "Hello, this is Lee J. Howard, and I'd like to come by and meet you. I know my card's on file, but I'd like a chance to tell you in person what I do and how I might help

your functions." She said, "Fine, can you come by at 5:30 today?" I met her, and I've already had one referral from that source. Making that appointment was part of yesterday's goals.

At this point, since I've been contacting people like this for a year, I already get a lot of calls. My daily goal is to call two people a day, and I try to *meet* with two people a week. This helps me meet my financial goal of playing four times a week.

But you've got to make a strong, positive impression. So, if you don't look as good as you think you should, go out and take a seminar on your presentation, hire someone to go shopping with you so the clothes you wear will look good on jobs, auditions, and meetings. If you don't have what you need, take the action to handle it. Make a list of all the things you need and work on getting them.

Here's an example of how calling on people works. I got a list of Atlanta's largest corporations, and I've called about ten of them. Sometimes it's hard to get to the right person, and I was beginning to wonder if this approach was worthwhile. Then, last week I got someone who might need music for corporate events, and we talked about that for a while. Then, out of the blue she started talking about the possibility of my providing music for other functions—for her church, her country club—so that call may pay off in several ways. If it does, it will be worth the first nine calls that may not produce any work.

I really like personal contact when I'm promoting my music. A friend of mine in Chicago, another musician, produced a really stunning brochure, did a mailing, and got virtually no results from it. His brochure is impressive, but I think nothing replaces personal contact. I am working on a mailing, though; I'm on the third draft of a letter I'll send to old clients as well as agents and meeting planners announcing the new band

I've put together. That mailing will *promote* my music, of course, but it will mostly just remind people that I'm around. Even if you do a great job for someone, you have to keep up with each client and stay in touch. Otherwise they may forget about you next time they need music.

I think it's also important to acknowledge clients and contacts — to appreciate what they do for you — not just for business reasons. So I make a special effort to acknowledge them in appropriate ways.

Q *What else is important in working toward your goals and promoting your music?*
A Along with everything else, a crucial element in meeting your personal goals is to build a strong structure of support. It's like a safety net that throws you right back up on the highwire, and it can be family, friends, or other musicians.

Goals are easiest to achieve when the *quality* of your life is what you want it to be, I think. So, if you're relaxed and peaceful, and feeling joyful and happy with what you do — not wishing that you'd done something else with your life — then that will be reflected in your performance and in the success of your career. When you show up on a job you can say, "Man, I'm really lucky to be doing this." That attitude really contributes to a job going well, even great. And people respond to your music if they can tell you really love what you're doing. That's a bottom line kind of thing for me. When I hire musicians of course I want musicality, but it's very important to me that they approach the job with the attitude, "I am thrilled to be playing on this job. I am thrilled to be playing music."

DOING IT ALL—WITH HELP

Now your marketing plan is complete, you've set up your home office, and you're busy organizing your filing system. Maybe you're even working with your computer learning to produce mailing lists and publicity pieces. You're accomplishing a lot, but when you consider all the things yet to do you get tired just thinking about it: promotional material to write, thank-you notes to send, tax returns to prepare, a logo to design, computer programs to learn, and—most important—jobs to book and play. Where's the time for fun?

"If successful freelance life is this frantic," you may think, "I'd rather go back to the poor old days with my garage band. At least we enjoyed the music without worrying about everything else." That's a real dilemma because there *is* a lot to do. Wouldn't it be great if you had a staff to help with all those nonmusical tasks? Here's the good news—you *can* have a staff of your own without too much trouble or expense. Competent professionals are available in your community who can make your life much easier, and their help may cost much less than you think. Furthermore, the quality of their work may surpass what you can do, and that's important.

SEEKING PROFESSIONAL HELP

Everything you do must be done well because you aren't just competing with other musicians, you're up against whoever sets the standards in business. In any area, that is, your competition will almost always be professionally trained people who have plenty of money to spend. For example, your publicity will be judged not by other musicians' brochures and letters, but by the prevailing standard for similar material designed and used by major advertising and graphic design companies. Quality is crucial.

Likewise, your demo tape can't be something recorded with your Walkman at last Saturday's gig even if that's what Band X uses. Your demo is really competing against the high-quality production and excellent musicianship of the recording industry—and prospective clients will expect your tape to sound that good. They won't stop to consider this, of course, but when your tape goes into their player, it had better measure up.

On a more mundane level, your tax return is another case where quality is important. Not only will it cost you money if you prepare it badly, overlook deductions, or make errors in calculation, but it can lead to an audit, a tax bill, or worse.

In other words, every aspect of your work must be done well, up to the standards that are set by other businesses. Sure, you can do it all—and you may enjoy it. But in case you're intimidated by so much work, your community offers plenty of professional help in every area, and you can hire other people to do many nonmusical tasks for you.

"Hire other people?" you ask. "I can hardly afford a new set of guitar strings—much less lots of high-priced professional help."

Count the Costs

You may be surprised at the real costs of hiring professional help—and you may not be able to afford *not* to seek them out. It's true that many graphic designers, for instance, have very high hourly rates, but it's also true that many don't. And your job may not take much of their time so that even a high rate doesn't mean a high bill.

What you *can't afford* as you build your business is to do a shoddy job of anything. Always try for the best quality possible, and if that means hiring outside professionals, then seek their help.

Money, in fact, may not be the real bottom line; you must also consider the quality of the job and the time and effort required. Perhaps you could prepare your own tax return, but it might take several days of torturous preparation, struggling to understand complex forms and indecipherable instructions. If your time is worth something—and it is probably worth a lot—why not hire an accountant? An accountant will surely do a better job than you could, keep you out of trouble with the IRS, probably save you money, and certainly reduce your tax-time hassle.

Perhaps such a competent accountant will charge two hundred dollars to prepare your return and give you general bookkeeping and financial advice. She'll do a better job than you could because she's the expert. And, if it took you two days to prepare your own return you'd be working for about twelve dollars an hour. Can you afford time away from your primary task—building your music clientele—to do that? Probably not.

The conclusion: you can often find pro-

fessionals who will deliver a better product and actually save you money in the process. Of course you *could* cut your own hair, change the oil in your car, and tune your own piano, but most people don't have time or the desire to be completely self-sufficient. And, you *could* write your own promo material, make your own publicity photos, engineer your own demo tape, sell your own music, and prepare your own taxes—and you'll probably do some of these things—but you won't likely do them all.

Remember, too, that spending money on your career is an *investment*—it's not simply money thrown away. If professional people can help you do a better job then your money is well spent. Sometimes it takes money to make money.

Who Can Help?

As you build your career, lots of professionals can help you. First, we'll look at *who* can help you, and then we'll discuss how to find these people. Professionals who can advance your career include:

Publicity professionals including photographers, writers, graphic designers, typesetters, and printers can help with the all-important task of publicizing your music. You probably won't use a PR or advertising agency because they are usually geared to the needs of larger companies—and they're too expensive. But you can often find freelancing writers, photographers, or designers who can provide superior, top-quality results for a very reasonable cost.

For example, in preparing your brochure, you may decide to write the copy yourself—perhaps after reading a book on publicity techniques for performers such as *Getting Noticed* (see Appendix B), but you might want professional help in designing the brochure. Thus, you'd profit from the help of a graphic designer who would have lots of ideas, highly developed skills, and all the tools needed for this specialized field.

You have a camera and you have friends who have darkrooms, but publicity photos are too important to leave to chance. You want the best one you can get, and somewhere in your town is a professional photographer who'll do a great job, work with you, spend time devising just the "look" you want—all for a reasonable cost.

You'll probably need a professional typesetter, too, to make sure your material doesn't have that "homemade" look. Typesetters know all about type styles; different faces, sizes, and weights; and they'll guide you to the right choices for a great-looking brochure, business card, and other material.

Attorneys, who can help with contracts and with the (hopefully) rare client who doesn't pay promptly. Before you sign management or recording agreements, you should certainly seek the advice of an attorney. You'll find that establishing a good relationship with a lawyer will be helpful in many ways. Perhaps you'll reach a point in your career where you should incorporate your business to lessen liability, decrease taxes, or just increase profits. Or maybe you're about to sign an exclusive contract with a promoter and you're unsure about all the fine print. Your attorney can help you. The lawyer's task is to ask "what if," to imagine what would happen if everything went wrong, and to protect you. Regardless of what other professional help you may need, you should establish a relationship with a lawyer. Maybe you'll never need her, but if you do, you'll know whom to call.

It's not necessary to retain the services of the largest, most prestigious law firm in town, and you'll probably want to avoid the hucksters who advertise on daytime television, too. Many small law firms or single practitioners will be happy to help you for an affordable fee. Young lawyers, especially, who are building their practices can offer excellent advice but will respect your pocketbook. Attorneys, like musicians, specialize,

so look for a general practitioner, or even an attorney who's worked with entertainment matters. Most musicians won't need (or be able to find in smaller towns) lawyers who specialize solely in entertainment matters, but usually a general attorney will be effective. Ask your friends, neighbors, and associates for referrals, or call the local bar association for a list of appropriate attorneys.

Accountants, like other professionals, should actually *save you more than they cost*. Simply discovering one overlooked tax deduction could save you many times the accountant's cost, and the other advice she could give might prove invaluable. Accountants will tell you what records to keep, give hints on the best way to record them, and help you improve your year-end profitability. Additionally, they'll keep you out of financial trouble—and that's important.

You don't need to use one of the "Big Eight" national accounting firms and you may not even need a CPA, but you should seek out a competent accountant. Don't use a store-front, part-time tax preparer who may have only had a few hours of training; your financial future is too important for that. Many musicians find a small accounting firm or a freelance accountant to be a perfect match with their needs.

Financial planners aren't just for the affluent. In fact, you probably need their help and advice more than rich folks do because each dollar is more important to you and you work hard to earn every cent. Financial planners can offer advice that will help your net worth increase year by year, and that's an important part of anyone's bottom line.

Unless you went to business school, you probably don't have a very good idea of how much insurance you need or of where to invest your savings. If you're like most musicians, nothing could be further from your mind than retirement . . . and if you do think of it at all, you assume that Social Security or something will take care of you. Time passes quickly, and you'll need to think about retirement much sooner than you'd imagine. With the advice of a good financial planner, you'll develop a simple investment plan that will prosper without requiring constant attention.

A secret that all businesspeople should understand is the value of time in investments. Even a simple savings account will grow through compound interest, and if your adviser can help you locate good investments with high returns, your savings could, over time, amount to lots of money. If you start saving while you're young, you'll have lots of extra years for your investments to grow—and you'll be amazed at how quickly your savings double.

Finding your way through the maze of IRAs, CDs, insurance options, stocks and bonds, and other investment possibilities is a full-time job, and a professional can be of great help. One warning, however: a pure financial planner sells no products—he or she only gives advice and makes suggestions. Many insurance agents and stockbrokers call themselves "planners," when in reality they are salespeople working for commissions. Be sure that the products you buy are reputable and that your adviser is as objective as possible. Again, do some research and read current business magazines, and you'll be able to judge the quality of the help you seek and receive. See Appendix A for ideas on useful publications.

All these professionals are in business, just as you are, to serve their clients. If you find a freelance designer, accountant, and independent financial planner, they'll understand the uniqueness of your career needs and problems because theirs are much the same.

Working with the Pros

How do you find an accountant or lawyer who'll be right for you? What if you've never hired a graphic designer before? How do you locate the right one? Here are some tips.

Ask around. Ask your colleagues, neighbors, and friends for recommendations. Don't necessarily try to use the same people used by big businesses, though, because they may be oriented toward unlimited budgets and complex issues. Instead, try to find a small operator, perhaps an independent like yourself, who is his or her own boss.

Sometimes a moonlighting artist or designer who works full-time for a big company will do small jobs on the side and can provide excellent work for a small fee. Designing your logo, for example, could cost hundreds or even thousands of dollars at a large graphic design house, but the same artist, working at home at night, might do the exact same job for a fraction of the big-company cost.

Ask to see samples. You won't need to see samples of a lawyer's work, of course, but you should always see *similar* work done by photographers, artists, and writers. Does the work look like what you want? Does the style match your ideas? Remember, the samples shown by these professionals should be their finest work, and you want the absolute best you can get—so if the samples aren't terrific, keep looking. You'll find someone who can do just the job you need, but it may not be the first person you interview.

Ask questions. Don't be shy. Maybe you've never hired an attorney before, and you're hesitant to ask her price. Don't be—go ahead and ask, "How do you charge? By the hour or the job? How much will a job like this one typically cost?" Don't be ashamed that you don't know the answers—you're not supposed to. She wouldn't know how much a band costs, either.

Keep asking questions until you're sure you understand and that the person you're hiring does, too. Go over and over your brochure ideas until you're positive that the designer knows what you mean. Ask the recording engineer everything you want to know, and don't assume anything; who pays to have the piano tuned before the session? Is mixing time included? Who will do the mixing? How many tapes do you get? How much are cassette copies? Is there a quantity discount? You have to ask.

Sometimes you may encounter someone who just doesn't communicate well with you—and you shouldn't hire that person. You must feel comfortable with any professional help you choose and not be reluctant to ask questions, make changes, or even argue a point, because these people are important to your career. In a sense, they are part of your success team, so if you interview a lawyer who won't answer you in plain English, find another one. If a photographer won't tell you exactly how many rolls of film his fee includes, find another one. You're the buyer here, it's your hard-earned money, and you should shop around until you are satisfied that you've found just the right team to help with your career development.

BOOKING AGENTS

One more category of outside professional is important to freelance musicians—the booking agent. These people locate jobs that need music, sell the clients, do all the paperwork—and, hopefully, hire you to play the gig.

Should you try to book all your music jobs yourself using the *PMMS*—or should you use a booking agent? Won't an agent keep some of the money that should go to you? After all, you're the one on the firing line, playing the job, and doing the work. Why should you share the income with an agent?

Most musicians ask these questions, yet most musicians work with booking agencies—at least sometimes. You'll find that a good, honest booking agent can be another member of your team of helpful professionals.

A good agent is, essentially, a highly trained salesperson specializing in the entertainment field. He devotes all his time to searching for clients, often big ones, and he has more resources than you do to complete the task. It makes sense, therefore, to understand exactly what agents do and to know how to use their expertise.

Musicians play for many reasons—including fun, artistic expression, profit, and personal satisfaction—but agents are in it for the money. Most agents are 99.9 percent businesspeople, interested in the bottom line. Like other clients, they don't care about your musical soul; they only want to know if they can make money with your music. So you should think of them just as you think of other clients and find ways to demonstrate that your music will fill their needs. They must believe that your talent will make money for them when they use their sales skills to find jobs for you.

Love-Hate Is Here to Stay

Sometimes—in fact, often—tension exists between musicians and agents because they are trying to do two different things. At the simplest level, the difference may be irreconcilable; the best you can do is to understand it and know where the agent's loyalty lies.

Musicians want to play music and derive as much satisfaction as possible from each performance. Perhaps making money is part of the goal, but it's not always first on the list. Many musicians' allegiance is, essentially, to their music, their art, and their craft. If you're following the ideas in this book, you know that commercial music requires compromise; but you also know that you must set your own limits—at some point, making music is what's most important to you.

Agents, on the other hand, are businesspeople whose loyalty is with their hard-earned clients. Their principal interest is in maintaining those clients and their business. When there is a musician-client conflict, the agent will *automatically* take the client's side, right or wrong. Why? Because that's where the money comes from. Musicians can easily be replaced, but if a client goes to another agency, that account and its revenue is lost.

By accepting the reality of this basic difference in orientation, you'll save yourself a lot of misapprehension and unpleasantness. Regardless of what they tell you, agents represent their paying clients—not you—unless you're a star or celebrity, and their aim is to keep those clients satisfied. Don't be shocked. That's their job.

So, at a convention where you're providing walk-up and awards music before playing the show, don't be surprised if the agent—on behalf of the client—asks you not to take a break but to play two-and-a-half hours straight. If that's what the client wants, that's what the agent wants. Sometimes such requests will be reasonable and you can accommodate them; sometimes they'll be unacceptable and you'll have to politely refuse or seek a compromise. But at least you'll know where the agent is coming from in such situations.

All this doesn't mean, of course, that agents are your enemies. It's just that if you understand what the bottom line really is, you can avoid needless conflicts and make your partnership more productive.

Establishing a Good Relationship
You'll get best results by finding booking agencies that handle your kind of music. Some agencies are completely rock/pop oriented, some book only college concerts, some specialize in Jewish weddings and other ethnic functions, and others book primarily large shows for major conventions. Some specialize in the six-night nightclub circuit, while others mainly book traveling shows for armed-forces installations around the world. So you may have to shop around to find an agent who books the kind of freelance jobs you're looking for.

But you should also spend a little time becoming known by the local agencies that *don't* specialize in your kind of music because they'll never turn down any business, and when they get that rare call for your speciality they'll call you. A rock-oriented agent may book very few harpists for weddings—but if he knows you're a terrific freelance harpist he'll think of you when he needs a harp. That's why *all* booking agencies should be at the top of your marketing lists.

Musicians and agents are often at odds because they are doing different things. However, you can minimize the friction and avoid problems by taking these steps in dealing with any agent.

■ *Communicate honestly and clearly with every agent.* Let them know *exactly* what you can and cannot do, and don't take a job if it's outside your area of competence. You'll only hurt yourself, and the agency won't hire you again.

■ *Discuss details and be sure you understand exactly what's been sold and promised.* Agents sometimes are careless with particulars, so insist on precise instructions about the job—where, when, whom to report to, whether there is a piano, who is providing the sound, what time rehearsal is, whether you must use the loading dock at the back of the hotel, whether you're doubling on sax *and* flute, how much you'll be paid for overtime, who authorizes overtime, and so on. Insist on a written contract or letter confirming these points. Usually, such small details determine the success of a job, and this aspect of the music business should not be left to chance. The agent is a go-between for you and the client, and you must pay close attention to be sure that all details are covered, understood, and agreed upon. Insist that the agent be honest with both you and the client. Sometimes, in the heat of a sales call, an agent will forget reality and promise the moon to close a sale. But the agent probably won't be at the job to take the heat if something goes wrong, so don't let an overzealous agent book your pop trio as a country group, or your seventeen-piece big band as a rock group.

■ *Always have a clear understanding with agents about money.* Is the price quoted net to you or does the agency's commission come out of it? Will the client pay the agent directly, or should you pick up a check? Will the agent pay you immediately following the job, or will you have to wait weeks or even months until the agent has been paid by the client? If the worst happens and the client doesn't pay, will the agent pay you anyway? Or if the job is canceled two days before the performance, will you be paid? Misunderstandings about money have ruined many relationships, including those between musicians and agents. If you have a firm, clear — better yet, written — understanding about these matters, you'll both be happier and more prosperous.

■ *Never ever try to "steal" a client from an agent.* When you play a job booked through an agent, you should refer any inquiries generated by that job to him. Never hand out your own card at an agent-booked job; carry a few cards from the agency. Good agencies work very hard to find and book jobs, and you'll quickly find yourself blacklisted if you try to go around them to book yourself direct with their clients. (Of course this doesn't mean that you can't try to book your own music when you've discovered the prospective client. Just don't try to steal clients who "belong" to your agent. Agents won't forget.)

It Takes Money to Make Money

Why are agents entitled to part of your money? Simply because they've earned it doing things that you may not know how to do or may dislike doing. Besides, a good agent is an expert salesperson and can probably sell your talents better than you can.

There are lots of reasons that an agent should — in fact, *must* — get a percentage of the total. If your agent, Mark Smithers, has an office, then his overhead is much higher than yours. He has to pay substantial rent and utilities. His ad in the Yellow Pages may cost several hundred dollars a year — or a month, if it's a big one. Installing a business phone costs two to three times as much as a home phone: the monthly charges are also much higher. Nobody gives him letterheads, envelopes, invoices, typewriters, adding machines, computers, gasoline, business lunches, membership in the convention bureau (which may cost one or two thousand dollars), or his business insurance. His office copy machine probably cost two thousand dollars.

If Mark has a staff, his bookkeeping load is enormous, with federal, state, and local regulations to comply with and licenses and taxes to pay. He must hire a bookkeeper to compute withholding, unemployment, and workers' compensation. He must hire a secretary to type letters proposing your services to clients. He must hire and probably train salespeople to sell your musical services to clients.

And Mark may spend a hundred dollars in long-distance phone bills, business lunches, and postage trying to book your group for a job, only to lose the business to a competitor who quoted a slightly lower price for Band X. In short, it may cost even a small booking agency *five or six thousand dollars a month* just to keep the office operating. The cost of doing business is high, and the agent who finds work for you deserves the percentage that he gets. Thank him.

Don't begrudge him his fee. Much of the work Mark finds for you is work you'd never otherwise get, so you are gaining, not losing, by using his services.

Unfortunately, there are shady agents. Usually their poor reputations will warn you to be careful. Stay away from the ones who don't pay promptly or don't pay the agreed-upon amount. Avoid those whose jobs cancel frequently or who don't abide by standard agreements. Always insist on written confirmations; never depend on telephoned agreements. One bad experience with a booking agency should warn you to watch your step. Two such experiences should end your relationship. Most booking agents, however, especially the established ones who prosper, are hard-working and honest businesspeople who need your music as much as you need their sales talent.

Long-Term Agreements

Eventually, many musicians are offered some kind of long-term agreement, perhaps by an agent, promoter, would-be manager, or record company. What should you do if Mark Smithers, whose agency has booked you on lots of jobs, wants you to sign an exclusive contract so that all your performances must be booked through him? He promises lots of work—well-paying, of course—if you'll just "sign an exclusive."

Maybe you're flattered by Mark's interest in your music, and you've always liked him, anyway. Why shouldn't you go ahead and sign? Remember this important principle:

Rule to Remember:
Never sign any long-term agreement without your lawyer's advice.

The important word in this rule is *"your."* It doesn't mean "any lawyer's advice"; it means *your* lawyer's advice, because your lawyer will be looking out for your interest.

The agent's lawyer will be watching out for *him*, not you.

"Is all that really necessary?" you ask. "After all, my attorney's advice isn't free. Why should I pay for him to give me his opinion of the contract? I can read, can't I? And I trust Mark Smithers."

You can read, of course, but you are a musician, not a legal expert—and your lawyer is trained to look for problems, loopholes, weaknesses, and threats of any sort to your well-being. He's one of the professionals whose help you need as you build your career, and this is a perfect case where he must be consulted.

What kind of problems can an attorney help you avoid with that long-term agreement? Consider:

■ Does the exclusive contract *require* the agent to book you a certain number of jobs for a specified rate of pay? Or does it just require him to try? Does it promise you a specified income?

■ What if your old college roommate wants you to play for his wedding, free? Would your exclusive contract force you to pay the agency a commission on your own gift to a friend?

■ What if your record doesn't sell as well as the producer expected? Is the producer or record company still obligated to spend a certain amount of money and effort on publicity and advertising?

■ What if you break your arm and can't play the planned series of concerts? Could you be liable for the producer's lost profits?

■ What if the proposed series of concerts fizzles out? Will you be released from the contract if the promoter fails to deliver the promised crowds?

■ What if clients approach you directly? Will you be obligated to pay a commission to the agency from your profits? This is not an uncommon problem for freelance players — if you have a long list of regular clients, will this agreement force you to share them with the agency?

■ What if a producer promises elaborate lighting and sound systems, but fails to deliver them? Can you force him to live up to the agreement? Was it written (and enforceable), or just verbal?

These are only a few of the kinds of questions that should be *legally* settled, *to you and your lawyer's satisfaction*, before you sign any long-term agreement. It's not that you should mistrust those who show an interest in your career. It's just that agents, producers, promoters, and record companies are primarily looking out for themselves, *and that is not the same thing as looking out for you. You have to do that yourself.*

GOOD TEAMWORK PAYS OFF

Establishing a good relationship with appropriate professionals in your community can really benefit your career. Of course you won't just go out and randomly select advertising, accounting, and legal firms from the Yellow Pages; you'll carefully shop around and find the kind of professionals who understand your needs, communicate well, are affordable, and do great work.

Booking agents are probably the outside professionals with whom you'll do the most business because they exist to sell music and entertainment, and, whether or not you work with other professionals, you'll want to establish a good relationship with as many agents as possible. What you're after is a productive team effort, with each partner doing what he or she knows (and likes) best.

You're a musician, and you want to spend as much time as possible with music. You're also an independent businessperson, but with the proper team of outside professionals, you won't have to devote all your time on nonmusical chores — and you won't be doing everything by yourself. You'll have your own team of helpers standing behind you, and your career won't be a solo act but a group effort.

THIRTEEN

PUBLICITY AND SELLING

With your marketing plan in operation and your business sense activated, you're ready to face the next logical—and very important—step. You're ready to spread the word and tell all those carefully chosen prospects exactly how your music can help them. That means creating publicity material and making sales calls.

"But I couldn't sell anything!" you moan. "I'd be scared to death to go into an office and brag about my music. I don't think I could ever talk someone into signing a contract."

Of course you don't *have* to make sales calls. You can just mail out a few brochures and hope they do the job, but they won't. Or, you can let booking agents do all the selling for you—and in some cases that will bring in all the jobs you need. But who's going to sell your abilities to the agents?

The fact is, at some point you have to sell your own music because no one else cares as much about it as you do. Selling and publicity aren't difficult, and you'll probably enjoy the process more than you'd expect. If you're well prepared there's no reason to be scared of sales calls—in fact, they can be fun. And you know you'll enjoy playing the jobs you book—and depositing the checks.

Before you make those calls, however, you need to prepare your publicity material.

PUBLICITY MATERIAL—WHAT YOU NEED

To really explore different aspects of publicizing your music, you should read a book or two on advertising or public relations, such as *Getting Noticed* (see Appendix B), because this field is complex. You'll find that you can spend as much time and money as you have available in preparing a publicity kit, but often, simple and straightforward material will do.

When creating and using publicity material, the aim is to *sell* yourself and your music. Therefore, your material should be carefully crafted and designed to reinforce the image you want to project. Ideally, your letterhead and logo will stand out in a prospect's mind, and when you telephone her, she'll remember who you are just from the quality of your publicity material.

Not every musician will need every one of the items discussed here, and you may need something that isn't listed, such as a résumé, for example. But in general, for most freelance musicians and bands, well-prepared publicity material includes a logo, business stationery, a photo, a brochure, a sales letter, a tune list, and a demo tape.

A logo. This is the starting point for all your printed material. It's a graphic symbol that represents you and your music, and it will be part of the design of everything you produce. A logo can be an illustration, a graphic symbol, or even just a particular style of type. Most musicians will work with a graphic artist to develop a logo, but you can do it yourself if you're artistically inclined.

Perhaps the shape of your instrument will suggest an idea, or a combination of your initials make a nice design. The logo can be as simple as your name, set in a distinctive style of type. Whatever you choose, however, the logo will be your identifying mark, a symbol that stands for you and your music. Professional help in designing such an important graphic element may be very worthwhile because you'll use it for years, and books listed in Appendix B will give you ideas, inspiration, and technical advice.

Business stationery. Basic stationery needs include business cards, letterhead, envelopes, invoices, and contract forms. Choose a paper type and color that is distinctive but not odd — it's hard to read type on bright red paper, for instance — and use the same paper for all your publicity needs. A white or light color is usually appropriate, and it is very helpful if your paper color matches a standard correction fluid color.

If you're working with a graphic artist, ask her to incorporate your logo, name, address, and phone number into a design for your stationery. If you're doing it yourself, use the paste-up skills from a book on graphic design to produce neat "camera-ready copy." Shop around before choosing a printer because prices for the same services vary, but be sure all the quotes are for the exact same paper stock.

If you're likely to move and get a new address or phone number, don't have thousands of letterheads printed. Even though prices drop for large quantities, you'll have little use for business cards with last year's phone number on them, so buy judiciously. Avoid the kind of cards that leave a blank for your phone number to be filled in on the spot; that won't impress any prospects with your reliability.

A photo. Eight-by-ten glossies are still the norm, though smallers sizes — five-by-seven, for example — work for mailings. Black and white is usually acceptable. Your photo should be of excellent professional quality, and it should match the feel of your kind of music. You can have photos inexpensively duplicated, with your name added at the bottom, by one of the businesses listed in Appendix C.

A brochure. This can be as simple as a piece of paper printed on both sides and folded, or it can be expensively produced in color on slick paper. If you want a top-quality brochure, you'll probably need the help of a graphic designer. However it's designed, though, the brochure should describe your music in general terms without mentioning prices or any other facts that might change.

As you write the copy for your sales material, remember the old advertising adage, "Sell the sizzle, not the steak." That is, emphasize the benefits of your music, not the music itself. Tell how your music helps a party, what it does for the client, how it makes the audience happy, and so on. Don't tell what kind of equipment you have — the client won't care — but *do* tell how you can make a party happen and get people dancing.

A sales letter. Many bands use a "Dear Prospective Client" letter in addition to, or instead of, a brochure. This should be *typed,* not typeset, and should be a more personal explanation of how your music can help a client. Personalized letters aren't always necessary, and a well-written form letter carries lots of impact. (Of course, if you're bidding on a major account you'd write a personalized sales letter because it would be worth your time in that case.) If you have a computer, you can personalize form letters, too, with the prospect's name and address. However, even with a computer help-ing you, such personalization takes time, and you'll probably just use the stock "Dear Prospective Client" format, at least for your larger mailings.

Study the examples that come in your mail; the letters in those "junk mail" pack-ages were written by highly paid experts, and they wouldn't be used if they didn't work. Your library has a selection of terrific books on writing effective sales letters. Fol-low them, and write your own hard-hitting sales letter.

One thing you'll learn from studying those professionally produced "junk mail" letters: they *always* include a "P.S." That's because studies show that the postscript is the most-read part of a letter. So, repeat your main selling point briefly in a P.S.

A tune list. When they ask, "What kind of music do you play," give them your up-to-date song list and they'll know. Perhaps this list should be divided into categories, and it should certainly be updated frequently; pop music especially changes quickly. Like all your publicity material, this list should be neat and graphically appealing, but it need not be professionally typeset. Your computer printer or typewriter will produce the needed quality.

A client list. Not every musician will need this, but if your target market includes lots of businesses, prepare a list of past business clients. If you've played dozens, or hun-dreds, of successful engagements for large and small businesses such a client list will add impact to your promotional material. Make it match your target; a business list won't mean much to a bride, nor vice versa.

Testimonials. If you have a collection of "thank-you" letters from clients, why not use them? Ask permission of the writer, of course, and then have the letters repro-duced at a quick-copy shop. Perhaps you can

have them reduced, so that several can be printed on one page. Some experts think it's more effective to reproduce the entire origi-nal letter than to just use extracted quotes because, while you could make up quotes, you probably wouldn't make up an entire letter and devise a fake letterhead. Of course, you can get more selected quotes on a page, and a number of good ones will have a strong impact on the reader.

How do you get testimonials? The sim-plest way is to ask for them. After playing a good engagement, when your client is happy, ask if she would write you a letter of commendation for your files. She'll be flat-tered that you asked. Or, you can ask your clients to complete an "evaluation form" after each engagement, and you'll get lots of positive feedback—assuming, of course, that you do a good job.

Miscellaneous printed materials. Some active bands publish a newsletter—often just one 8½ by 11 inch sheet printed on both sides. The newsletter updates clients about what the band has been doing, personnel changes, new tunes, and any important achievements. Mostly, of course, the news-letter gently reminds clients of your exis-tence.

Postcards are another weapon in the publicity arsenal. They're inexpensive to produce and mail and can alert clients or friends of the band about upcoming engage-ments. Keep your mailing list updated, and you can send out postcards often. It's an ex-cellent technique for raising your profile without breaking the bank.

Demo tapes. Both audio and video tapes are helpful, and they should be of the highest possible quality. With digital technology, it is possible to make your own audio demo, but again, it must be as good as the competi-tion—and the competition is the radio, not Band X. Include a representative sample of the kind of music you do, and plan to update your tape when necessary. You may want to make several specialized tapes for different kinds of clients—perhaps a middle-of-the-road tape for conventions and a more rock-oriented tape for younger prospects.

If your act is a show, a videotape will be essential. But for many bands it may not be worth the money, though it seems that video is an increasingly important sales tool. You should monitor the situation in your area and make a video if your competitors are effectively using them. This is one item you probably shouldn't try to do yourself; get professional help, and be sure your video is really well done. Well-produced videotapes can be expensive, but if you shop around you'll probably find a reasonably priced freelance producer. Pay as much attention to the audio as to the video, because ultimately, your product is your sound.

Should you try to prepare this promotional material yourself? It depends on your pocketbook, time, and abilities. Visit the library and read up on advertising and simple paste-up techniques. You may find that you and your computer can produce excellent work, but you may prefer to search out reasonably priced professional help. Either way, be sure you have the material you need and that it is of competitively excellent quality. Don't skimp here; your reputation is at stake.

Using Publicity Material
When you're fully equipped with boxes of fresh, new letterheads, business cards, and demo tapes, you're ready for action. Using your final *PMMS* list as a guide, send an introductory packet of information to all the prime prospects you've identified. Enclose a short personal letter introducing yourself, and explain that you'll soon be calling to meet them in person. You'll find that the combination of a letter *and* a phone call (or visit) has more impact than either separately. Make a note in your datebook when this material is mailed, and plan a follow-up

sales visit within a couple of weeks.

This first mailing should include all your publicity material (except the videotape, which is too expensive to use in large quantities). Later mailings may be just a follow-up letter or a new bit of information about your band, such as a revised tune list or even a newsletter. Think of the initial mailing as an introduction only, and realize that most of your material probably won't be read. That, unfortunately, is the fate of most mailings, but even if every word isn't absorbed by the prospect, your name will at least be familiar when you call. Further, the prospect will know you're a professional because your promo package is so well done.

Keep complete publicity packages with you all the time, especially at the jobs you play—there's probably room for a couple in your instrument case, purse, or briefcase. When people express an interest in your band, give them the complete publicity kit—and they'll be impressed with your efficiency.

Never run out of business cards, and give one to everyone you meet who expresses an interest in your music. If you don't have your publicity material with you, get that person's card and send your promo material to him promptly. Always follow up immediately while the prospect still remembers who you are. Think of business cards as seeds, which may sprout in weeks, months, or even years.

SALES BASICS FOR MUSICIANS
Your library and bookstore have a good selection of excellent books on salesmanship. Read several of them (see Appendix B for suggestions), and you'll learn from master salespeople. It really doesn't matter if they're discussing selling cars, insurance, or music because the techniques are the same and you'll gain from their experiences. But to get you started, here are some exercises you can do to improve your sales pitch.

The Susan Bennett Show

"Great entertainment, great music, and lots of fun!"
"It makes me want to sing along."

That's how audiences respond to –

The Susan Bennett Show.

The president of one of Atlanta's largest entertainment agencies calls it, "The best show in the area."

They're talking about Atlanta's new after-dinner entertainment package that's available in a size and format to suit your particular needs – and that offers top quality entertainment at a realistic cost. It's **The Susan Bennett Show.**

The Show – Susan's show combines terrific singing with lots of audience participation, skillful impressions, and upbeat tunes that are sure to have the audience clapping along. In fact, Susan will have some of your group singing with her – on the microphone – and three live wires from the audience join her on stage to sing backup, do some soul dancing, play "air guitar" – and more. Have your cameras ready!

Susan's impressions are uncanny, from a medley of country tunes to her version of *Cabaret.* One of the most popular parts of the show is *Those Were the Days,* where the "guest singers" include Julie Andrews, Dolly Parton, Marilyn Monroe, Ethel Merman and several others. Close your eyes and you'll be amazed at the voices she creates.

The Artist – Susan Bennett is perhaps Atlanta's busiest vocal talent. She is co-leader of The Gibson/Bennett Band – a fixture at top corporate and social events in Atlanta, and she maintains a full-time career in the demanding recording industry. Susan has done hundreds of radio and TV

Sager, and Roy Orbison. She has often performed the National Anthem on network television before National Hockey League games, and she was cast in a CBS television movie, *A Time to Triumph.* Her industrial film credits include work for IBM, Georgia-Pacific, and Kinder-Care. In her spare time, she teaches aerobics.

The Band – Unlike many performers who rely on pickup bands, Susan's show always has the same backup group - **The Gibson/Bennett Band.** These four musicians have worked steadily together for years, and have developed a client list that reads like the Fortune 500 – from Chevrolet and Ford to Mellon Bank and Arthur Andersen & Co. The band not only does an expert job at backing Susan's show, but is the perfect choice for an entire evening of music.

The band is available in two standard, rehearsed formats. The four-piece **Gibson/Bennett Band** is the basic unit, versatile and reasonably priced. For an even bigger sound, the seven-piece group adds the excitement of three horns and a guitar.

The Plan – When you plan an event, include T Gibson/Bennett Band and **The Susan Bennett S** to guarantee a memorable evening. The band c provide elegant dinner music and the best da music around – or you can book just the show way, you'll have a great evening to remem

And, if you need to add custom elements t like the 1920s segment Susan created for Chicago Bank, that's no problem. If yo really special requirement – like the 3 tribute to Judy Garland that Susan pro American Medical Systems, even tha pared.

MUSICAL SERVICES OF THE GIBSON/BENNETT BAND

When you're planning a business or social function, you may have a variety of musical needs, and the simplest solution is to book as many of them as possible with the same people.

The **Gibson/Bennett Band** is the ideal core for whatever function you're planning, and you'll be able to relax and deal with experienced, professional musicians who will understand what you want to achieve with music.

Here are some of the musical services we offer:

The Gibson Bennett Band, of course, is the starting place v This is a versatile, high-quality, four-piece featuring both sophisticated listening and upbeat danceable music.

Single piano music is often needed to add a nice backg touch to parties and dinners. Both Susan and Jim excellent pianists, and can provide electronic ke if no acoustic piano is available.

Duos are another background music possibility. We piano and bass, or piano and guitar--both of w soothing and relaxing for cocktails or dinner

Susan Bennett and Jim Gibson can also work as a duo, featuring both Jim's keyboard virtuosity extraordinary vocals. This combination is m entertaining than just typical background appropriate for elegant dinners and recept

Strolling banjo or guitar call for Rick Hinkl Rick is a walking encyclopedia of pop mus surprises the band with the obscure songs for cocktail parties, and Southe where a banjo sets just the right tone

Piano/bass/drums trio music offers jazz in a liste and Jim's piano playing is reminiscent of both Garner and Oscar Peterson. This format is great for early part of an evening, and with the addition of Susan the trio becomes a terrific dance band.

We offer, then, a range of musical services that are centered around the cohesive **Gibson/Bennett Band,** but that are appropriate for early, and spin-off, functions where the full band might not be needed.

We'd like to work with you. Let us know how we can help.

THE Gibson/Bennett BAND

PARTIAL TUNE LIST

MEDIUM AND UP-TEMPO STANDARDS

Bill Bailey
Cabaret
I Get a Kick Out of You
Hello, Dolly
All of Me
Fly Me to the Moon
In the Mood
Boogie-Woogie Bugle Boy
Chattanooga Choo-Choo
Mack the Knife
Ain't Misbehavin'
T. D.'s Boogie-Woogie
Lady Is A Tramp
A Foggy Day
Sentimental Journey
Tuxedo Junction
String of Pearls
Don't Get Around Much Anymore
Puttin' On the Ritz
You Gotta Have Heart
Bye Bye Blackbird
Chicago
Makin' Whoopee
On a Clear Day
On the Street Where You Live
Stompin' at the Savoy
Out of Nowhere
There Will Never Be Another You
Rock-a-Bye Your Baby
September in the Rain
Near You
Have You Met Miss Jones

LATINS, BOSSA NOVAS ETC

Wave
Girl from Ipanema
One Note Samba
Look of Love
Little Boat
Desifinado
Carnival
Guantanamera
Besame Mucho
Frenesi
Green Eyes
Miami Beach Rhumba
Poinciana
Brazil
Dindi
Mais Que Nada
Rio de Janero Blue
Tea for Two
Cherry Pink
Never on Sunday
Quiet Night
St. Thomas
Call Me
Summer Samba

'50's and '60's ROCK AND ROLL "BIG CHILL TUNES"

The Twist
Peppermint Twist
Twist and Shout
Twisting the Night Away
Old Time Rock and Roll
Blueberry Hill
Do Run Run
Louie, Louie
Shout
Jailhouse Rock
Hound Dog
Heard it Through the Grapevine
Shop Around
I've Got You, Babe
Same old Song
Proud Mary
Joy to the World
Midnight Hour
Love Potion Number 9
Rescue Me
Do Wa Diddy
Walkin' the Dog
Good Lovin'
Brown-Eyed Girl
All My Lovin'
Eight Days a Week
Surfin' USA
Be Young, Be Foolish . . .
My Girl
Heatwave
It Takes Two
Shotgun
Wooly Bully
Harlem Shuffle
Whole Lotta Shakin'
All I Have to Do is Dream
Don't Be Cruel
Hey, Baby
Johnny B. Goode
Just One Look
Knock on Wood
Lion Sleeps Tonight
Love Me Tender
My Guy
Peggy Sue
Rockin' Robin
Sea Cruise
Stagger Lee
Stay
Tossin' and Turnin'
Twilight Time
Under the Boardwalk
Up on the Roof
Will You Love Me Tomorrow
Natural Woman
Way You do the Things You Do
When a Man Loves a Woman
With This Ring

Other categories not listed include: Jazz, Blues, Dixieland, Show Tunes, Polkas, Waltzes, Horas, Novelty, Sing-a-Long, and Honkey Tonk. Of course, our repertory includes dozens of tunes in each of these areas.

MUSIC FOR EVERYBODY

THE **Gibson/Bennett** BAND

HOW THE GIBSON/BENNETT BAND CAN MAKE YOUR
SPECIAL EVENT A GREAT SUCCESS

Dear Prospective Client:

If you're planning an event that needs music, you probably have a
good idea of what you want. Perhaps you envision an evening of
sophistication and elegance, with music setting the mood and
carrying the party along. Maybe you'd like the music to pick up
as dinner ends, and then you want your guests to pack the dance
floor for a party to remember.

However . . . getting from plan to reality isn't easy, and for
many people hiring a band is a difficult task. Most people have
little experience with musicians, and no idea where to find a
good band.

Here's where we can help. As one of Atlanta's busiest bands,
we know what kinds of music each event needs. We're experts at
working with clients, feeling out the crowd, and making every
party a success--because we do it several times each week.

The Gibson/Bennett Band is a four-piece group--keyboards (both
electric piano and synthesizer), bass (and optional guitar),
drums. We feature three-part vocals, an up-to-date repertoire
(that also spans several decades), and very high musical
standards. (Also, we're a "real" band--you'll always get the
same four people--and we're the players on our demo tape.

What do you look for when you hire a band?

That can be a difficult question, because you may not know
exactly what your event will be like. Will it remain
sophisticated? Or will it be a lively affair, with a
dance floor? Will you need mostly rock and roll? Or
band music? Until the party itself, you may not know

The first thing you've got to have at any priv

BUSINESS EVENTS AND THE GIBSON/BENNETT BAND

When you're planning a business event, don't overlook the many
benefits of music. Whether you're planning a kick-off breakfast
for a hundred, or a banquet for thousands, the Gibson/Bennett Band
can help you achieve your goals.

We've played hundreds of business and convention dates of every
conceivable kind, and we know how music fits your overall plans.
Because of our experience we're able to work closely with you, and
our musical quality and flexibility will help you relax and enjoy
your own function.

Here are suggestions for how our music can help:

Sales Meetings often need cheerful, peppy walk-in music to
set an upbeat mood, theme music, and music for awards.

Awards Ceremonies are important to motivate your people, and
our music can support your goals with fanfares, drum
rolls, walking music, and other exciting fills. We're
adept at working from scripts, with headphones, or just
'winging it.' Also, Susan is a professional "voice
talent," and can work with you as a presenter.

Dinners and luncheons are more elegant and sophisticated with
good background music. The music is crucial, but it
can't be too loud, and we're sensitive to that.

After-dinner entertainment can be a highlight of your meeting,
and the Susan Bennett show involves the audience and is
lots of fun. The show can even be custom-crafted to fit
your industry or theme.

Hospitality functions need music to break the ice, establish
a cheerful mood, and encourage clients and staff to
mingle; these events may start quietly--and end with a
packed dance floor.

Dances are a great place to unwind with your business
associates, customers and friends. We play the best
quality music, with the right mix for all ages and
backgrounds.

Theme parties can be elaborate, and we're adept at matching
our music to the evening's motif. We can start with
specific music to match the party's focus, and gradually
shift to more general dance music. We've done 'twenties,'
'fifties,' shipwreck, horsetrack, M*A*S*H, and many more.

One common scenario is to begin quietly, perhaps with single piano
music for the cocktail hour. Then, we'll add bass and drums for
light dinner music, and an awards ceremony. Finally, Susan joins
the band for an after-dinner show and/or dance.

That's a great evening of music, and it's simple to arrange. We
can work closely with you to assure that both your CEO and the
newest salesperson on your staff has a good time--and that's quite
an achievement.

We've done it for hundreds of business, convention, and social
clients, and we'd like to add you to our list. Let us know if we
can help you plan a successful meeting.

WEDDING INFORMATION SHEET

The Gibson/Bennett Band

We look forward to working with you to make your wedding a
pleasant event. Of course, each reception is different and all
these questions won't apply to every one, but the information on
this sheet will help us keep your party flowing smoothly.

Please return this form to Susan or Jim. If you have questions,
or would like to discuss anything further, please call. We'll be
in touch with you to double-check everything shortly before your
wedding.

If we're supplying music for your ceremony, we'll get that
information separately.

Date of Reception:_____ Time:_____

Do you want the Bridal Party formally introduced?_____

Bride and Groom to be introduced as:_____

Song for first dance:_____
(We suggest doing the first dance early in the evening,
when you are introduced, to officially start the dancing.)

Will there be other special dances?_____

Will there be toasts?_____ When (approximately)?_____

By whom?_____

Will there be a traditional cake-cutting?_____ When?_____

Will there be the traditional bouquet/garter routine?_____

As you leave, will there be birdseed, rice, flower petals, or
colored paper for the guests to throw? Which?_____

Where will they be located?_____

Approximately what time do you plan to leave?_____

Please add your general instructions and comments on the back of
this form. We'd especially like to know what kind of music you
like (and anything you dislike, as well), and what kind of party,
in general, you'd prefer. Thanks for working with us!

Why People Need Your Music

Since you're used to making lists by now, make another one to guide your publicity and sales efforts. Title it "Why Clients Need My Music." This will be a list of what your music can do for clients and how it will help them—a checklist of why people *need* your music. Brainstorm and put yourself in the client's place to imagine what he'll want the music to do. Make as long a list as possible. Here are some ideas to get you started.

■ Music creates an appropriate atmosphere

■ Live music demonstrates affluence

■ Music makes an event memorable

■ Music entertains

■ Music breaks the ice, encourages mixing, mingling, and talking

■ Music brings people of different backgrounds together

■ Music sells

■ Music inspires

■ Music makes people feel good

■ Music attracts crowds

■ Music recalls nostalgic memories

■ Music is soothing therapy

■ Music even helps people fall in love

You'll come up with more benefits of your music, but you get the idea. Make as long a list as possible of all the things your music can do, and use these ideas when you're writing sales letters, brochures, and talking to clients. All salespeople know that prospects are interested in themselves and their own problems. If you can show how your music helps them, you'll book more jobs, so work on your benefits list until you've discovered every possible way your music can be used.

Develop Your Own Sales Ideas

Another exercise that will help you prepare an effective sales presentation is to do another bit of role playing and put yourself in your prospect's place. Ask, "Why do I need music?" "What kind of group am I looking for?" "How will music help (or hurt) my function?" Once you realize what the client needs, you'll be able to show how your music matches those requirements better than your competitors could. Of course, you should be honest in your presentation.

Here are some ideas for selling points; you'll think of more. Use a sheet of paper or the "Personal Sales Ideas" work sheet on page 143 to list your own ideas about how your music meets clients' needs. That's the approach you'll take in selling your music. *Don't think about what you want or need for this list—concentrate on what the client requires.*

To sell your music, devise creative ways to convey the following information, showing how you're right for the job and better than the rest. Don't be shy—go ahead and blow your own horn.

You're professional. This is what you do for a living and you provide better quality than part-timers can produce. Point out that quality is more important than ever these days, with audiences trained by TV and radio to expect great music. And, since you're a full-time musician, you spend more time keeping up with what's popular and you'll know all the tunes the audience will request.

If, on the other hand, you're a part-time player, you could argue that you aren't a jaded, bored professional. Point out that you play because you love music and that your enthusiasm and energy will make up for any lack of full-time experience.

Remember that *service* is really your business—you're providing music to fulfill a client's needs. Remember, too, the sales adage that a good salesperson is more interested in what the client wants to buy—perhaps a good time at a party—than in what you're selling—perhaps a four-piece combo.

You do a good job. You understand that your success is based entirely on doing a good job for every client, so tell her that's what you strive to do. Don't just imply this point—tell your prospect, simply and directly, that your success depends on doing a good job for her, and that you will be on her team, working with her to make the event successful.

Sometimes decisions aren't easily made, particularly when a committee is involved, so give your prospect all the information you can to convince her to support you in that committee meeting. Or offer to make a presentation to the entire committee, if necessary.

You care about the client's needs. Show that you understand this particular client's requirements well—that you've done your homework—and that you can provide exactly what's needed. Give examples of similar successes for similar clients. References won't hurt, either, so go prepared with names and phone numbers of previous, satisfied clients.

Convince a corporate prospect that you'll make her look good to her boss and co-workers. Anyone who hires a band is, to some extent, taking a risk; your task is to convince the client that you'll make the event so successful that she'll be a heroine for hiring you.

Use all those thank-you letters from your file. Perhaps you should make photocopies to leave with the client, or put them in plastic sleeves in a notebook for him to review during your sales visit. If your client list is impressive, use it.

You have the latest equipment. Explain, if it's appropriate, that your equipment is the best. Prospects won't really be interested in many details, but you should point out that part of your success is based on keeping up with current technology—that you have "today's sound" because you have today's equipment. Offer to let the client use your state-of-the-art sound system for speeches, toasts, or whatever, thus saving the cost of renting another public-address unit.

If the job you're going after requires virtuosity, expound on your virtuosity—if you have it. If variety is the key, explain that you can play the full spectrum that's needed—if you can. If a raucous party is the goal, don't talk about your years at Juilliard, but tell them about all the toga parties you've done. It's just a matter of emphasizing the match between your music and the client's needs, but don't exaggerate or lie. If you can't provide what's needed, you'll do a lot better to recommend someone who can.

You're responsible. Underline that you'll not only be on time, but early. Many clients assume that musicians are not dependable, so assure them that your band will be ready. In fact, offer to be set up early if you're willing to do that or if they require it. (Some musicians have an early set-up fee, but sometimes you'll have to give a bit of extra time to make a client happy.)

Your cost is reasonable. If the cost of your music seems to bother the client, point out how low it really is when it's divided by the number of guests at the function. "Well, Mr. Jones, if you consider that our thousand-dollar fee really only amounts to about two dollars each for your five hundred guests, it's not really very much for a great evening's entertainment, is it?"

Or, discuss the cost of the music when compared to the rest of the function's expenses. A corporate dinner, for example, may cost thousands—or tens of thousands—of dollars when you add in the flowers, decoration, bar bill, hors d'oeuvres, dinner, and so on. Remind the client that the right music can make the party a success and that the flowers or even the wedding cake may cost more than your fee.

Be specific, give examples, and show the prospect exactly what you mean. "Well, Mrs. Smith, most weddings we play for seem to have two- to four-thousand-dollar budgets for flowers and decorations, and it's not unusual for the wedding cake to cost five hundred dollars. But when you think about it, the music is really more important to the success of the party. Don't you agree?"

Make Your Sales Plans in Detail

You've just made two more lists, "Why Clients Need My Music" and "Personal Sales Ideas," as presales exercises, and this newly gathered information will be the raw material for your sales calls. Use it in your thinking, writing, and talking to emphasize your qualifications. Frequently go over these lists to remind yourself how good you are and what a good job you'll do for all those prospects you've located. Now, here are the steps you'll take in going out to meet the clients who will pay you for performing.

Plan your approach. Before your first sales call to a prospective client, think in detail about what you have to offer. Read over your "Benefits of My Music" list (see page 143), and know how your music will help this client. Have the details firmly in mind, too—exactly what you have to offer, how much it costs, and how the client can book it. Review these ideas several times before your sales call, and be sure you know your product.

Read the interview with Dr. Kessler on page 148, and notice the emphasis she puts on rehearsing your sales pitch; it's not just a theory, but it's what full-time, successful salespeople actually do. Maybe you should write it out in advance, but don't try to memorize it—just remember the points you want to cover and talk conversationally with the prospect. If you try to memorize a sales pre-

sentation you'll likely worry, forget parts of it, and probably make a poor impression.

With the information you've gathered you'll be prepared with pertinent selling facts. Practice your sales pitch on your spouse or friends. Have them ask you hard questions, because the client will. "Well, Chris, your band sounds interesting, but we've always used a DJ for our Christmas party. Since your band costs twice as much, how would it be better?" Practice answering such questions until you're fluent with persuasive answers. Remember that your goal is sales, not sales calls, so prepare to make a strong presentation at every opportunity.

Confidence in the quality of your music will show in every presentation, so if you're not sure of your ability, go back and work on your product until it's the best possible quality. When you *know* you're the best and *know* that your music will help the client, you'll be a convincing salesperson. You might try writing out a specific proposal before your sales call if you know what kind of music the client needs. Leave a copy with the prospect and, needless to say, keep a copy for your files. Specify what you are offering, for how long, and how much it will cost.

Another important step is to write a short, personal letter of introduction to each prospect before your sales call. Send your brochure and perhaps a tune list. Explain who you are and that you'll be calling for an appointment soon. Mention that your visit will be short, that you'd like to meet the prospect, drop off some material, and describe what you can do for him. Such a letter should be less than a page long. A sample is on p. 144.

Make an appointment. Never drop in unexpectedly on a prospect. Assume that your potential clients are busy and that their time is valuable. You must follow standard business practices when dealing with business-

PERSONAL SALES IDEA WORK SHEET

Don't be shy here. Go ahead and brag. Point out every possible advantage of your music. If you don't tell them, how will they know? Remember, you aren't the only musician around who's selling your kind of music, so it's important that you *know* what sets you apart from, and above, the others. Use this page or notebook paper to *write the information down.*

What my music can do:

How my music serves Clients' needs:

What's best about my music:

What others have liked about my music:

Why my music is a bargain:

Why I'm better than my competition:

Other advantages:

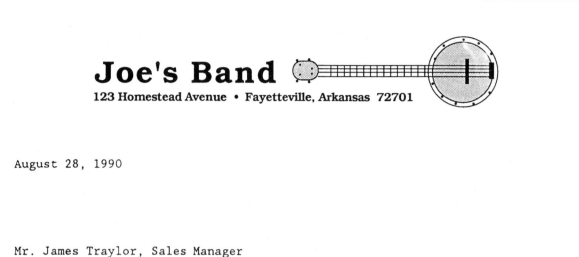

Joe's Band

123 Homestead Avenue • Fayetteville, Arkansas 72701

August 28, 1990

Mr. James Traylor, Sales Manager
Amalgamated Consolidated, Inc.
123 Main Street
Fayetteville, Arkansas 72701

Dear Mr. Traylor:

As sales manager for Amalgamated Consolidated, you're certainly looking for
ways to make your quarterly sales meetings exciting and effective. Inspiring
the sales force year after year, however, must be a difficult task.

As the leader of one of Fayetteville's most successful bands, I'd like to talk
to you about how we could help you produce more exciting and successful sales
meetings. We do a lot of corporate work and regularly perform for many of
Arkansas' largest companies. We've used this experience to develop a set of
ideas that will, we believe, help motivate your salespeople--just as we've
done for General Acquisitions, Multi-World Enterprises, and Corporate Buyouts,
Inc.

I'll be calling for an appointment to meet you soon. I'd like to ask for ten
minutes of your time to show you how we can pep up any meeting, and drop off
some descriptive material about our group.

I look forward to meeting you soon, and thank you in advance for the chance to
talk with you.

Sincerely,

Joe Jones

Joe Jones

people, so call ahead for an appointment.

Ask for your prospect by name whenever possible, and if you've written an introductory letter you can say that the prospect is expecting your call; after all, you told him in the letter that you'd be calling in about a week. If you know only the company name, use your experience and common sense to reach the music buyer. If you are calling on a hotel, for example, you'll probably need the catering or sales department. In a large corporation, you'll deal with the public-relations, meeting-planning, or protocol staff.

If you know the event you'd like to talk about, simply ask the operator to connect you with the person in charge of that project, whether it's a Christmas party or an annual company meeting. With good telephone manners and friendly persistence you can usually reach the right person. Get the proper spelling and pronunciation of your contact's name (and note whether it's "Miss," "Mrs." or "Ms."). Jot the name down as you talk, and don't forget it.

Large companies spend thousands of dollars training their salespeople in effective use of the telephone. They know the value of good telephone etiquette, and it's just as valuable to you. Work on your approach to convey an air of friendly confidence. Speak up and don't mumble, but don't rush breathlessly into your prepared speech either. Once you have the right person on the phone, identify yourself and ask if the prospect has a moment to talk to you. "Ms. Jones, this is Susan Cameron. I'm with the 'Harvest Moon Band,' and I wondered if you have a minute to talk about music for your Christmas party?"

Be punctual. When you have an appointment, be on time or a few minutes early. Whatever you do, don't be late. Allow for rush-hour traffic and parking problems. Many businesspeople are suspicious of musicians and artists. So, when you call on them, you must show that you can abide by their rules because the game is being played on their court. Punctuality is crucial. Why should a client believe that your band will start on time if you're late for your initial meeting?

Be appropriately dressed. How will your prospect be dressed? Use that as a guide, and don't flaunt your independence from business conventions by dressing too casually; it will set the wrong tone for your meeting. Be neat and clean. Businesspeople read books like *Dress for Success*, and they often pay very close attention to appearance, so be sure yours is right for the sales call.

Talk about your prospect's music needs. Ask questions and really listen to the answers. Remember the ideas on active listening discussed in Chapter Four, and put them into practice; a prospect may give you valuable information about his needs, but you'll have to understand what's being said. You may even have to read between the lines or change your approach in the middle of a sales call based on what the client tells you.

Maybe you can help the prospect solve a problem. In fact, good salespeople actively seek potential problems that they can solve for the client. So, look for areas where you can actually help, and make suggestions. Maybe the client hasn't thought about the advantages of dinner music before the show until you suggest it. Maybe you could do a fifteen-minute minishow while the client's staff rearranges the room for an audiovisual presentation. If you see a place where your music or even someone else's music will help the client, mention it; that's what salespeople call being "proactive."

Asking questions will keep the focus on the client's needs, and your skillful questions can suggest new uses for your music: "Mr. Jones, have you thought about how effective it would be to have music during that morning sales meeting you're planning? We've provided music frequently for Amalgamated Insurance and Bigtime Manufacturing, and it really adds excitement to the morning. Plus, the music helps keep things moving, and it fills pauses and gaps. We could work with you as you develop the script for the meeting." And so on. You're not being pushy, but you're making helpful suggestions based on what you know the client needs.

Try to avoid the word "I" as much as possible, and emphasize "you" because that's what your client is ultimately interested in—what *he* wants, what you can do for *him*.

To repeat an important point—be honest. If a prospect needs something that you can't provide, tell him so. Never book a job you can't perform well just because you need the money. Both you and your client will lose, and bad news travels fast. Sometimes your best sales technique will be to refer the client to another musician: "Well, Mr. Jones, I'm not really very good at the kind of classical music you want, but I can refer you to a couple of excellent players who are." Mr. Jones will be impressed by your professionalism, he'll appreciate your honesty, and he'll remember you when he needs what *you* do.

Use backup material. Give the prospect your brochure. Show him your videotape. Tell him about other clients you've worked for successfully. Give him references (but be sure they're willing to be called on as such). Let him read a few good thank-you letters from satisfied clients. (Don't give him your brochure until you've finished your sales pitch, however; you want him to listen to you and not be glancing at your material.)

State your price. Tell the prospect confidently, not apologetically, what you charge. To speak with self-assurance in stating your price, you must determine beforehand the monetary worth of the job you are proposing and be prepared with a contract form. Don't

be timid. Be ready to talk about money—that's what businesspeople deal with every day, and many of them work with very large amounts of it. Your charge, while significant to you, may be a very small part of the event they're planning, so don't feel like you have to apologize. Music is your business.

Take the initiative. When you've told him what you can do for him, ask for a commitment. Don't be vague or wishy-washy. Your sales pitch should have convinced him that he really *needs* your music.

This is what salespeople call the "close"—getting the client to sign on the dotted line. When you've finished your presentation and know that your proposal fits his needs, take out a contract form and say, "Now, Mr. Jones, why don't we get the specifics down in writing so I can hold this date for you? Saturday nights go quickly, you know, and we'd hate for this one to get away, but we do work on a first-come, first-served basis." Put a little pressure on Mr. Jones at this point; after all, you're doing him a favor by showing him how your music fulfills his needs. If he doesn't act now, he may procrastinate until you—and even Band X—are booked.

When you go out to sell your music, you're really *educating* your prospects; you're showing them how your music can *help them achieve their goals*. You aren't talking them into buying something they don't want, so there's no need to feel guilty, embarrassed, or uneasy. (Of course, if your quality isn't good or you're the wrong band for the job, you may not feel so positive about your sales calls. But in that case, you have other problems to solve.)

Don't prolong the meeting. When you've finished your presentation, leave. No further sales pitch is wanted after you've gotten a "yes," "no," or "not at this time." Don't overstay your welcome, don't be too aggressive, and don't talk negatively about other musicians. A good relationship with a client can take time to develop and is worth more than any single job.

Learn to deal with rejection. Sometimes, despite your best efforts and the fact that your band really is the best one for the job, your sales efforts won't succeed. Clients will have various reasons for not hiring you or hiring other bands, and some of those reasons will be poor ones. Perhaps they've used Band X for four years and don't want to change even though you're clearly better. Perhaps the boss' son-in-law is Band X's soundman. Perhaps Band X's agent is giving a kickback to the client. Who knows? Sometimes you'll just have to be satisfied with a "no." Like any good salesperson, though, you must learn not to let rejection slow you down.

The best way to deal with a client who doesn't hire you is to:

1. *Be polite and friendly.* Don't tell him that he's stupid for hiring another band. If you insult him or get angry, you'll never do business with him. Just smile and say, "Well, I know you'll have a great party with Band X, but I hope you'll give us a chance at the next one." Leave it at that.

2. *Follow up.* Send an occasional letter or brochure to this client to let him know you're still interested in working for him. Don't pester him, of course, but gently remind him once in a while that you'd like to play for his next party. Sooner or later you'll get the chance.

3. *Move on.* There's more than one fish in the sea and if you've completed you *PMMS* you have an extensive list of potential clients. Don't fret about the ones who aren't responsive, but move right down the list to the next one. To some extent, selling is a numbers game, and the more prospects you have, the more jobs you'll sell.

Follow Up

After each sales call, successful or not, follow these steps:

■ *Write it down.* Immediately after leaving a prospect's office, write down all the important details you discussed. *Don't trust your memory.* If you need to contact the client or prospect in the future, write a reminder on your calendar or put one in your tickler file.

■ *Send a note of appreciation.* Write a short thank-you note to each prospect you see whether she buys music from you or not. If she hired you, send a contract with the note. If she didn't, write the note anyway. She'll have a more positive impression if you show your appreciation for her time. Treat each prospect like a valued client you'll be working with for five or ten years; you're building a career, so a little extra effort now will pay dividends for a long time.

■ *Continue to follow up.* Keep in touch with potential clients whether they are businesspeople, agents, or other musicians. Buyers get in ruts, too, and you need to remind them of your availability. But don't be a pest. An occasional phone call, mailed brochure, or short sales visit will keep your name before good prospects. Easy, but regular, does it.

The best attribute a salesperson can have is a sense of quiet self-confidence. If you really believe in your music and are convinced that it will honestly help your clients, you'll convey a relaxed, positive feeling. If, on the other hand, you aren't sure about your music, you simply won't be able to convince many prospects. Boost your self-confidence by reviewing your personal inventory and the work sheet in this chapter—and don't be afraid to work on your craft if it needs improving. Once you know that you're the best, your selling efforts will be much easier.

SALES TECHNIQUES FOR MUSICIANS
INTERVIEW WITH DR. SHEILA KESSLER

Dr. Kessler is a psychologist, a former university counselor, and a business consultant. She has done marketing and sales training for Fluor Daniel, Inc., the world's largest engineering firm, and is currently a Corporate Account Representative for Microsoft Corporation. She lives near Los Angeles.

Q *What sales techniques would be useful to musicians?*

A A very good technique for individuals is to sit down and talk to yourself, in a way. Write down what you consider to be your strong points; write a description of what you do. This helps to give some definition of what you do—you have to know yourself and be sure of what your strong points are.

Actually writing this information down is very important. Think of it as writing an ad—how would you describe who you are and what you do? Just thinking isn't the same thing at all as writing down your thoughts.

As you decide what to say, remember that you're the expert in music; you're the one who knows what's good. I've looked at hundreds of successful sales proposals, and one interesting thing the most successful salespeople do is to gently *educate* their prospects, teaching them the value of what is being sold, because the prospect probably doesn't really know the details of your business. Of course, it's important to avoid seeming to be "the expert" and you certainly don't want to be condescending, but sometimes a good sales proposal will show, explain, and teach.

Another thing is that good salespeople always have a pad with them, and they write down what they've just heard and discussed when they leave a meeting or even a conversation. Short-term memory only lasts about half an hour and then it's gone. So if the person you've just met has two children or is going to the beach next week or whatever, your relationship will grow if you remember those details for your next meeting or conversation—and you'll never remember them if you don't write them down.

Finally, the best salespeople write short "thank-you" letters after meetings. Since it's not standard practice and everybody doesn't do it, it really makes you stand out when you take the time to write that short note to your client or prospect. It's a simple thing, but it works.

Q *Are there especially useful ways to use the telephone?*

A Strangely, people who are normally considerate forget about common courtesy when they make phone calls. The first thing you should think of when you make a call is that it may not be convenient for the other party to talk at that moment, so you should always ask, "Is this a good time to talk?" or even, "Do you have a minute right now?"

Another simple technique is to always jot down the main points you want to cover in that phone call and maybe some important questions. That way, you won't forget to get the information you need, and you won't have to call back and ask again. That doesn't mean you'll read your questions from those written notes, of course, but it will help you focus the conversation.

An interesting and very simple technique for enhancing telephone communications is to smile before making a phone call. That sounds a little silly, to sit by your own phone alone and smile to yourself, but it really relaxes the voice and helps put you in a pleasant mood. You can even laugh before the call.

FOURTEEN

ONWARD AND UPWARD

Your *PMMS* is working, and your sales efforts are paying off. The band is booking more and more jobs, and every successful engagement leads to one, two, or more referrals. Your business is growing in an almost geometric progression, and there is at least the possibility that you'll have more work than you can handle. How do you manage such success? Can you finally just lay back and relax?

This book has concentrated on the business aspects of your music, discussing the sales ideas and marketing techniques that are important to every freelance musician. These are the practices that will help you build your reputation, your career, and a healthy bank balance.

But there's a lot more to music, of course, than booking jobs and taking care of taxes. You've got to actually play the job — and you have to keep your musicality moving in the right direction. Sometimes professional musicians need to stop and take a music appreciation course to keep themselves interested in, and excited by, music.

Terms like "stress" and "burnout" apply to musicians just as to other professionals — even more, in fact, because there's often such a gap between what you'd *like to do* musically, and what you're actually doing. If you recognize this tension, you can manage it and keep it from destroying your career and even your love of music.

PLAYING THE JOB

One way to reduce potential stress is to actively manage every playing job. You're in charge — it's your gig — and you can direct it in positive directions. You can, believe it or not, make your client, your musicians, and yourself happy, and you can all have fun on almost every job. How do you do that?

First, be sure that all your musicians know what you're trying to do, and that they share a positive, success-oriented attitude. If you're all thinking and working together, every job will be more successful. It's not easy, but this is what you've worked for — the moment on the stage, making music and filling the dance floor, entertaining the audience, pleasing the client. You've spent hours in preparation working on your professionalism, practicing your music, and marketing your product in a businesslike way — and now you're on stage. This is it; there's no place to hide.

The approach you *don't* want to take is the old-style, jaded musician attitude that you see on so many faces at commercial jobs. Everyone's familiar with the stereotype: the once-talented but now burned-out musician who's tired, bored, and perhaps angry, spreading gloom and negative feelings wherever he goes. Can you avoid this fate?

It is possible to do a good job, enjoy the music you play, and please the client, all at the same time. Actually, the hardest part of the music business is behind you—finding and booking engagements is more difficult than playing those jobs. Making music should be the fun part, and if you work to insure that everything goes well you'll be more confident and relaxed. When you know you're doing a good job, you won't feel stressed out and you'll actually be able to enjoy making music. That's your goal—the confident, "in-charge" feeling that comes from professional competence.

Successful musicians develop an innate "job sense" that helps them almost automatically know what to do. This awareness alerts you to the client's needs, keeps you tuned-in to how the party is going, and tells you how to behave and what to do next. The best way to develop such "job sense" is to be responsible for the success of the job. If you're the one who deals with the client, you'll quickly adjust your music to match his needs.

A musician with well-developed "job sense" knows that *the success of a job often depends on nonmusical factors.* It's not just what you play. It may be whether your shoes are shined or whether you start on time. Interestingly, if you attend to the details of the job, the music will often flow naturally; sometimes it doesn't really matter what you play, and you'll have greater freedom if you keep the client happy about all those petty but crucial details.

Do's and Don'ts for Every Job

Here are some ideas that apply to all freelance music jobs. While they won't guarantee success, they'll get you started.

Know what you're supposed to do. This isn't as easy as it sounds, but if you've practiced active listening as discussed in Chapter Four, you should be in good shape. Did your client say she wanted classical music? Did she mean Beethoven or Cole Porter? Or does she think classical music is anything

written before 1950? Some clients are musically naive, so ask questions and be sure to define any musical terms the client uses.

Remember that the *intangibles* and *indefinite* are important. Is the client trying to hire a band to please his boss? Is she trying to impress her guests with her sophistication? Or is the goal a rowdy, good-time atmosphere? If you can accurately assess the client's needs, *stated or not,* you'll have a much better chance of fulfilling them. Watch for nonverbal cues, rely on your experience, and *ask questions* to get a good fix on what's really important to each client.

Details are crucial. To repeat, the quality of the music doesn't always determine the success of a job. Often it's the little things, the insignificant details so easy to overlook, that the client will remember.

So—be early to the job. Check the lighting, the sound, the piano, the location of the service elevator, parking, whether the electrical outlets work, where you can store your equipment cases, and where the dressing rooms are.

Tune instruments, replace broken strings or drum heads, and test sound systems *before* the job begins. Nothing is as irritating to people enjoying a quiet dinner, for example, as loud guitar tuning or repeated "Testing 1, 2, 3 . . ." Testing and tuning are crucial, but do them early before the job begins. And practicing or excessive playing before a job often looks like showing off and seems unprofessional. Remember, you aren't a garage band anymore.

Make sure that the house lights won't be turned off just when you start reading the most important music of the evening, and be certain that turning off the house lights won't also turn off your electricity. If you're using light-trees that consume lots of power, find out where the circuit-breaker panel is and be sure that the lights are on an ample circuit; ask the building engineer, if there is one.

Find out if the musicians are invited to eat and drink with the guests, who authorizes overtime, what the boss' favorite song is, what the newlyweds' first dance will be, and who will make the first toast. If you're to make announcements, check to be sure you can pronounce the names; don't guess at this but ask in advance because people will always remember if you get it wrong.

Always double-check with musicians you have hired concerning time, place, instruments needed, doubles, rehearsals, proper dress, and pay. Remember to have extra music-stand light bulbs, guitar cords, bow ties, drum sticks, and whatever else is most likely to break or be forgotten. Keep an extra set of such items in the trunk of your car because the time will come when you'll need them.

It's unfortunate, but even though your music is perfectly chosen and performed, the client may remember only that you started ten minutes late or that the sax player wore a blue shirt instead of white. Often there are photos or videos to remind the client, so watch out for those details.

Rule to Remember:
Often, it's the small, nonmusical details that make—or break—a job. Little things can mean a lot.

Communicate during the job. Check periodically with the client to be sure that everything is going well. Sometimes she won't complain until it's too late, or for some reason she may feel awkward about interrupting your performance to request a change. The selection of tunes, stage demeanor, volume, lighting, tempo, and so on can be changed if necessary. Remember, in commercial situations you're hired to fulfill a particular need, not necessarily to express yourself musically.

A cliché is appropriate here: The boss may not always be right, but he's always the

boss, and sometimes you'll need to be an actor. If your client wants to hear "New York, New York" again, play it again. Grin and bear it, think about the money you'll make from that tune, or play it in a different key for practice.

In any case, try to avoid the musician-client hostility that sometimes develops. The easiest way to keep everyone happy is to keep talking. Communicate with your client; he's not the enemy. Keep in mind that you're on the same team with the same goal in mind—a successful event. Work together to achieve it.

Keep it all under control. When you're asked to do the impossible—and you will be, sooner or later—don't react angrily. The client or audience probably doesn't understand the technical reasons why your trio can't sound like Bon Jovi's latest hit. Don't try to explain by talking about overdubs, studio musicians, backup singers, and so on; the client will probably think you are just making excuses. It's easier to explain politely that you don't know the requested song and suggest something similar that you *can* do. Nobody knows everything—except teenaged audiences.

One way to stay in control is to have the next tune always in mind, and start it as soon as you finish the previous one. That will keep people on the dance floor, and it leaves no time for them to badger you with impossible requests. Wasting time between numbers will make the audience restless and give them time to think of hundreds of requests that you can't do.

Follow up. Write a short thank-you note to the client after the job (unless you booked it through an agency). Let her know that you appreciate her business and that you'd like to work with her again. Enclose your card. If you're sending an invoice, a thank-you note will soften its impact. In any case, the extra few minutes spent following up will be appreciated.

Your client has no doubt paid you a considerable sum of money. Don't vanish without a trace. You'll need her again.

Maintain enthusiasm. A professional level of competence is certainly important to your success as a freelance musician, and you should work to be as good as you can be. But your attitude and demeanor are also important. If you regard playing music commercially as a chore, your attitude will inevitably be communicated to your listeners and they'll resent it. If you're taking their money, they can rightly expect your cheerful best. That doesn't mean that you should be a clown or a buffoon or that you should act silly, but a glowering, nasty attitude is never called for. There is a middle ground.

If you're bored with a particular job, don't show it; try to be enthusiastic instead. This isn't easy to do, but it's worth the effort and you'll feel better, too. Think about your last visit to the doctor. Was he interested in your ailment, or did he act bored with your situation? What was your response to his interest in your problem? Your client wants and deserves an interested attitude from you, just as you do from the other professionals you deal with.

MANAGING YOUR CAREER

As you continue to build a network of prospects and clients, you'll find that active management is still necessary. Even if all you have to do is answer the phone and mail out contracts and even if everyone in town knows you, you'll still have to work at it. You can't really relax and let your career coast because coasting is always downhill. You have to fight the competition, of course, but you also must guard against stress and burnout. Here are some ideas to keep you moving in the right direction.

Stay involved. If you reach the point where you have a manager, producer, or agent who's taking care of your details, you'll still need to be alert. Keep up with all aspects of the business, use your common sense, and don't succumb to the music-industry hype.

Most musicians won't have professional management, so they'll continue to do everything for themselves. Once you're successful, remember what got you there and keep doing it. For example, maintain your *PMMS* and continue your marketing efforts. Write sales letters and thank-you notes. Keep building your network of contacts actively, because if you slack up on your efforts, someone else will take your place.

Stay up-to-date by keeping up with changes in the music world. How will electronics affect what you do? Computers? Synthesizers? You can't hide from new technologies, and they won't go away.

Music changes rapidly, propelled by a vast industry that thrives on trendiness. Keeping up can be very stressful, especially if you don't like or understand what's popular. You can reduce such stress, however, by not judging new music until you understand it. Remember all those musicians who said rock music wouldn't last? (And remember those rock musicians who said rock would obliterate everything else?) If you don't keep up with the music in your field, you'll be left behind—you can count on it.

An excellent way to stay in tune is by reading in your field. Appendix A lists many excellent magazines that cover specific areas of music, and you will profit from reading them. You won't find all of these magazines at newsstands; you'll probably need to subscribe, but it's worth it to know what's developing in your kind of music.

Practice is always important. Learn new tunes and current styles, because the more you know, the more you can sell.

Another important reason to practice is

that being good, *and knowing that you're good,* increases your self-confidence and helps reduce stress. Perhaps the most uncomfortable position in music is knowing that you can't do what you're being asked to do—whether it's reading a show or playing a current hit. If you're in the spotlight—and all musicians are—and you're embarrassed by lack of ability or knowledge, you'll know firsthand what real stress is. Working on your music, and continuing to work on it through the years, is the best way to assure confidence, both on and off the stage.

Avoid burnout by varying your activities. Music is important to your life, of course, but it's not everything. If you reach a point where the stresses of self-employment and the pressure of constant performing combine, burnout might result in boredom, dissatisfaction, and tension. How do you avoid it?

Start by remembering that you are more than your music. Your life can and should include many nonmusical activities, and your sense of self-worth should be based on more than just your playing. A healthy person knows he is more than his professional abilities.

Involvement also means that you should look outside yourself for interests and activities. Join neighborhood organizations, professional clubs, churches or synagogues, or other groups. Don't do this for business reasons but for personal ones; you'll benefit from knowing and working with lots of people in lots of situations. Hobbies other than music will also help you maintain a healthy, well-rounded mental attitude.

Stay healthy if you can, and you'll be more productive and happier. Physical exercise is important. Long hours in a nightclub, breathing smoke-filled air, maybe drinking too much, probably eating junk-food snacks are anti-health forces. They must be con-sciously countered by taking steps to stay healthy.

Maybe you should jog or walk, swim or bike, join a health club, or lift weights. What's important here, as with your career, is that you set a goal and stick to it.

Maybe the most important thing in your life is your music and you'd be happy jamming all day, every day, with your band. Even if that's your interest, you'll feel better and play better if you keep your body in good shape.

Set goals. As Dr. Worthy and Lee J. Howard discussed in their interviews, goals are important both to your career and your sense of achievement. Feelings of forward movement and accomplishment remain important as time passes. Are you content to just do the same old jobs, year after year? Is drifting along good enough for you? If you set goals and work toward them, you'll know where you're going and in what direction you're heading.

Remember, if you don't have a goal, any road will do—and a sense of aimlessness is very bad for self-employed people. You don't need to map out every week's activities or plot month-by-month stages of career progress, but you should develop a personal goal. Read a book or two on goal-setting, and practice what they preach. You'll be happier if you know where you're going.

Don't stop working on your PMMS. You've spent hours devising your own marketing plan, and it will help you find more work. When success comes, don't change your tactics but work just as hard (or even harder) to maintain it.

Keep adding to your *PMMS* as you acquire new skills and discover job possibilities. Continue to call on new clients and reinforce your relationship with old ones. Keep up with changes in your community and in music so you're always on top of what's going on.

MAKING THEM LOVE YOU

You've invested lots of effort in producing a marketing plan—and, just like big corporations, you want the customers to love you. When they need music, you want them to think immediately of *you*. You want to do such a good job that there'll be no question in their minds about who to hire next time. How do you do that?

An article in *Fortune* magazine (March 13, 1989) discusses how major corporations deal with the same problem. In a list of "Keys to Staying Close," the magazine suggests these ways of keeping customers happy—and they're just as relevant to musicians as to automakers. *Fortune* suggests:

■ Thinking of yourself as the customer

■ Making every employee aware of your vision

■ Listening to customers

■ Staying in touch after the sale

If you do those things, all of which we've discussed in this book, you'll be taking care of business and making sure that those loyal customers will be taking care of you for years to come.

I hope the marketing methods described here will work as well for you as they have for me. If you use them, I'm sure you'll succeed. But don't just think about it. Do it.

Good luck!

A SAMPLING OF USEFUL PUBLICATIONS

Keeping up with your area of music and developments in financial management, trends, taxes, business, computers, and other subjects of interest will be easier if you stay in touch through magazines and journals. Here are some good ones, but your library won't have them all. Many specialized magazines and newsletters are only available through subscription, and you can write for information. Some of the more popular magazines aren't listed here since they're available everywhere.

The American Harp Journal, 6331 Quebec Dr., Los Angeles, CA 90068. Covers activities of the American Harp Society.

American Music Teacher, 2113 Carew Tower, Cincinnati, OH 45202. Useful information for music teachers.

The American Organist, 815 2nd Ave., Suite 318, New York, NY 10017. Official journal of the American Guild of Organists.

Banjo Newsletter, Box 364, Greensboro, MD 21639. For banjo players and enthusiasts.

Bluegrass Unlimited, Box 111, Broadrun, VA 22014. Emphasis on bluegrass and old-time country music.

Chamber Music, 215 Park Ave. S., New York, NY 10003. Covers the field of chamber music.

Changing Times, 1729 H St., NW, Washington, DC 20006. Covers personal finance, trends, and consumer information.

The Church Musician, 127 9th Ave., Nashville, TN 37234. For church musicians.

Clavier, 200 Northfield Rd., Northfield, IL 60093. For pianists, organists, and teachers.

Compute!'s PC Magazine, 324 W. Wendover Ave., Greensboro, NC 27408. Magazine containing IBM/clone disk containing several useful programs per issue.

Downbeat, 222 W. Adams St., Chicago, IL 60606. Covers jazz and contemporary music.

Frets Magazine, 20085 Stevens Creek, Cupertino, CA 95014. For acoustic string players.

Guitar Player Magazine, 20605 Lazaneo, Cupertino, CA 95014. For all guitarists.

Guitar World, 1115 Broadway, New York, NY 10010. For guitarists, with emphasis on current music.

Home Business News, 12221 Beaver Pk., Jackson, OH 45640. Focus on ideas for home-based businesses.

Home Office Computing, 130 Broadway, New York, NY 10003. Practical articles on running a high-tech home office.

Instrumentalist, 200 Northfield Rd., Northfield, IL 60093. For band directors, teachers of instrumental music.

International Musician, 1501 Broadway, New York, NY 10036. Published by the American Federation of Musicians; sent to all members. Covers union and general professional news.

Keyboard Magazine, 20605 Lanzaneo, Cupertino, CA 95014. Covers all keyboard news, including electronic developments, new equipment, and all styles with emphasis on current music.

MCS — Music, Computers, and Software, 190 E. Main St., Huntington, NY 11743. The name says it all.

Modern Drummer, 1000 Clifton Ave., Clifton, NJ 07013. For all percussionists.

Modern Recording and Music, 1120 Old Country Rd., Plainview, NY 11803. Covers recording news and techniques.

Money, Time-Life Building, Rockefeller Center, New York, NY 10020. Covers personal financial issues.

Music and Sound Output, 220 Westbury Ave., Carle Place, NY 11514. Covers music business for musicians and sound people.

Music Educators Journal, 1902 Association Dr., Reston, VA 22091. For professional music educators.

Music Magazine, Suite 202, 56 The Esplanade, Toronto, Ontario, Canada M5E 1A7. Emphasizes classical music.

The Music Trades, P.O. 432, Englewood, NJ 07631. For music retailers; covers industry developments.

Notes, 120 Claremont Ave., New York, NY 10027. Publication of the Music Library Association. Publishes scholarly articles and reviews.

Personal Computing Magazine, 10 Holland Dr., Hasbouck Heights, NJ 07604. Focuses on hands-on business applications of computers.

The Piano Stylist, 352 Evelyn St., Paramus, NJ 07653. Includes music and lessons in pop and jazz, featuring well-known players.

Publish! The How-to Magazine of Desktop Publishing, 501 2nd St., San Francisco, CA 94107. Emphasizes how-to's of desktop publishing for beginners and professionals alike.

Suzuki World, 79 E. State St., Athens, OH 45701. For music teachers involved in the Suzuki method of instruction.

Symphony, P.O. 669, Vienna, VA 22180. Of interest to the symphony community.

A FEW HELPFUL BOOKS

Your library or local bookstore has excellent books on financial management, sales techniques, financial and tax planning, self-motivation, and, of course, music. These are only a sample of the many helpful resources you'll find. Don't forget that books offer an enormous amount of help for very little money—and they bring enjoyment, too.

Billboard Annual International Buyer's Guide, Billboard Publications, annual.

Business Letter Writing Made Simple by Irving Rosenthal and Harry Rudman. Doubleday, 1968.

Complete Book of Tax Deductions by Robert Holzman. Barnes and Noble, annual.

Complete Guide to Managing Your Money, Consumer Reports Books, 1989.

Controlling Stagefright by Peter Desberg and George Marsh. New Harbinger Publications, 1988.

Directory of Music Research Libraries by Rita Benton. University of Iowa Press, continuing publication.

The Do-It-Yourself Business Book by Gustav Berle. John Wiley and Sons, 1989.

Getting Noticed by James Gibson. Writer's Digest Books, 1987.

The Grant Game by Lawrence Lee. Harbor Publishing, 1981.

Guerrilla Marketing Attack by Jay C. Levinson. Houghton-Mifflin, 1989.

How to Get Free Press by Toni Delacorte, Judy Kimsey, and Susan Halas. Harbor Publishing, 1981.

How to Make Newsletters, Brochures, and Other Good Stuff Without a Computer System by H. Gregory. Pinstripe Publishing (P.O. 711, Sedro Woolley, WA 98284), 1988.

How to Master the Art of Selling by Tom Hopkins. Warner Books, 1982.

How to Sell Anything to Anybody by Joe Girard. Stanley H. Brown, 1979.

How to Sell Yourself by Joe Girard. Warner Books, 1979.

How to Set Up an Office at Home by Robert Scott. Scribner's, 1985.

How to Teach Piano Successfully by James Bastien. Kjos Publishing, 1977.

If They Ask You, You Can Write a Song by Al Kasha and Joel Hirschhorn. Simon and Schuster, 1979.

Library Research Guide to Music by John E. Druesedow. Pierian Press, 1982. (Check library's reference department.)

The Magic of Thinking Big by David Schwartz. Simon and Schuster, 1983.

Making Money Making Music No Matter Where You Live by James W. Dearing. Writer's Digest Books, 1985.

Marshall Loeb's Money Guide, Little Brown, 1988.

The Memory Book by Harry Lorayne and Jerry Lucas. Ballantine, 1974.

Musical America Annual Directory, ABC Leisure Magazines, annual.

A Musician's Guide to the Road by Gary Burton. Billboard Books, 1981.

Need a Grant? The Individual's Guide to Grants by Judith B. Margolin. Plenum Press, 1983.

The New Freelancer's Handbook by Marietta Whittlesey. Fireside, 1988.

Perfectly Legal by Barry Steiner and David Kennedy. John Wiley and Sons, annual.

Secrets of Closing the Sale by Zig Ziglar. Fleming H. Revell, 1984.

The Songwriter's and Musician's Guide to Making Great Demos, by Harvey Rachlin. Writer's Digest Books, 1988.

Songwriter's Market, Writer's Digest Books, annual.

Stop Forgetting by Dr. Bruno Furst. Doubleday, 1972.

The Student's Memory Book by Bill Adler. Doubleday, 1988.

Sylvia Porter's Your Own Money, Avon, 1989.

Running a One-Person Business by Claude Whitmyer. Ten Speed Press, 1989.

Touch Typing Self-Taught by Nicki Montaperto. Barnes and Noble, 1983.

The Unabashed Self-Promoter's Guide by Dr. Jeffrey Lant. JLA Publications, 1983.

A P P E N D I X   C

MUSIC-RELATED BUSINESSES

This is a small sampling of the thousands of businesses serving musicians. Their catalogs will provide price and quality comparisons. Remember that buying equipment locally should build a good relationship with retailers, and you may sometimes need their advice and assistance.

Ability Development, Box 887, Athens, OH, 45701. Catalog of music learning aids, with emphasis on Suzuki methods, books, and instruments.

Jamie Aebersold Records, 1211 Aebersold Dr., New Albany, IN 47150. Catalog of play-along records, especially jazz-related. Phone 800-456-1388.

Sam Ash Music Stores, 124 Fulton Ave., Hempstead, NY 11550. Telephone: 800-4-Sam Ash. Large discount music store, good for price comparison.

Ray Bloch Productions, 1500 Broadway, New York, NY 10036. National booking agency and convention-service company, with several regional offices around the country.

Crutchfield, 1 Crutchfield Pk., Charlottesville, VA 22906. Phone 800-521-4050. Catalog of home office products and supplies.

Day-Timers, Inc., P.O. 2368, Allentown, PA 18001. Variety of datebooks and time management tools.

Dexter Press, Rt. 303, West Nyack, NY 10994. Large color printing company. Can print color postcards, slick flyers, brochures.

Dover Publications, 31 East 2nd St., Mineola, NY 11501. Catalog of hard-to-find books, musical scores, and copyright-free music illustrations.

Envelope Sales Co., Normandy, TN 37360. Prints letterheads, envelopes, and other stationery at competitive prices.

Everything's Music, 1155 Belvedere Rd., West Palm Beach, FL 33405. Catalog of music-related items.

Friendship House, 29313 Clemens Rd., Suite 2G, Cleveland, OH 44145. Catalog of music-related items, novelties, and gifts.

Kendor Music, P.O. 278, Delevan, NY 14042. Supplies charts for big-band and smaller groups.

Letraset USA, Inc., 40 Eisenhower Dr., Paramus, NJ 07652. Catalog of press-on letters and graphic aids. Available at local art dealers—or write for catalog and nearest dealer's name.

Mass Photo Co., 1439 Mayson St., Atlanta, GA 30324, or 1315 Waugh St., Houston, TX 77019. Produces publicity photos from your original.

Meadow Creek Music, P.O. 18262, Louisville, KY 40218. Supplies charts of all sorts to big bands and combos.

Music Gifts, Box 351, Evanston, IL 60204. Catalog of music-related items.

National Repro Service, P.O. 70, Kimberly, WI 54465. Photo reproduction, posters, labels, cards, even personalized guitar picks.

Nebs Computer Forms, 12 South St., Townsend, MA 01469. All kinds of supplies for the computerized musician.

Tara Publications, 29 Derby Ave., Cedarhurst, NY 11516. Publishes books of Jewish music.

SELECTED MUSIC ORGANIZATIONS

There are hundreds of organizations for musicians, from groups promoting a particular instrument to national labor unions. In fact, the *Encyclopedia of Associations*, an annual reference book your library should have, lists over three hundred music organizations devoted to every aspect of music.

Many of these groups publish newsletters or magazines, handbooks or membership lists. Write to any organization you're interested in for membership information because this is an excellent way to keep up with your area of music, broaden your professional contacts, and make new friends. Addresses do change, so consult the current edition of the *Encyclopedia of Associations* for current specifics.

Amateur Chamber Music Players, 545 8th Ave., New York, NY 10018.

American Choral Directors Association, P.O. 6310, Lawton, OK 73506.

American Federation of Musicians, 1501 Broadway, New York, NY 10036.

American Federation of Television & Radio Artists, 1350 Avenue of the Americas, New York, NY 10019.

American Guild of Organists, 815 2nd Ave., Suite 318, New York, NY 10017.

American Guild of Variety Artists (AGVA), 1540 Broadway, New York, NY 10036.

American Harp Society, 6331 Quebec Dr., Los Angeles, CA 90068.

American Music Scholarship Association, 1826 Carew Tower, Cincinnati, OH 45263.

American Society of Music Arrangers, P.O. 11, Hollywood, CA 90078.

Balalaika and Domra Association of America, 2225 Madison Sq., Philadelphia, PA 19146.

Big Band Academy of America, 6565 W. Sunset Blvd., Suite 516, Hollywood, CA 90028.

Black Music Association, 307 S. Broad St., Philadelphia, PA 19107.

Blues Foundation, 352 Beale St., Memphis, TN 38103.

Chamber Music America, 545 8th Ave., New York, NY 10018.

Country Music Foundation, 4 Music Square E., Nashville, TN 37203.

Fretted Instrument Guild of America, 2344 S. Oakley Ave., Chicago, IL 60608.

Gospel Music Association, 38 Music Square W., Nashville, TN 37203.

Guitar Foundation of America, P.O. 1090A, Garden Grove, CA 92642.

International Bluegrass Association, 326 St. Elizabeth St., Owensboro, KY 42301.

International Clarinet Society, Dept. of Music, Southwest Texas State Univ., San Marcos, TX 78666.

International Double Reed Society, 626 Lakeshore Dr., Monroe, LA 71203.

International Horn Society, 1213 Sweetbriar Rd., Madison, WI 53705.

International Piano Guild, P.O. 1807, Austin, TX 78767.

International Polka Association, 4145 S. Kedzie Ave., Chicago, IL 60632.

International Rhythm and Blues Association, 11616 S. Lafayette Ave., Chicago, IL 60628.

International Rock 'n' Roll Music Association, P.O. 50111, Nashville, TN 37205.

International Society of Bassists, School of Music, Northwestern Univ., Evanston, IL 60208.

International Trombone Association, School of Music, North Texas State Univ., Denton, TX 76203.

Jazz World Society, P.O. 777, Times Square Station, New York, NY 10108.

National Academy of Jazz, 12501 Chandler Blvd., No. 107, North Hollywood, CA 91607.

National Academy of Songwriters, 6381 Hollywood Blvd., Suite 780, Hollywood, CA 90028.

National Flute Association, 805 Laguna, Denton, TX 76201.

National Old-Time Fiddlers' Association, 618 Ivy St., Truth or Consequences, NM 87901.

North American Saxophone Alliance, School of Music, Univ. of Georgia, Athens, GA 30602.

Pedal Steel Guitar Association, P.O. 248, Floral Park, NY 11001.

Percussive Arts Society, 214 W. Main, Urbana, IL 61801.

Pianists Foundation of America, 210 5th Ave., New York, NY 10010.

Rhythm and Blues Rock and Roll Society, P.O. 1949, New Haven, CT 06510.

Society for the Preservation and Encouragement of Barbershop Quartet Singing in America, 6315 3rd. Ave., Kenosha, WI 53140.

Sweet Adelines, P.O. 470168, Tulsa, OK 74147.

Violin Society of America, 85-07 Abington Rd., Kew Gardens, NY 11415.

SPECIAL EVENTS AND HOLIDAYS

By checking into the reference books below—your library should have them (probably in the reference section)—you can come up with a special event for each day of the year to celebrate with music. There are, as *Chase's Annual Events* notes, presidential proclamations, national days, state days, sponsored events, astronomical phenomena, historical anniversaries, birthdays, and events from folklore.

What nightclub owner, apartment-complex manager, or country club social director could resist the lure of a party to celebrate the Kentucky Derby (May), Thailand's Elephant Round-Up (November), or the South Carolina Governor's Frog Jump and Egg Striking contest (April)? If you want an excuse for suggesting a party, these books will give you plenty of official reasons for any day and many weeks of the year.

The American Book of Days by Jane M. Hatch. H.W. Wilson Co., 1977. Exhaustive list of birthdays, official holidays, and other celebrated events.

Anniversaries and Holidays by Ruth W. Gregory. American Library Association, 1975. Excellent list of fixed and movable celebrations.

Chase's Annual Events by W.D. and Helen Chase. Contemporary Books, annual. Lists over 4,500 events for every sort. At least seven entries per day.

Festivals Sourcebook edited by Paul Wasserman. Gale Research, Detroit, 1977. Descriptions of thousands of fairs, festivals, and community celebrations listed by subject of the event.

Most dates change each year with calendar changes, and new events are added from time to time. To whet your appetite for this kind of job-creating research, here is a short selection of events for January and February, 1989. There are many more entries available for these months, but this list will show you the wide variety available.

January
1 National Oatmeal Month
1 Polar Bear Swim (Colorado)
1 Emancipation Proclamation
4 Trivia Day
7 Millard Fillmore's Birthday
8 Battle of New Orleans
8 National Man-Watcher's Week
9 Joan Baez's Birthday
13 Cuckoo Dancing Week
13 Friday the 13th
16 Martin Luther King Festivities
20 Hat Day
20 Yuma Fiddler's Contest (Arizona)
21 National Hugging Day
22 National Popcorn Day
27 Jerome Kern's Birthday
27 Mozart's Birthday

February
1 Black History Month
1 National Macadamia Nut Month
2 Groundhog Day
4 Halfway Point of Winter
4 Dan Quayle's Birthday
5 Chinese Lunar New Year Festival
5 Weatherman's Day
10 International Strange Music Weekend
   (Olive Hill, KY)
11 White Shirt Day
14 Valentine's Day
20 Lunar Eclipse

20 Presidents' Day
21 Northern Hemisphere Hoodie-Hoo Day
23 George Frederick Handel's Birthday
26 Levi Strauss' Birthday

You get the idea. Suggest a blue-jean brunch to celebrate Levi Strauss' birthday, or a chamber music concert for Mozart's birthday. The possibilities are endless.

INDEX

OTHER BOOKS TO HELP YOU MAKE
MONEY AND THE MOST OF
YOUR MUSIC TALENT

The Craft & Business of Songwriting
John Braheny
A powerful, information-packed (and the most up-to-date) book about the songwriting industry which thoroughly covers all the creative and business aspects that you need to know to maximize your chances of success. 322 pages/$19.95, hardcover

The Craft of Lyric Writing
Sheila Davis
Davis, a successful lyricist, composer, and teacher, presents the theory, principles, and techniques that result in lyrics with timeless appeal. 350 pages/$19.95, hardcover

Successful Lyric Writing:
A Step-by-Step Course & Workbook
Sheila Davis
A practical, self-contained lyric writing course, complete with exercises and lyric writing assignments designed to stimulate your creativity and build writing skills. 304 pages/$18.95, paperback

Getting Noticed:
A Musician's Guide to Publicity & Self-Promotion
James Gibson
Gibson helps performing musicians create effective yet inexpensive publicity materials, then use them to *get noticed* and *make money* with their music. 224 pages/$12.95, paperback

Making Money Making Music
(No Matter Where You Live)
James Dearing
Dearing shows you how to build a successful music career in any community—playing clubs, performing radio and TV jingles, operating a record studio, teaching, and selling lyrics through the mail. 305 pages/ $12.95, paperback

The Performing Artist's Handbook
Janice Papolos
Practical know-how classical musicians need to progress in their professional music careers. 219 pages/ $12.95, paperback

The Songwriter's Guide to Making Great Demos
Harvey Rachlin
From how to judge if a song is ready to be pitched to exactly how to produce a multitrack recording, covers every step of the process of making great demos. 192 pages/$12.95, paperback

Writing Music for Hit Songs
Jai Josefs
Professional songwriter Jai Josefs shows how to musically craft successful popular songs. His easy-to-understand explanations are illustrated with more than 170 musical examples from today's top artists. 256 pages/$17.95, hardcover

Making It in the New Music Business
James Riordan
The coauthor of *The Platinum Rainbow* shows how to achieve success as a recording artist by building your own path to success. 377 pages/$18.95, hardcover

The Songwriter's Guide to Collaboration
Walter Carter
A complete guide to all aspects of co-writing songs, from working relationships to legal and financial arrangements. 178 pages/$12.95, paperback

How to Pitch & Promote Your Songs
Fred Koller
For songwriters who want to make a full-time living with their music, a step-by-step self-employment guide. 144 pages/$12.95, paperback

You Can Write Great Lyrics
Pamela Phillips Oland
Inside advice from one of today's top songwriters on how you can write lyrics with commercial appeal and focus on writing songs that have what it takes to succeed. 192 pages/$17.95, paperback

Protecting Your Songs & Yourself
Kent J. Klavens
A practical, thorough, easy-to-read guide to copyright, contracts, taxes, and other songwriting legal topics. 112 pages/$15.95, paperback

Playing for Pay:
How to Be a Working Musician
James Gibson
Gibson shows you how to develop a well-organized and strategic "Personal Music Marketing System" that will help you make money with your music. 160 pages/$17.95, paperback

Beginning Songwriter's Answer Book
Paul Zollo
An essential resource for songwriters, with detailed answers to the 218 questions most often asked the National Academy of Songwriters. 128 pages/$16.95, paperback

Gigging:
The Musician's Underground Touring Directory
Michael Dorf & Robert Appel
2,000 contacts to help you/your group book a regional or cross-country tour and/or get airplay for your records. 224 pages/$14.95, paperback

1990 Songwriter's Market
edited by Mark Garvey
This annual directory is designed to help you make the right contacts! Includes 2,000 listings of music publishers, record companies/producers, advertising agencies, audiovisual firms, managers, booking agents, and play producers. You'll also find helpful articles on the business of songwriting, interviews with professionals in the industry, and lists of clubs, contests, and associations. 528 pages/$18.95, hardcover

A complete catalog of all Writer's Digest Books is available FREE by writing to the address shown below. To order books directly from the publisher, include $3.00 postage and handling for one book, 50¢ for each additional book. Allow 30 days for delivery.

Writer's Digest Books
1507 Dana Avenue
Cincinnati, Ohio 45207

Credit card orders call TOLL-FREE
1-800-289-0963

Prices subject to change without notice